Autoworkers
Under the Gun
A Shop-Floor View of the End
of the American Dream

Gregg Shotwell

Foreword by Jerry Tucker
Afterword by Lee Sustar

(H)
Haymarket Books
Chicago, Illinois

Published in 2011 by Haymarket Books
PO Box 180165
Chicago, IL 60618
www.haymarketbooks.org
773–583–7884

ISBN: 978-1-60846-142-4

Trade distribution:
In the US, Consortium Book Sales and Distribution, www.cbsd.com
In Canada, Publishers Group Canada, www.pgcbooks.ca
In the UK, Turnaround Publisher Services, www.turnaround-uk.com
In Australia, Palgrave Macmillan, www.palgravemacmillan.com.au
All other countries, Publishers Group Worldwide, www.pgw.com

Cover design by Eric Ruder
Cover image of a gear in a car enginge © Nataliya Hora, 2011.

Published with the generous support of Lannan Foundation and the Wallace Global Fund.

Printed in the United States by union labor.

Library of Congress cataloging-in-publication data is available.

10 9 8 7 6 5 4 3 2 1

SUSTAINABLE FORESTRY INITIATIVE

Certified Sourcing
www.sfiprogram.org
SFI-01234

Contents

For Sheila, my wife, to whom I owe my life and all the blessings it may contain: Sonia, Camille, and Colin

In memory of Caroline Lund, Dave Yettaw, Pablo Lopez, and Camron Austin

Soldiers of Solidarity

We the People are at war.
We need to develop Soldiers, not career opportunists.
It will take time and patience.
There will be setbacks and victories.
Given time and effort,
the law of multiplication will prevail.
If one goes out and trains two soldiers,
and they go out and do the same,
and this continues, we will have our army.
We the People are the Union.

—Miguel X. Chavarria, UAW Local 22

Foreword

Intelligent discontent is a mainspring of civilization. Progress is born of agitation. It is agitation or stagnation.

—Eugene Debs

This unique volume by rank-and-file autoworker Gregg Shotwell is a collection of urgent, well-documented "struggle-in-progress" protests over how the US auto industry management, particularly General Motors, and the United Auto Workers (UAW) union leadership engaged in a concerted effort to support an anti-worker industry agenda. That agenda enhanced profits and encouraged offshore investments at the expense of domestic autoworkers' wages, benefits, working conditions, and dignity. This collection exposes in detail the results of the union's role reversal from adversarial defender of solidarity to champion of "corporate-think."

Not only is this collection a catalog of attacks on autoworkers—attacks that are continuing today—but it is also a hopeful testament to the ability of a small, though growing, number of workers to understand what lies behind these attacks and to organize to fight them. As such, it tells a story that has largely been ignored by the mainstream media.

For scholars interested in the decline and fall of both the US auto industry and the UAW in the period from the 1980s to today, Gregg Shotwell's detailed accounts of compelling events over the past twelve years will provide a literary slide show of otherwise unavailable materials. It details workers' reactions to the sustained attacks by the auto bosses—who acted with the complicity of union bureaucrats.

The US auto industry and the UAW have a storied past. They have been the subject of much public exposure and media coverage over the years, ranging from the widely reported sit-downs in Flint, Michigan, in

the late 1930s, which institutionalized the once-fractious industrial relationship, to the present shallow reporting of "routine" events in workers'
unequaled decline in economic and social power. The once constructively
adversarial relationship between those heavyweights is gone, replaced
these last thirty years by the calculated morphing of the union into a corporate junior partner.

Academics used to devote considerable attention to the rise of the
UAW as a wage and benefit pacesetter for millions of autoworkers and
other unionized industries and workers. For a number of years, the auto
union was also studied as a progressive force in politics and a major supporter of social struggles. Those scholarly inspections fell off significantly
in the 1970s. Now—as the UAW during the past thirty years has presided
over the most destabilizing job and income loss in industrial history—
outside analysts observe little and write less about our union's forced
march to the rear.

The limited exposure of the details of autoworkers' downward economic spiral is most often provided by progressive outlier publications like
Labor Notes and, with much more limited circulation, shop-floor newsletters,
blogs, and websites produced under the threat of retaliation and rebuke by
the UAW and corporate leadership. These organic, pained protests of individual UAW members or self-organized groups of rank-and-file workers
give voice to the call for a democratic union and collective struggle against
concessions and the culture of "jointness" that envelops today's UAW.

For the past twelve years, one of the foremost sources of dissent and
comprehensive analysis inside the UAW has been a widely circulated publication titled *Live Bait & Ammo*, created by Gregg Shotwell, who at the
time was a veteran GM fuel injection plant machine operator in southwestern Michigan.

Gregg's journey to becoming a preeminent voice from within the
ranks of the UAW and an open critic of the policies and practices of both
General Motors and its UAW partner began inauspiciously enough. Between 1994 and 1996, Gregg wrote articles for the official local union
newspaper of UAW Local 2151 in Coopersville, Michigan. But when the
union officialdom found his observations and probing questions incon-
sistent with their defense of the UAW administration's agenda, they shut

him down as a contributor. He promptly rolled out an even more probing underground series of articles and distributed them throughout his plant.

Local 2151 members began to rely on Gregg for the unabridged and "spin-less" version of events and a preview of the next indignity they could expect from management and, all too often, the union's claim of impotence. On the strength of his communication skills, and with virtually no campaigning, Gregg was elected as a delegate to the 1998 UAW Constitutional Convention in Las Vegas. That experience, coupled with his attendance at the 1999 Collective Bargaining Convention, provided a troubling picture of the future for workers like him and his parts-industry comrades.

His 1999 Convention Report (originally *Live Bait & Ammo* #10), included in this book, lays bare what he witnessed. Gregg saw how the corporate "partnership" agenda, secured on the false altar of corporate "competitiveness," and the absence of democracy in the union's processes compromised the ability of the union leadership to steadfastly defend its members' income security, job security, and working conditions.

Brother Shotwell's attendance at the Bargaining Convention was enough to confirm for him his earlier parochial observations in the Coopersville local: GM was recklessly moving its capital away from US production and jettisoning its component parts supplier divisions, including the Coopersville plant, which would now become part of the newly created Delphi Automotive Systems. The UAW's role in this dispersal process had become suspiciously complicit, and the most fundamental questions in the minds of the affected rank and filers went unanswered. With keen powers of observation, a burglary victim's sense of indignation, and fine-tuned writing skills, Shotwell set out to fill the vacuum.

While at the UAW Convention, Gregg had met and talked with a number of the original New Directions Movement (NDM) local union leaders from around the country, including NDM supporter and legendary UAW cofounder Victor Reuther. Gregg also found comfort in the prophetic literature that had defined the founding of the NDM in the first place.

For Brother Shotwell, the twin chickens of bedding down with the company and running a "one-party state" union had clearly come home to roost. Shotwell decided to use his considerable communications skills to turn a spotlight on the doublespeak and "concessions save jobs" hypocrisy of the corporate/union axis, and the era of *Live Bait & Ammo* was fully under way. His self-assigned research included a more thorough evaluation of the NDM, which was much derided—and feared—by the UAW's ruling Administration Caucus.

In the mid-1980s, just as the stealthily conceived labor-management partnership was becoming systematically adapted to all the structural layers of the UAW in the auto industry, a movement of principled opposition emerged. Rising from the lower Midwest/Southwest UAW Region 5, hundreds of UAW local union officers and activists challenged the top union leadership's calculus of unbridled collaboration.

The union had long been managed like a "one-party state." Now, the bosses'—and capital's—so-called competitiveness agenda were supplanting what small measure of democracy and rank-and-file accountability had existed prior to the 1980s. The dissident bloc was called the New Directions Movement because of a statement its local leaders had issued, "Calling for a New Direction," on the part of the International Union. New Directions challenged politically by running for executive board offices and with a wave of newsletters and printed materials with well-constructed arguments against folding the union's agenda into that of the employer. The movement's primary publication was the *Voice of New Directions*, which at one point was being mailed to more than seven thousand subscribers, and was routinely copied (often on employer copying machines) and distributed in many plants. In some local unions, NDM supporters created their own alternative newsletters or underground publication systems.

The UAW leadership spent untold millions trying to bury the NDM and its supporters. They engaged in harsh retaliatory tactics toward known supporters of New Directions. For example, they set up a massive patronage program throughout the union, often underwritten by the auto employers through "jointness" slush funds, to appoint Administration Caucus loyalists to cushy off-line jobs negotiated between management and the UAW at the International Union level. These were particularly common in auto locals where an NDM presence was growing.

This all-out assault on internal democracy and rejection of membership accountability, coupled with the growing wave of layoffs and plant shutdowns throughout the industry (as the union leadership stood by in mute acceptance), took its toll on the advocates of changing directions among the ranks. Like the legendary labor songwriter Joe Hill, the New Directions movement never really died. It dispersed into smaller, renamed strands and pockets of dissent within a woefully abused and drastically shrunken auto industry workforce.

Live Bait & Ammo, to date, numbers more than 150 distinct editions. This book features a selected and representative number of these unique and lively testaments. *LB&A*s have reached thousands of autoworkers as well as other interested workers and readers by way of e-mail, the Soldiers of Solidarity website, secondary senders in many plants and cities, and untold hard copies distributed in numerous workplaces. They are always topical and well researched, with accurate quotes and citations. They are crisply written—with a piercing wit, words that rattle the conscience, and phrases that impale their targets. Gregg Shotwell has abilities reminiscent of America's most notable social muckrakers, and it's not a stretch to call Mark Twain to mind as a reference point.

However, no one should get the impression that Brother Shotwell is just a computer-bound literary craftsman with a deeply ingrained sense of class grievance. Gregg was a moving force in the creation of the UAW Soldiers of Solidarity, is a frequent speaker at activist worker meetings, and is a consistent advocate of workers taking control of predatory workplaces with "work-to-rule" strategies and other collectively applied shop-floor tactics.

Most UAW members who speak out against the policies and practices of the union leadership, regardless of how politely, will experience one form or another of retaliation. Over the years, the intrepid author of *Live Bait & Ammo* was no exception. However, a strong following of rank-and-file supporters, many in the immediate perimeter of his work area, took a hand in protecting him. He readily defends his role as a leadership critic. This is illustrated in an excerpt from *LB&A* #47: "I don't deny that I critique the union and challenge its leaders. Standing up and speaking out is what being a union activist is all about. I even sign my name. It's called self-respect. That's what I like about being a union member—I don't have to walk around with my tail between my legs and pretend I like it."

Everything Gregg writes is a straight-ahead testament of views that workers have come to share about the downward spiral of perpetual concessions and the ever-present terms of surrender a "partnered-up" union leadership prefers to the option of fightback and struggle. Here are his words on the union's impotence in the face of internal corporate restructuring, from *LB&A* #50: "In recent years many plants formerly owned by the Big Three were forced into separation agreements. The restructuring has instigated massive concessions, intolerable working conditions, and a gross neglect of ergonomic standards. The corporations are breaking the union into smaller, more isolated, and thus more manageable pieces. Without a worldview independent of the capitalists, the union has no strategy other than the Three Cs—cooperation, collusion, and capitulation."

Few critical contributors to the debate on the corporate/union strategy of "jointness" and its dangerous acceptance of "competitiveness" as the union's agenda can provide so clear an analysis as Brother Shotwell. Here, in *LB&A* #83, he makes his case:

> Competition between workers will decimate, not solidify, our ranks.
> A Competitive Operating Agreement is a Trojan horse loaded with three lethal concessions:
> (1) the expanded utilization of temps, which is in effect two-tier;
> (2) the importation of nonunion labor into the plants;
> (3) the manipulation of union members as "team leaders" in supervisory roles.

Gregg Shotwell has compiled a prolific body of work in defense of his coworkers and their families and, by extension, working-class communities everywhere. This *Live Bait & Ammo* anthology will consolidate those vital messages for longtime and new readers alike. Gregg has a unique gift: he's an excellent writer and a keen analyst of events, and he cares deeply about the victims of social injustice.

Gregg Shotwell's vision, sharp analysis, and durability may distinguish him as a critic, but he is not alone. More and more rank-and-file workers are informing themselves and taking up the tools of uncensored communications. They are collectively combating institutionalized oppression as well as those profiting from it. The steady production of *Live*

Bait & Ammo over the years, and now the publication of this anthology, serves to inspire and impassion that growing cadre. To Gregg and those intrepid others, I can only repeat the words that apply to any meaningful struggle for justice: "Carry on, carry on!"

Jerry Tucker
Former UAW Executive Board Member
and one of many cofounders of
the New Directions Movement

Introduction

I hired into GM and joined the UAW in 1979. I didn't know much about how unions worked. I soon learned. At six thirty one morning, we were sitting around sipping coffee and trying to wake up to a new day of the same old shit. A foreman who was new to the area told us to get up and get to work. "Right now," he said. "I'm the boss." We said, "Yes sir, boss." We went right to work. Thirty minutes later, every machine in the department was down. Then skilled trades came out, tore the machines apart, left parts all over the floor, and went off to look for the missing parts. They didn't come back. There was no production that day. Every department behind us went down like a domino.

The next morning, the same foreman said, "Good morning, gentlemen." Then he left us alone to do our jobs.

The shop floor was our turf. We controlled the means of production because we were the masters of the means. We didn't plan this direct action. It was automatic. It was natural. We called it "showing the boss who's boss." That's what old-timers taught me about unionism.

About twenty years later, I started writing in earnest. I came up with the name *Live Bait & Ammo* first of all, because I live in southwestern Michigan and those are essential ingredients. Secondly, I considered that it was bait for the bosses—both company and union—and information that workers could use to defend themselves, and therefore, ammo.

Initially, I wrote for fellow workers in my own UAW Local 2151 in Coopersville, Michigan, but as the Internet became more accessible, distribution proliferated. I remember asking Richard Benavides at the Saturn plant in Tennessee if he wanted me to mail a few *Ammos* so he could give them to his coworkers. He said, "Don't bother. A thousand copies hit the floor this morning." I guess I struck a chord.

The vacuum of leadership in the upper echelons of the UAW provided an echo chamber for *Live Bait & Ammo*. When I organized the first Soldiers of Solidarity (SOS) meeting in Grand Rapids in November 2005 with the help of Eric Dent, the president of UAW Local 1231, who opened the union hall for our rank-and-file gathering, autoworkers came from five states and eight different companies. The word was out. Delphi was the lead domino in the restructuring of the auto industry.

UAW bureaucrats accused SOS of being divisive. My favorite accusation was that I am a socialist. The capitalists eat our lunch every day, and we are supposed to be afraid of socialists? GM is partners with China, and the UAW red-baits *me*?

I worked ten years under the gun of union and management intimidation. I prevailed because of the support of fellow workers. I worked and wrote under their protection. One day, I complained that a foreman was bird-dogging me. My committeeman, Dennis Krontz, stood in my work area like a soldier at attention for an entire shift. Local union officials tried to dissuade him, but he stood his ground. Dennis dogged the bird dog down.

I believe *Live Bait & Ammo* resonated with autoworkers because I never said anything they didn't already know in their hearts. I just put it down in plain English and backed up assertion with fact.

I don't have a political orientation like some of my socialist friends who are all better educated than I am. Whatever knowledge I have, I picked up from my coworkers. I was fortunate. When I became interested in autoworker rebellion in the late nineties I discovered a variety of shop-floor fliers: *Kick the Cat* by Camron Austin at Caterpillar in Decatur, Illinois; *Nuts and Bolts* by Tom Laney at the Ford assembly plant in the Twin Cities; *The Barking Dog* by Caroline Lund at the NUMMI plant in Fremont, California; *The Contender* by Gene Austin at the GM truck plant in Pontiac, Michigan; *The Rocker* by Steve Derickson at the Ford plant in St. Louis; *War Zone* by Mike Griffin, a veteran of the Staley lockout in Decatur; *Outside Track* by John Felicicchia, a volunteer organizer at Toyota in Georgetown, Kentucky; and the *Voice of New Directions*.

By 1998, when I distributed *Live Bait & Ammo* #1, the dissident UAW caucus New Directions Movement (NDM) was on its last legs. I was fortunate to meet some of those fighters. They were accused of being radicals and were pilloried by UAW bureaucrats. In fact, it was the bureaucracy that implemented the radical restructuring of the UAW from a fighting union to a lapdog. The NDM dug in its heels in an old-fashioned stand-on-your-hind-legs unionism. They pushed for one member, one vote. (How radical is that?) They were strong, defiant, independent workers who defied the company-union partnership. They were just what I needed. I believe they were what the UAW needed.

After Delphi declared bankruptcy in October 2005, a reporter for the *Indianapolis Star*, Ted Evanoff, asked me, "In *Live Bait and Ammo* #10 you warned retirees, 'What's to prevent GM from slashing your benefits?' How did you know that back then?" I told him, I studied the UAW's New Directions Movement, which accurately predicted the destructiveness of union-management collaboration.

These *Ammos* were written on the run, for the issue at hand, and directed toward autoworkers on the shop floor. The original *Ammos* didn't have dates or titles. I just numbered them and left them on tables in the break areas. In retrospect, they follow the arc of restructuring in the auto industry and the UAW bureaucracy.

The selection of *Ammos* contained in this book begins, in chapter 1, with a report on the UAW Bargaining Convention in 1999, where the Delphi spinoff was the hottest issue. Delphi encapsulated outsourcing, lean manufacturing, auto industry restructuring, two-tier wages, decreasing job security, and the threat to pensions. The convention report is essentially the voice of New Directions and foreshadows the outcome, up to and including, the bankruptcy in 2009. Work-to-rule is also introduced early, in chapter 1, in "Strike Back." It recurs, and then plays rhythm and bass throughout the Delphi bankruptcy.

The SOS organization described in chapter 2 appears to erupt spontaneously when Delphi declares bankruptcy, but in fact it was a resurgence of New Directions, body and soul. Its most instrumental leaders were former members of NDM.

"The Cost of the Status Quo Is Always More," also in chapter 2, reveals that vulture capitalist Wilbur Ross, who worked side by side with Delphi CEO Steve Miller, publicly admitted that the UAW couldn't control the workers, aka Soldiers of Solidarity.

In chapter 3, "A Cat Named Job Security," "Highball the Strike," and other *Ammos* chronicle resistance to the 2007 UAW negotiations that delivered two-tier wages, a Voluntary Employees' Beneficiary Association (VEBA), an underfunded trust to cover retiree health care, and the desecration of the UAW legacy.

Finally, in chapter 4, bankruptcy: "The Perfect Capitalist Disaster." A worker eats and is satisfied, but the gods of capital are always hungry.

Forty years ago, workers controlled the shop floor. It was our turf. In some locales that turf extended beyond the factory gates. The culture of struggle walked out into the streets. The tradition of rebellion and resistance sat down at the bar, the theater, the VFW Hall. Direct action dined in restaurants. Solidarity went to church. Union values prevailed in communities like Detroit, Flint, and Anderson, Indiana. Workers were empowered, and the shop-floor dynamic spread like a song about a boy who could play guitar just like ringing a bell. A bell of freedom, a bell of joy, a bell that celebrated the strength and wisdom of the working class.

And if what I say rings true to you, it's because I'm not saying anything you don't already know. The power of organized labor can change the world. These shop-floor fliers are reprinted here in edited form by Haymarket Books as a testimony to the men and women who rebelled against corporate unionism, and as a reveille for the new generation of rank-and-file workers reorganizing in the industrial ravages of a *de*structured economy. I hope these *Ammos* will help new hires learn, as I learned from autoworkers back in the day, how to "show the boss who's boss."

Acknowledgments

A writer works alone; nonetheless, it is a collaborative craft. I listened to the voices and ideas of my coworkers. I collected their observations and insights and turns of phrases. Sisters and brothers whom I never met distributed *Live Bait & Ammo* in their plants.

After Delphi declared bankruptcy, I traveled all over for SOS meetings and protests. My wife, Sheila, traveled with me everywhere, distributing fliers and carrying picket signs. She is a soldier's soldier.

I could not have been more fortunate than to work with Lee Sustar, my editor. I met Lee at the 1999 Bargaining Convention. He has been a brother-in-struggle to me ever since. Thanks are also due to Juanita Cadman, the smallest person with the bravest heart. She designed the SOS website, paid for it out of her own pocket, and maintained it knowing full well that people with power are vindictive and ruthless. Her smile is a priceless light in dark times. Thanks to Skip Hanline for his research on joint funds. The waves on the ocean thought they were relentless until Skip stood on the pier. Thanks also to Allen Nielsen for his printing press and indefatigable spirit; Tom Adams for his groundbreaking dissertation, *UAW Inc.: The Triumph of Capital*; Bob and Melodee Mabbit for multimedia exposure of SOS activities; Mark and Tonyia Young for FactoryRat.com; Theresa Barber for maintaining the FactoryRat site; Jack Kiedel for WarriorsofLabor.com; Todd and Amber Jordan for FutureoftheUnion.com, an instrumental website for SOS; Don and Stacey Kemp for opening their hearts and home to SOS; Jane Slaughter for the title; and Elly Leary, Dianne Feeley, Wendy Thompson, and all the staff at *Labor Notes* for unremitting dedication to the rank and file.

When I first wrote to New Directions requesting information, Dean Braid sent me a whole box full of documents and videos. Dean lit the fuse. He supplied lighter fluid as needed. Finally, to Jerry Tucker. When I was researching work-to-rule for *LB&A* #43, I called Dave Yettaw. He told me that I should call Jerry Tucker, which to me was like saying, "If you want to learn about songwriting you should call Bob Dylan." Dave gave me Jerry's number. I called, and Jerry generously gave me a personal tutorial. In the worst of times Jerry was there for me. I am not alone in this regard. That's who he is. Jerry never told me what to do, but after talking to him I felt I knew what I had to do next. That's the gift of a true organizer. If you listen closely to *Live Bait & Ammo*, you will hear Jerry's bass in the background guiding the wild rhythm section with a firm hand.

The challenge of acknowledgment is to include the enormous number of soldiers who contributed wit and wisdom, blood and gristle, boots on the ground, and time above and beyond the call. You were burrs in the boss's saddle. You were kindling for the camaraderie of revolt. You inspired *Live Bait & Ammo*, and if there's a spark of true unionism left in the UAW, it's because of you.

Chapter One

The Delphi Spinoff
and the Lords of Lean

Between 1990 and 1998 there were strikes at twenty-two General Motors plants. Most were successful struggles against mandatory overtime and production issues, forcing the company to hire new workers at many of the struck plants.

The showdown between the company and the union came in the summer of 1998 over GM's plans to disinvest from two parts plants in Flint, Michigan, where the UAW first showed its power in the famous 1936–37 sit-down strikes. Because those plants made parts used in most GM vehicles, production across North America came to a halt. As labor journalist and author Kim Moody noted, "The union inflicted enormous damage on the company, which lost almost three billion dollars in profits and twelve billion dollars in sales during the fifty-four-day conflict. Strikes in just two plants had closed twenty-seven of GM's twenty-nine assembly plants and over one hundred parts plants in the United States, Mexico, and Canada."*

The UAW's 1998 Constitutional Convention in Las Vegas was held in the midst of the strike, and UAW president Steve Yokich vowed to step up the pressure on the company to protect the jobs of workers in GM parts plants and fight outsourcing and downsizing. Nevertheless, the UAW settled the strike when GM agreed to return equipment to the struck plants and invest in new production, leaving wider issues unaddressed.

---

* Kim Moody, "At General Motors, 'What Means This Strike?,'" *Against the Current* 76, September–October 1998.

But soon after the agreement that saved jobs in two parts plants, GM announced that it would spin off its entire parts division as Delphi Automotive Systems. This chapter includes Ammos *that cover rank-and-file activists' fight against the spinoff and the struggle against Delphi's demands for job cuts and lower-tier wages for new hires.*

UAW Bargaining Convention: End the Silence
(March 1999)

I drove to the Bargaining Convention with one concern in mind: the Delphi spinoff. No single event in my twenty years as an autoworker has caused so much anxiety and disruption. Is it the beginning of a calculated dismemberment of the union?

The big question on everyone's mind is what will the UAW do, and why haven't we heard anything? The "no news is good news" slogan does not apply. We got the news. It's bad. We're waiting for a response from the UAW. The cold silence coming out of Solidarity House is ominous.

As I drove to Detroit I felt angry. Angry at the silence of the International UAW. Angry at the lack of action and direction. Angry about capitulation and concession. Angry because the International UAW seemed so remote and unresponsive.

Two thoughts ran through my mind: *When leaders are ethically but not legally obligated, they will take advantage of you for their own selfish ends. Then, they will demean you in order to justify their behavior and suppress their guilt.*

UAW Bargaining Con, Day One: Stop the Spinoff
UAW International president Stephen Yokich opened the convention by saying, "If we don't address things that face us honestly and up front, we have a real problem." I've been taking notes long enough to know that remark will come back to haunt him. Then he claimed he had no prior knowledge of the Delphi spinoff. Where's he been? On the shop floor we've been talking about it since 1995. "And that's what pisses me off about GM,"

he said. Yokich doesn't tell us anything. That's what pisses us off about him. Yokich revealed that when GM decided to sell off American Axle, they came to the International beforehand and together they "worked out a pattern agreement." An agreement that dislocated hundreds of families.

He said modular assembly was "another word for outsourcing." He hadn't addressed the modular issue until Suman Bohm confronted him at a UAW subcouncil* meeting and former UAW Local 599 president Dave Yettaw published an article in the *Flint Journal* about the damaging consequences to working families and their communities. Up to that point, Yokich had been silent on the issue. Rick Haglund, a syndicated columnist, said, "Union silence is considered by management to be a positive sign." I believe it went further than tacit approval. The Lordstown and Lansing plants had already begun whipsawing (the practice of locals competing against other locals to make concessions). Does anyone believe that Yokich was unaware of those negotiations?

He said we needed to make outsourcing a "strikable issue." Delphi is the largest maker of modular automotive systems in the world and the spinoff is the most massive outsourcing plan in history. So when do we strike? He said we needed to find ways to restrict overtime. Yokich claimed, "A forty-hour (workweek) restriction would create 86,000 jobs in motor vehicle assembly alone." So what are we waiting for? He railed against the corporations for moving jobs overseas, but still no mention of how the UAW would confront the Delphi spinoff.

There were about two thousand delegates and an army of UAW International Reps jammed into Cobo Hall. Microphones were spaced throughout the hall for delegates to address the assembly. While International Reps speaking from the podium were always clearly audible above the din of the crowd, speakers from the floor were difficult to hear. Many of the delegates called on to speak were merely lapdogs for the Cooperative Caucus. I won't repulse you with alliterations of their lapping sounds.

It was a welcome relief when Suman Bohm approached the mic. Suman is the bargaining chair at the GM assembly plant in Delaware,

---

* A regional negotiating committee of UAW members who have a common employer.

and a cochair of New Directions, a dissident caucus that opposes union-management partnership. Her passion and courage sharpen conviction like oil and stone.

She spoke out against outsourcing. She demanded the International "put the brakes on modular assembly." She said it "would kill us" and was nothing more than a "union-busting" scheme. She denounced GM for closing Buick City and sending the work to China. "Production in China is designated for export to America."

Mark Paine, from an engine plant in Cleveland, said, "Despite overall job growth, union jobs are disappearing." He denounced whipsawing. He said his local jumped through all the hoops, "embraced the Modern Operating Agreement and every other program they came up with," and now they're "scheduled to be phased out." It was a familiar refrain: the cooperation strategy is a failure. We aren't partners, we're rubes. We've been conned into turning tricks for promises while corporate executives laugh at our antics.

When Dave Yettaw took the floor, I could sense the hair standing up on Yokich's neck. Yokich was bristling before Dave ever opened his mouth. Yettaw, who came out of retirement to lead the delegation from Flint Local 599, is a resourceful challenger and a prominent leader in New Directions. Unlike Yokich, he doesn't resort to angry outbursts and profanity to make his point. You may not agree with Yettaw, but one should respect his willingness to stand up for what he believes. That's a lot more than you can say for most of the tail-wagging, wet-nosed lapdogs that pass for convention delegates.

Yettaw calmly asked that GM be made to "live up to the 95 percent job security agreement that was negotiated three years ago." He warned that modular assembly would be devastating to all of us and would result in "outsourcing on a scale we've never seen before." He advocated for temporary workers who pervade the industry. He said, "This union stopped [former Chrysler CEO] Lee Iacocca from spinning off Accustar, and we can stop Delphi and Visteon from being spun off, too."

Dave Koscinski from Local 1866 said:

My members are living the fears of the unknown every day as Delphi is spun off from GM. Brothers and sisters are leaving at an alarming rate through retirement and transfers, causing family hardships. Delphi counts on bargaining a contract that calls for lower wages and benefits, including a two-tier wage and benefit package. Management says the spinoff will be good for everyone. I don't believe it will be good for the UAW. It will divide the parts sector from the assembly sector, thus reducing our bargaining leverage. I support Steve Yokich when he said that GM must retain majority interest in Delphi. We must stop the trend of spinoffs and sales. I urge the UAW to take a hard line against GM and Delphi and all the other spinoffs and sales.

I sensed a raw nerve in the crowd. They'd been pushed around too long. They were anxious about outsourcing, modular assembly, and downsizing. The atmosphere was ripe for a campaign to stop the Delphi spinoff.

Willy Hubbard, president of Local 550, stepped to the mic. His voice sounded like the howling wind off Lake Michigan we call The Wolf. The UAW has negotiated positions to "give us a voice in quality, health and safety, and benefit decisions. One of the things that disturbs me the most is that some of these appointees think they are CEOs of the union."

It was eerie. Cobo Hall was quiet as a church when he spoke.

"We have to return the respect to the floor and remind them they are union reps, not CEOs. These programs were designed to give members an equal voice. The only way we can make sure we live the life as well as work the life of union is by voting for appointees." His speech hit the floor like a cluster bomb. A number of appointees had to be evacuated on stretchers. But they had only fainted.

I'd never spoken at a convention before, or to such a large crowd. It's scary, but I had to take a chance. I thought, I'll keep it short and to the point. I waved my Local 2151 sign in the air. Yokich called on me.

When a delegate steps up to the mic, their image is projected onto two giant video screens. I looked like the fifty-foot man. I felt like stomping down to the Renaissance Center and kicking some corporate butt. Instead, I made a short, impromptu speech:

Brother Yokich, you compared American Axle to the Delphi spinoff. But there is a difference. American Axle was sold. Delphi will be owned and controlled by the exact same group of people. It's a paper shuffle, not a real transfer of assets. Workers at Delphi see the spinoff proceeding full speed ahead, but we do not see or hear the opposition of the UAW. The UAW's silence and lack of visible resistance to the spinoff is perceived as consent. As a result many workers are being scared into early retirement or hasty transfers that destabilize families and disrupt communities. If the spinoff of Delphi is successful, other spinoffs will follow and an undertow of competitive forces will shatter our solidarity and shred the principle of pattern bargaining. Stop the Delphi spinoff in its tracks.

Brother Yokich said, "Next."

Then Suman Bohm got the floor again. She said, "We are losing tens of thousands of jobs to outsourcing because outsourcing language in our National Agreement is too weak. The language is so full of pro-company loopholes that the company could be brain-dead and still get away with taking our jobs. In the '99 contract we must make outsourcing a strikable issue on the local level. We have to get away from two-tier wages, and make sure all new hires are brought up to par after ninety days, not three years. We have to help our brothers and sisters in the parts sector." She explained that union density has fallen from 75 percent to 15 percent in the parts sector. "This is ridiculous. We have to help them get what they deserve, which is wages and benefits equal to our own." Suman doesn't pull any punches.

Edward Mosley, a big man from Local 34 in Atlanta, said, "We are closing. . . . The governor offered GM incentives to keep us, but GM said it's not about money. So this is about us. Wherever we go we're going to be union. We're not going to go down without a fight." I didn't know it then but two days later I would shake Brother Mosley's hand and thank him for his support.

Dean Braid from Local 599 was one of the last speakers of the day. Dean has worked for twenty years at Buick Engineering. He pointed out that *Ward's Automotive* magazine has awarded Buick the best engine in its class for the last five years. J.D. Power & Associates recognized Buick City as the best-quality assembly plant in the world. Nonetheless, GM is closing it and moving production to China.

Dean said the corporation is playing games with people's lives. "We know we cannot trust GM, and jointness doesn't work without trust. I believe we need to follow the lead of the Canadian Autoworkers and create what they call 'a culture of struggle.' I believe we need to disengage from the UAW culture of cooperation that has failed to save jobs."

We adjourned for the day.

The Cooperative Caucus wines, dines, and dances the delegates every night. I imagine it's hard to remember where you came from when you're gazing down at Detroit from the top floor of a swank hotel with a free drink in your hand. Karl Marx said religion was the opium of the masses. I always thought religion was rather hard. I wonder what Marx would have thought of the Cooperative Caucus. Free food, drinks, and a chance for an appointment in Solidarity Heaven beats the hell out of religion for mind-numbingness. I didn't go.

Instead I drifted down to the back room of the Anchor Bar on Fort Street, where New Directions and other dissidents gathered. I liked it. It was humble. It was real. I've always been attracted to people with bad attitudes and passionate convictions. I felt right at home. Robert Bohm from the National Writers Union fought me for the last word. He might have won. It's hard to call the winner in a brawl like that. But either way, I sharpened my wits and went back to my room determined to come out fighting tomorrow.

UAW Bargaining Con, Day Two: Unconventional Truth

Dave Yettaw was one of the first speakers. He said the era of one replacement for every two retirements should end. We need "one for one." Again, he advocated for temp workers who have no voice (though some have been paying dues to the UAW for four years). "None of us would be here today if we'd been temps for thirty years. Part-time America is not going to work." Then he directed our attention to the hundreds of retirees who were gathered in front of Cobo Hall. "I would like to ask the chair to invite them in with their signs and placards so the leadership could see the issues that are critical to them. Thank you."

Yokich fumed like the little engine that could. "If you'd been paying attention, you'd have seen us marching with them this morning."

"I was there," Yettaw replied.

"Sit down, David," Yokich snapped. "I was there," Yettaw repeated.

"You're all done talking. Cut the mic."

"The leadership was out there marching with them because they fought for our union," Yokich was screaming. "We were glad they were here!"

Whenever Yokich gets mad, the mob jumps to their feet and cheers like a World Wide Wrestling audience. They enjoy the expression of belligerence. It gives vent to their pent-up feelings of frustration and rage. It's a knee-jerk reaction instigated by hired clappers, that mercenary army of International appointees planted throughout the arena. But it's thoughtless mob reaction, it doesn't answer the question.

Dick Shoemaker, the UAW's VP of the GM department, took over as chairman of the convention. Shoemaker reminds me of my eighth-grade math teacher, Sister Mary Francis. He has that pinched, pasty look of an old woman who is saving herself for Jesus and torturing children to bide her time until He comes. Can you imagine Shoemaker working on the assembly line? I think every International Rep should work one month out of each year on the door line at Saturn. What do you think of that? Saturn lineworker Tom Hopp hanging doors with Dick Shoemaker?

The next speaker of note was Justin West from Local 2488, the Mitsubishi plant in Normal, Illinois. He began by expressing appreciation for a statement made by our president, Steve Yokich: "If we don't address things honestly, we have a problem." (I knew that line would come back to bite him.)

> Part of the new jobs for UAW workers you spoke of includes "full time supplemental workers" (temps) who do not receive the benefits and rights that even two-tiered workers receive. This is one of the results of the so-called victory at Caterpillar. In reality the only victory was that the union survived.
>
> To those who view the Cat struggle as a victory,* I urge you to take the blinders off and be honest and up front with our membership. I was there when the line in the sand was drawn in Peoria, Illinois. Caterpillar crossed it repeatedly, and society and government allowed them to do

---

* At the Constitutional Convention the year before, Yokich said the UAW had won the Caterpillar struggle: Referring to the strike at Caterpillar, Yokich said, "Don't let anyone tell you we didn't win that." Then he swung a left hook at a shadow and yelled "Goddamnit!" (*Live Bait & Ammo* #3, July 1998).

it. We all, as leaders in the labor movement, need to change that. Go home, brothers and sisters, educate and organize.

John Reichbaum from Local 2400 in Cleveland had the best line of the whole convention. He said, "Strike, strike, strike! If we want what we are talking about here today, we'd better let them know we do not intend to go into these negotiations on our knees and come out on our bellies. We're not going to back up or stand our ground where we're at. We're going to push forward and get everything, including COLA [cost-of-living adjustments] on pensions." Now that was worth standing up and cheering about.

It was a tough act to follow, but I felt prepared. I'd been listening to my coworkers long and hard. I got my chance.

> Yesterday, Brother Yokich said he was surprised by the announcement of the Delphi spinoff. I don't know why. No one on the shop floor was surprised. We've been talking about it since 1995. Indeed, on page 413 of the '96 Agreement with GM, it states that the Human Resource Center was renamed the Center for Human Resources and reconfigured to accommodate a "restructuring within the corporation," namely, "Delphi Automotive Systems."
>
> The Center for Human Resources, the tax-exempt, nonprofit corporation, which administers the Joint Programs and Relocation Allowances, had to be renamed and reconfigured in order to satisfy the legal ramifications of the spinoff with the IRS. We saw the corporate offensive coming from a long way off. What we haven't seen is the counteroffensive of the UAW against the giant modular assembly outsourcing scheme called Delphi.
>
> Ed Northern, Delphi's guru of lean, has visited our plant three times since the announcement of the spinoff and he will be back again after Easter. But we haven't seen or heard anyone from the International contradict the news that it's a done deal. All we've heard is that we can retire under a GM contract if we get out before October 1999. That's not a deal, it's an ultimatum, it's a threat.
>
> Three top-level managers in our plant have retired since the announcement of the spinoff and two quit to work for furniture factories. Our bargaining chairman retired midterm. What does it tell us about the future of Delphi when the people in the know jump ship? We don't want a good deal. We want the damn deal stopped.

If the Delphi spinoff is a done deal, then Visteon is a done deal, Accustar is a done deal, and modular assembly is a done deal because Delphi is the biggest assembler of modular automotive systems in the world.

Stop the Delphi spinoff dead in its tracks or just come out and tell us the truth now. End the silence. Give us the information we need to make the best decisions for ourselves and our families. If it is a done deal, we demand a national pattern contract for all parts plants, no matter what name they go by or how they are reconfigured on paper. We need wage and benefit parity—not prevailing wage, which is nothing more than a code name for wage cut. How can we hope to organize parts plants if all we have to offer is prevailing wage? They've got prevailing wage and it stinks. We want parity with the Big Three for all parts plants. Furthermore, we must demand portable pensions that travel with us wherever we go without losing credit, because we don't know who we will be working for tomorrow, or what name they will go by, or where or how they will dislocate us.

Brothers and Sisters, if you work for one of the Big Three today, beware. Modular assembly will take the skill out of assembly and undermine your bargaining power. The corporation has an agenda to emasculate the union. Stop the modular assembly outsourcing spinoff schemes now.

Shoemaker responded. He said the name change "had nothing to do with the Delphi spinoff." It was simply for "IRS regulations." Eventually, we learned that the stock split was tax exempt as per a special dispensation from the IRS.

There was consensus among delegates to abolish two-tier and the overutilization of temps. When Fred Willbanks from Flint Local 599 addressed this issue, he was true to form.

I stand in opposition to the watered-down, weak language on economic issues. It is immoral and wrong that after ninety days, workers are not made permanent with full recall rights. It is immoral and wrong that not all workers have full medical benefits. It is immoral and wrong that some workers don't get equal pay for equal work. Furthermore, we need portable pensions for the industrial gypsies. We must knock off the spinoffs. Stop modular assembly. It will reduce our standard of living. It will diminish our base of support for future pension and health care benefits. Some people in this union have COLA on pensions, and some don't. We all deserve COLA on pensions.

That night, as I walked through the bar to the meeting room, someone pointed out an assistant to President Yokich seated in a booth strategically situated to observe everyone who entered. I wondered what else he did for a living. I wondered if that was our dues dollars at work or another example of the flexibility of joint funds. I wondered why Yokich needed a spy when we were the most wide-open, up-front, outspoken union members at the convention. The schmuck wasn't there when we left.

Reaching a consensus with a roomful of dissidents is a contradictory proposition of invariable odds, but we all agreed that Delphi encompassed a host of hot-button issues: outsourcing, lean production, restructuring, two-tier, job security, and pensions. We agreed to focus on the spinoff. None of us expected to get called on. We'd have to use every maneuver at our disposal to gain the floor. We agreed whoever gained recognition would raise the issue.

Erwin Baur, an eighty-three-year-old UAW rebel, pulled me aside and graciously took the time to coach me. "Forget your notes," he said. "Speak from your heart. Think on your feet."

UAW Bargaining Con, Day Three: Legal vs. Ethical

First thing in the morning, Malcolm Marts from Local 1976 demanded a point of information. Yokich reluctantly agreed to follow Robert's Rules of Order and recognized the member's right to ask for a point of information. "What's your point, brother?"

Malcolm responded: "The last three days I've received more information from the *Wall Street Journal* than I have from our leadership. I was hoping President Yokich could spend some time explaining the strategies that are in place to save Delphi jobs."

"Well, brother," Yokich responded, "We do have a strategy but I sure as hell ain't going to explain it to the *Wall Street Journal*. I'm going to explain it to the people sitting across the table. You've heard my statements on Delphi. I believe GM should keep a majority of the stock at GM and not completely sell Delphi. I explained that yesterday if you were listening."

The mob applauded but it was clear that Malcolm had jerked the president's chain.

Claudia Perkins from Local 651, Delphi Flint–East, made a speech that sounded all too familiar. "Delphi's approach to workplace organization is called lean, but it's really downsizing. Employees aren't involved in the decision-making process until after management has created a big mess. Then they ask for input. We are the experts. Why is that so hard for management to comprehend? When we attempt to give input, we are blown off by management. Then they try to cram jointness down our throats. We need stronger contractual language to help curtail the way management approaches lean. We are coming up short in the so-called process of jointness. We need to improve job security for our members."

Another base hit. Two on and nobody out. It was going better than I expected. Yokich attempted to skip to the next region when Dean Braid from Local 599 in Flint yelled for a point of information so loud and so long that Yokich could not ignore him.

"Only a point, not a statement," Yokich snarled.

"Most members I talked to said they wanted to knock off the spinoff of Delphi. I want to know, how many such resolutions were submitted?"

"I don't understand," Yokich said. "Most members you spoke to?"

"Yes, most members I spoke to at this convention are against the spinoff," Dean said.

"So are we," Yokich said.

"I understand that, but you said publicly that you would allow up to 49 percent of it to be sold. Isn't that what you said?"

"I said: I told GM they have to keep 51 percent of the stock. That way after the IPO [initial public offering of stock], they are still part of the GM system."

"My point of information is: how many resolutions were submitted to stop the spinoff?"

"I got to tell you something. I don't think we had any. But I thought somebody should take a stand, and I took a stand early."

The bases were loaded. Dean Braid had set up Yokich like a golf ball on a tee.

When Yokich moved to Region 1-D, I waved my sign like a checkered flag at the Indy 500. He called on me. I felt like a pinch hitter going to bat with two out in the bottom of the ninth. I'd seen Yokich slice and dice opponents. The mob reaction was on his side. I had to take the knife away. Then it came to me: *rope-a-dope.*

"President Yokich, sir," I stammered, "I humbly ask you, please, be patient with the passion I feel about the issue of which I am about to speak." I acted jittery. "I feel very strongly about this issue because it affects my livelihood, my future, and the welfare of my family." I hesitated, visibly struggling with the words and emotion. "I feel very strongly about this issue because it affects my union brothers and sisters. For example, my union brother, Tom Bradfield, seated next to me. Tom is an elected delegate, a health and safety rep, a dedicated union member. He has worked for General Motors for twenty-seven years at four different plants. He doesn't know today if he will retire with a GM pension because of the Delphi spinoff. He deserves a GM pension. Thousands more workers are in a similar position."

The crowd was drawn in. Yokich dropped his guard.

"Brother Yokich, I know that a resolution to stop the Delphi spinoff was submitted because I wrote that resolution and my local supported it. I am certain that every Delphi local in the country submitted similar resolutions, because it's in all our best interests."

At this point Yokich interrupted and did a little rope-a-dope of his own. When Yokich dislikes a speaker, he interrupts, he tries to make them lose their train of thought. I waited calmly, gathering my thoughts until he was done interrupting. I needed to win the delegates' support. I had to compel them to buy in at a gut level. I stepped back up to the mic.

"It's important that we stop the spinoff. It's important to all of us. If we allow GM to spin off Delphi, GM Powertrain, you're next. Ford-Visteon, you're next. Accustar, you're next. Independent parts suppliers, do you expect a pay raise if our wages are cut like Delphi intends? You assembly workers, where will your bargaining power be when your numbers are cut in half and you're snapping automobiles together like LEGO blocks?"

A brother seated somewhere nearby said, "Preach, brother, preach." His words hit like a shot of adrenaline straight to my heart. I raised my voice.

"Last summer, after a seven-week strike, the leaders of GM and the UAW agreed to have more high-level talks. They agreed to meet more often. They agreed to communicate openly and to improve the relationship. One week later, GM announced the spinoff. It was a slap in the face. It was an insult. It was a declaration of war. Forty-six thousand UAW-Delphi autoworkers are mad as hell. And the eyes of forty-six thousand Delphi autoworkers are focused on this convention today to see what our response will be. I ask the assembled delegates to rise, rise in solidarity and support for the Delphi autoworkers."

I held my breath. All the delegates stood up and applauded. The Delphi spinoff struck a unifying chord. The only people who didn't stand were the members of the International Executive Board seated on the stage. When the applause receded, I said thank you and walked away.

"I guess you just haven't been listening to the leadership of this union," Yokich said. He was mad.

I started to walk back to the mic. If he was going to talk like that to me, I was going to talk back. I wanted to tell Brother "Cut-the-Mic" that he hadn't been listening to the membership.

"No, no, you're not going back to the mic," Yokich said. "I just want to tell you, I don't know how many damn times you have to say it for people to believe you. If you think you're mad as hell, if you think Delphi is mad, you should have been with me when I got the phone call. Then you would know what mad as hell means, and I sure as hell didn't use the word hell."

The crowd jumped to their feet clapping and yelling, "Stop the spinoff! Give 'em hell!" My grin reached up from the bottom of my feet. What luck. We just got two bangs for the buck. It was the biggest spectacle of the convention. Everyone was focused on the spinoff.

Afterward I thanked Big Brother Mosley from Atlanta for the shot of adrenaline—"Preach, brother, preach." I told him it was just what I needed. We shook hands. "You were telling the truth," he said. Moments before I spoke, Justin West, from the Mitsubishi plant in Normal, Illinois, told me, "I wanted to ask the delegates to stand in support of the Delphi autoworkers, but he wouldn't call on me." It was his idea and it was brilliant. I felt a little apprehensive that Tom Bradfield might be upset with me for making an example of him publicly. He shook my hand. He thanked me. He said, "Everything you said was true, Gregg."

Then Dave Yettaw demanded a point of information.

"When we were in Las Vegas," Dave began.

"What is your point of information?" Yokich interrupted.

"Joint funds."

"Wait a minute, David."

"At the [Constitutional] Convention in Las Vegas, you said bring it to the Collective Bargaining Convention."

"What's your point of information?"

"The joint funds are used to fund many programs throughout our national contract."

"I know what joint funds are used for. I'm not going to allow you to make a statement on a point of information."

"I want to ask that they be reported out in the form of an LM-2 because it's a separate entity of which our union is a part."

"David, it's a separate corporation and not a part of this labor organization and that's why it's not reported out on our LM-2. We've gone over this completely with our lawyers." *When leaders are ethically but not legally obligated, they will take advantage of you for their own selfish ends.* "As a union structure, we are required to report out everything we do in an LM-2. But not as a separate corporation."

"I think it should be reported," Dave said.

"Turn off mic five," Yokich commanded. *Then, they will demean you and disrespect you in order to justify their behavior and suppress their guilt.*

"Thank you," someone in the crowd yelled, "Solidarity!"

"Well, if you don't like the answer," Yokich snapped back, "I'm sorry, it's the truth."

"I don't like the answer, 'Shut off the mic!'"

Yokich refused to debate or consider a legitimate point of view. Unions are required by federal law to list all financial information on a form called an LM-2. These forms are available to all members of the union. While joint funds support many programs negotiated in our national contract, the funds are controlled by a corporation separate from GM and the UAW. GM supplies all the money for this separate corporation, but the method of funding is negotiated in our national contract. Half of the board of directors of this tax-exempt corporation are UAW

VIPs. These people control the programs and the money. About a third of our International staff receives salaries, allotments, and expenses from this separate corporation. In other words, GM funnels money into the hands of UAW reps through the conduit of this separate corporation. I'm sure the lawyers have fixed the deal and sealed approval with a kiss. The question Yettaw raised, and which Yokich refused to answer, was: is it ethical? And if so, why has the UAW adamantly refused to supply UAW members with information about the uses of joint funds and resisted forming any provisions for oversight?

Information about joint funds wasn't the only thing Yokich didn't want delegates to hear. Gene Austin from Local 594 GM Truck and Bus was never given an opportunity to speak, despite the fact that he was seated a mere nine rows from the podium. Gene Austin led a battle against corrupt local union politics that set the standard for integrity and became a blueprint for the victory of union democracy. The International Executive Board refused to recognize Gene. We deserve to hear from leaders like Gene Austin. For that reason, I asked him to contribute to this report:

> I want to speak on the issue of settling all local contracts before the national.
>
> When the national contract is ratified before the locals have agreements, the bargaining position of the local unit is undermined. There have been incidents in the past when the International has settled the national contract before all locals have settled their contracts and as a result, some locals found themselves victimized by local-level management because the International could no longer strike all or any number of the multiplant employers.
>
> It is the duty of the International to give local unions all the support necessary to ensure fair and equitable settlements of their local agreements. Local 594 endured the hardship of an eighty-seven-day strike because the leverage just wasn't there. Even locals that have the power to shut down an entire corporation, as did Locals 651 and 659 last summer, have been held hostage by the unforgiving corporation. The strength of each local union is greatly enhanced by association with the UAW International Union. Each local union depends largely on the International Union's ability to negotiate with major employers or amalgamated groups of employers. It is not only necessary to settle all

local contracts before each national contract is signed, but it is also necessary to consider an entire industrywide work stoppage to exert the power we need to win good contracts for our families.

Unions exist for the purpose of collective activity. The UAW's strength depends upon united action. The greater the unity, the greater the strength. The UAW membership is an organized industrial army. A strike is industrial warfare. The Big Three is our major enemy. No general wants to fight a battle with divided forces. The combined strength of the entire UAW membership in an industry-wide strike is more likely to bring a quick decisive victory than piecemeal actions against individual auto plants. A national, industry-wide strike is more likely to win the hearts and minds of the American people and galvanize public support. Most gains from UAW strikes in recent history have been extremely limited, failing to reflect the organized might of our union. This is because we consistently employ relatively feeble forces in battles with limited objectives.

We have been told that by striking one of the Big Three we can pit one against the other, damaging the struck corporation's sales by threatening it with a permanent loss of its share of the market when customers get acquainted with the products of its competitors. We also have been led to believe that a strike against one of the Big Three is strengthened by the members who stay on the job and continue to pay into the strike fund.

Bitter experience has taught us that those concepts are errors. The Big Three build stockpiles before a strike and do not lose sales. The idea that a large strike fund must be maintained to win a strike supports back-to-work sentiment when strike benefits are exhausted, deliberately withheld, or limited. Some of our strongest unions do not have strike funds! The one-at-a-time strategy causes demoralization. Those who are on strike suffer to create a *pattern* which will benefit members who did not strike. The so-called *pattern*, as we have seen, is itself limited because the strike has been limited. Such weaknesses encourage management and help prolong strikes.

Therefore, I ask that this assembly join with me and demand that the International Union not settle the national contract until all locals are settled, and insist that we abandon the self-defeating, strike-breaking tactics of one-at-a-time struggles and mobilize the membership for an industry-wide strike to achieve our goals at the bargaining table.

Now you know why Steve "Cut-the-Mic" Yokich wouldn't call on Gene Austin.

The Lord of Lean
(April 1999)

Ed Northern, Delphi's leading cheerleader, has been humping the stump from Texas to New York. His road show has all the homely charm and contagious enthusiasm of a tent revival. While the alleged ravages of sinful waste wreak havoc all about the land, Ed holds forth the global anthem of saving grace, "Lean! Lean! Lean!"

An evangelistic fever carbonates his speech. "Lean" is repeated with hypnotic cadence like a Hindu mantra in a backwoods accent that lends the simple four-letter word an unmistakably nasty twist.

It's a weird mix and a heady brew. He promises salvation on the cross of competition and emotes optimism with a moonshiner's grin. His vision of deliverance is more reminiscent of the Hollywood version than the Biblical one. You can almost hear pigs squealing in the background.

Recently, I spoke with a Mexican Delphi worker at a Labor Notes conference in Detroit. She makes less than a dollar an hour. That's not the sad part. The sad part is that Delphi tells her she has to be more competitive. A coyote has more conscience than a Delphi executive.

CEO J. T. Battenberg said that Delphi would be the "listening organization." We got a taste of what he meant when the road show hit Coopersville. Ed Northern and his entourage breezed into the meeting twenty minutes late and spent the next thirty minutes competing to see who could say the magic word—"lean"—most often. Ed won. Then we had four minutes of questions and eight minutes of rhetorical answers, that is, answers that repeat the questions. You don't have to do the math to see that the numbers tell the tale of just who exactly will do the listening.

I figured I'd only have one chance to question the Lord of Lean, so I tried to pack it all into one shot. "Union members are on the front lines of any value-added work, yet we are the last to find out about any changes in organization and process. How do you propose to improve the relationship between management and union when the experts, the people who actually do the value-added work, are ignored; when only managers are permitted to participate in the decision-making process; and the local union leadership is left out of the equation?"

Then I heard something I never thought I'd hear from a management person. Ed Northern said, "I agree with everything you just said. That was a great question." Too bad the answer wasn't great, but that's easy to explain. Delphi has a business plan that Ed can expound upon until all the oxygen in the room is gone. But when it comes to the union, the agenda is hidden in a foil of smiles, hype, and phony camaraderie. Get real.

Since 1992, Delphi has reduced its UAW workforce by 42 percent, and Merrill Lynch expects that trend to continue. Since the announcement of the spinoff, those numbers are increasing daily. That's the real agenda.

If you want to predict the future, you study history. In light of the wisdom gained thereby, you examine the present. The seeds of the future are evident in the here and now. Delphi plans to grow the business by gutting the union. Another union member piped up, "The last time you were here, you said, 'I don't close plants. I build plants.' Where and how soon are you going to build plants in the US?"

Northern started backpedaling fast on that one. He hurriedly explained that because of the successful implementation of lean manufacturing, we now have a lot of vacant floor space. He pledged to fill that floor space before he laid any concrete. He took a deep breath, blinked twice, then claimed he was going to "triple the business." He said that Delphi was going to be "adding Social Security numbers this year."

"You mean workers?" someone asked.

"Yes, workers," Ed said.

"American workers?"

"Yes, American workers."

"You mean hourly workers?"

"Yes, hourly workers."

"UAW workers?"

"Yes, UAW workers. That's hard to believe, isn't it?"

Yes Ed, it certainly is hard to believe.

When union members in Rochester, New York asked him how he felt about the hundreds of workers retiring and transferring out of Delphi, he replied that he wanted them to go because they were "not the kind of workers that Delphi needs." He wants workers "who use one hand to do their job and the other hand to help their coworker." When asked if they were going to replace vacating workers he said, "No, it's called cost savings and lean manufacturing."

Yes, Ed, it is hard to believe a person who continually changes his story.

While Northern spewed his unsubstantiated pie-in-the-sky predictions of unlimited expansion in the good old USA, Donald Runkle, president of Delphi, was busy hosting the official dedication of Delphi's newest and largest technical center located in the heart of Juarez, Mexico. Delphi employs about two hundred thousand people worldwide. More than 40 percent of those employees are in Mexico. Just the facts, Ed.

Northern's pompous prediction to "triple the business" is verbal snake oil. Since the announcement of the spinoff, three of our top-level managers in Coopersville have retired, and two more went to work for furniture factories. How are we supposed to believe our future is hopeful when those in the know jump ship? If he couldn't convince them to stay aboard, what can he expect of us? We know the score. When his pipe dreams don't come true, workers will take the hit. He'll feel no guilt for letting the axe fall on thousands of working families.

In this glorified era of casino capitalism, growth is engendered by hype and hyperbole; the counterfeit standard of the bottom line is used to justify a reckless, unconscionable war against workers worldwide. Success is measured in numbers with no regard for the damage to overworked families and their communities plundered for tax breaks and then stranded with abandoned lots of industrial wreckage and toxic waste. *Globalization* is just a four-bit word for sweatshop; "lean" stands for Lay off Every American Now.

Lied To, Cheated, and Betrayed
(March 2000)

Union members at Delphi have been lied to, cheated, and betrayed. All our years of credited service with GM have been turned over to Delphi, a company that didn't even exist before 1999. This information wasn't mentioned in the contract's *Highlights*.

At the contract information meeting, we were assured that our years of credited service at GM were secure, and that if we transferred back to GM within the next four years we would retire with a GM pension. Don't worry about it, we were told.

Now we're informed that effective May 28,1999, all credited service becomes Delphi. We never dreamed this was legal. We were lied to, cheated, and betrayed. Does anyone believe that Yokich and Shoemaker didn't know this deal was in the cards long before negotiations began?

Yokich opened the Bargaining Convention by saying "If we don't address things that face us honestly and up front, we have a real problem." You said it, President Doublespeak. When the leadership of our own union sets out to deceive union members and protect the corporation, we certainly do have a real problem. It spells company union. It smells of corruption. It tells a tale of sellout. It's riddled with lies, prevarication, and complicity.

At the Bargaining Convention Yokich reiterated: "I told GM they have to keep 51 percent of the stock. That way after the IPO they are still part of the GM system." We made him repeat it over and over. He said, "You've heard my statements on Delphi. I believe GM should keep a majority of the stock at GM, and not completely sell Delphi." He said if they didn't, "there'd be hell to pay." Now we, the union members, are paying.

On the last day of the Bargaining Convention, when I brought up the threat to our pensions once again, and the assembled delegates stood up and applauded in solidarity, he said, "If you think you're mad as hell, if you think Delphi is mad, you should have been with me when I got the phone call. Then you would know what mad as hell means, and I sure as hell didn't use the word hell." I'll bet he didn't. He probably said, "Golly, gee whiz, what can I do to *help*, sir?"

At the Bargaining Convention, I pointed out that the International had known about the intention to spin off Delphi since 1995 and had maneuvered to protect joint funding. GM-Delphi pumps millions of dollars into the pockets of UAW officials in the form of padded expense accounts and unreported salaries under the cover of joint funds.

Yokich and Shoemaker protected the cash cow, but failed to protect union members' pensions from a corporate jettison. I confronted Shoemaker in front of the assembled delegates: "Tell us the truth now. End the silence. Give us the information we need to make the best decisions for ourselves and our families." Instead he chose to protect the interests of the corporation and the "Rollover Caucus."

Workers who had thirty years of GM seniority now have zero years of GM pension credits. I know "GM gypsies" who have transferred nine times, hopscotching from plant to plant across the country in a desperate attempt to maintain unbroken seniority and guarantee their pensions who now have no GM seniority at all.

We were never told the truth: because Yokich and Shoemaker knew we would have voted the contract down, because there would have been a stampede at the National Placement Center, because it was not in the best interest of the corporation for so many workers to transfer or to threaten a strike.

Meanwhile Frank Joyce, the PR man at Sold-our-dignity House, will be promoting Yokich's image as a luminary in preparation for the ordination of the Stephen P. Yokich Golf Course at Black Lake. This is the president who rolled over on 441 unfair labor practice charges, abandoned fifty discharged union members, forgave back dues to scabs at Caterpillar, and then called the debacle a victory. The president who cut off strike benefits for locked-out workers in Henderson, Kentucky, and literally busted their union; the president who treats union members at Saturn like Beck resisters;* the president who rolled over on the wholesale out-

---

* A reference to the 1988 US Supreme Court's *Communications Workers v. Beck* decision, which allows workers to withhold the portion of union dues beyond what is necessary for employee representation.

sourcing of Delphi and Visteon; the president who cut the mic rather than listen to elected convention delegates will be lauded as a hero in the pusillanimous pages of *Solidarity* magazine.

What does "pusillanimous" mean? Just let it roll off your tongue. It tastes just like it means.

Brother Yokich, while lap dogs and lackeys pamper your ego, know for certain, other union members use your name in quite another context: one more commonly associated with dogs, scoundrels, and punks.

This is just the beginning of revelations. Who knows what else we haven't been told? At a meeting in Coopersville, I posed a question to J. T. Battenberg, CEO of Delphi: "Since 1992, you have reduced the UAW represented workforce at Delphi by over 40 percent. Do you expect that trend to continue?" He paused, thoughtful, bemused, then said, "I don't know."

The honeymoon is over, folks. The Batt's got our balls in a paper sack. No more union-friendly overtures, no more placating people's fears with promises.

Battenberg said, "We had to reduce labor-intensive industries." Then the Batt added, "We're getting beat by the UAW because they've organized shops on a second-tier wage so we can't compete." What's this, I thought, a parity parody?

Only 20 percent of Delphi manufacturing facilities are in the United States. They are not labor-intensive industries, and not all of them are UAW. The UAW is a small player on the global stage, and our influence is waning fast.

Battenberg assured us the pension plan was fully funded, but that belies the point. Contracts aren't renewed, they're renegotiated, and everything's on the table. As the UAW portion of Delphi shrinks, so does our bargaining power.

As a note of encouragement Battenberg added, "It's hard to differentiate who's who in the (Delphi-UAW) leadership, and that," he said with a smile, "is a very good sign." By that he must mean they all have brown noses and baggy knees.

Brothers and sisters, the Battman is so cool. You can see it in his composure, his slow thought, his gray deadpan eyes, his perfect haircut, and his introspective grin. He's sitting on top of the world. Nobody is going to pop his bubble. He actually told us to "think outside the box." I pondered those words of wisdom all day, and when my foreman asked me why I didn't make rate, I looked him dead in the eye and said, "Think outside the box," and walked away.

I felt smug as a rich man's son. Let's think outside the box of corporate containment and union cooperation. We know we can't trust the Rollover Caucus to take care of us. So let's get the hell out of the box they've locked us in. Let's stop accepting the competitive corporate agenda and reject partnership.

Strike Back
(January 2001)

When times get tough, the only class that is protected is the bossing class. Workers bear the burden of every slump in the economy while the chumps in ties shift their capital to more lucrative enterprises. If all else fails, they'll pack us off to war and profit hand over fist on every pound of patriotic flesh. Unemployed workers are stockpiled like sandbags to dam the rising tide of inflation. Meanwhile, cuts in social programs provide negative incentives for *lazy mothers* to get off their asses and find gainful employment in temp agencies where social commitment has no more currency than a peso in Decatur. As the old mine worker John L. Lewis once said, "Labor and management may be partners in theory, but they are enemies in fact."

The fact is workers take the hit and the bossing class takes a shit on our dignity. Teamwork, partnership, and "people are our most valuable asset" are all crap. Battenberg doesn't blink an eye when he severs the economic ties of thousands of families. No CEO in the nation will tighten his own belt. He'll tighten the harness on our necks instead. It's a recession, they say. Let's open the contract and make concessions. Work harder, faster, longer, leaner. For all the high-tech machinery and CNC,* produc-

---

* Computerized numerical control.

tivity increases still rely on whipping the horses in assembly and sweating the donkeys of supply. Forget the contract. Can the time study. Stick the gentleman's agreement up your competitive behind and press your nose to the grindstone. You're in for the Big Squeeze, baby.

When the economy slows down, workers need to keep pace with demand. It's a natural law of economics. The common man's sense of balance and equality. A working stiff's morality. When our brothers and sisters are laid off we should refuse as much overtime as possible. No more favors. No more rush jobs. Workers rule when they work to rule. Never forget how many times you were laid off, sold off, cut off, spun off. Never forget how many times you had to relocate your family. Never forget all the setbacks you endured at the hands of the bossing class. Strike back.

Where is it written the owners must never sacrifice? Where does it say only the rich may pursue happiness? Why do we let the dumb-ass boss decide how to divvy the workload and slice the pie? Why isn't full employment a workable reality? Who says democracy doesn't belong in the workplace? Why must the poor, the elderly, the disadvantaged pay for the excesses of the wealthy? Whoever calls this system Christian blasphemes. Whoever calls our country free and our government fair is blind to economic inequality and the barriers to social justice that courts call "injunctions." Workers are outlaws in America. It's no damn wonder they don't want us to own guns.

Strike back.
Strike back because your brothers and sisters are laid off.
Strike back because you hate the bastards.
Strike back to redeem your dignity.
Strike back for full employment.
Strike back to abolish inequality.
Strike back because your job is a bore and your boss is an ass.
Strike back for freedom.
Strike back to restore the balance of power.
Strike back because you are human and care about life.
Strike back to break the corporate chokehold.
Strike back to get the leeches off our backs.

Strike back for more democracy.

Strike back because they never listen to you.

Strike back to control the means of production.

Strike back because Medicare doesn't cover prescriptions for your mother.

Strike back because politicians retire in splendor.

Strike back because injunctions are only against unions and never against management.

Strike back because judges are the lackeys of industry.

Strike back because no one believes in the system.

Strike back to show we can strike back.

Strike back.

Fry the Corpos in Their Own Grease
(September 2001)

Concessions forced on Delphi workers were always destined for application throughout the auto sector. This Ammo *was written for Ford workers, but the principles are universally relevant.*

When Ford CEO Jac Nasser can't bring home a million bucks a day, he feels the pinch and when Jac feels the pinch you know who pays the price. But who can begrudge the Prince? He works hard. Although what he calls work most of us would call golf, or lunch, or lounging, or shooting the breeze, or trimming our fingernails and picking our teeth.

Ford Production System (FPS), the Blue Oval version of whipping the horses, seeks cost savings at the expense of workers' health, safety, and well-being. Nasser would deny the allegation. He just wants the horses in assembly to work up a lather so he can collect his daily sweepstakes. A million dollars a day's worth of lather is a lot of sweat, but we have to be competitive.

We agree. We want to be competitive, and in a spirit of competitiveness we propose that Ford executives get paid the same as their German and Japanese counterparts. We could thereby save hundreds of millions in one fell swoop. Fair is fair. Also, we will gladly agree to the Japanese team paradigm. We will wear uniforms, do jumping jacks together every morning, and sing the company song in smiling unison, if only our plant managers will emulate their Japanese counterparts and commit suicide when they fail. Let's go all the way.

Let's rise to the German standard and cut the work week to thirty-two hours with no loss of pay. Let's do like the Japanese and build a car you don't have to Fix Or Repair Daily.

Here's another competitive suggestion. How about we build trucks that don't roll over, ignition switches that don't burst into flame, or gas tanks that don't explode? Now wouldn't that be competitive? Imagine how competitive it would be to build the safest automobile as opposed to the cheapest stunt man vehicle.

How about we build a car that a person who cares about the environment could drive with pride? Do you think there might be a few million people in the world who fit that description? How competitive would that be?

Autoworkers are already bare-bones lean. Let's cut the real fat. Economist David Gordon, in his book *Fat and Mean*, writes: "In the 1980s, by common measures, the proportion of managerial and administrative employment was more than three times as high in the United States as in Germany and Japan." Despite all the lip-sync about downsizing, Gordon points out that the proportion of managers and supervisors in private nonfarm employment has grown during the 1990s, not shrunk. We have a higher percentage of supervisors than Germany, Japan, and Sweden combined. Why so many managers? 'Cause when you don't shake a carrot, you have to shake a lot of stick.

What sort of stick keeps employees motivated? The "bust unions" stick; the "threaten job security" stick; the "outsource" stick; the "hire temp and part-time workers" stick; the "speedup-multitask-just-in-time-rush-job" stick; the "continuous disapproval of your effort," "never quite good enough" stick. FPS, in a nutshell, is fear. There's no theory behind this whip-the-horses style management. Bereft of any credible thought process, their only recourse is to bulk up with a truckload of managerial personnel to police a workforce with no more morale than prisoners of war. It's a lowbrow, low-road, old-fashioned sweatshop dance step—about as smart as a pig in a wig.

Twenty percent of the purchase price of every product made in the United States goes to supervisors and monitors, not including secretaries, assistants, and featherbedders. In other words, when you buy a twenty-thousand-dollar vehicle, four thousand dollars goes to pay for the burden of supervisors whose sweat-less efforts add no value to the product. The Corpos protect their burdensome midriff bulge as if it were a precious pregnancy. Instead of cutting the fat to extract more profit, employers squeeze the lean workforce for another drop of sweat. They strangle the goose to pay for a boost in fast profits and executive bonuses. Next year they will have to find another sacrificial lamb. Today it's your plant, next year it's mine. The Big Three grind one supplier after another into the ground. What's good for management is death for workers. The Corpos whipsaw union members to the breaking point and then toss the injured onto the scrapheap like discards from a chop shop.

The Corpos compare our wages with workers in Third World nations, shrug, and say, "You can't compete. What can we do?" But the bulk of our trade imbalance is with Japan and Western Europe. As Gordon reports in *Fat and Mean*, "Apparently, economies where workers earn higher wages can flatten us in international competition at least as effectively as those with lower waged workers." We are getting our butt kicked in every corner of the globe because we go into the ring with a three-hundred-pound managerial gorilla on our back.

UAW proponents of competitive cooperation schemes are invariably non-value-added slackers: reps, office rats, FPS hacks, fops with clipboards and twenty-dollar haircuts. The type of people who believe we can only save jobs by eliminating jobs are the type of people who believe the planet is flat. Evidence means absolutely nothing to them. It's empirical fact that since the inception of competitive cooperation we have lost over seven hundred and fifty thousand UAW members. But flat-earth thinkers espouse that if we could just cut off another one hundred thousand, our jobs would be secure.

At the rate the UAW is losing autoworkers, the only UAW members left in another decade will be nodding and smiling in unison at the Stephen P. Yokich Solidarity House; manicuring the links at the Stephen P. Yokich Memorial Golf Course; bellhopping at the Stephen P. Yokich

Palm Springs Resort; handling baggage at the Stephen P. Yokich Airline; and hawking ads for the Stephen P. Yokich Radio Network. The only UAW members who support FPS and other such versions of sweat are those who benefit from it—appointees and reps who are paid for twelve to sixteen hours a day, seven days a week, even when they are on vacation.

Okay. We got it. There is too much fat. So let's pay Bargaining Committee members for hours they actually work rather than hours they roll over in bed. Let's put all the FPS appointees back on the line doing jobs that will not only add value but prevent repetitive trauma injuries and improve first-time quality. Wouldn't that be competitive? Imagine an assembly line that produced first-time quality, eliminated the lemon lot, and didn't injure workers. Let's put executive salaries in line with their German and Japanese counterparts and raise hourly salaries to the German and Japanese competitive standard. Fry the Corpos in their own grease.

The Fascist Production System encourages us to attack fellow union members, double workloads, snitch, brownnose, and exile dissenters. There's only so much room at the top, they say, but the bottom is starting to quake.

You Already Know the Answer
(April 2002)

The UAW gives members a harsh lesson at the Accuride wheel manufacturer, and sets an example for all parts workers.

In February 1998, Billy Robinson, the president of Local 2036 in Henderson, Kentucky, called Ron Gettelfinger for advice. At that time, Gettelfinger was the UAW Region 3 director. Billy explained that negotiations at Accuride were stalled. Gettelfinger said, "Take 'em out."

Forty days later, members of Local 2036 voted to reject the contract for a second time, but also to return to work unconditionally. In response, Accuride locked them out. It was apparent that Accuride was not interested in bargaining. Accuride intended to bust the union.

In June 1998, Gettelfinger ascended to UAW International vice president in charge of Ford. From that lofty perch he began to display all the *social movement* of a chicken crossing the road. First, he supported the strike and made a commitment to stand behind the workers "for as long as it takes." Then, he concurred with the UAW International Executive Board to cut off strike benefits. Then, he agreed to put the local under administratorship.* Then, at the hearing, he pretended not to know anything about Local 2036 or Accuride. (Well, maybe he wasn't pretending.) Then, he agreed to restore strike benefits at twice the normal rate. Then, he agreed to cut benefits for a second time. Then, he agreed to pull the local union charter if they didn't ratify [a concessionary contract]. On March 28, 2002, the UAW International sent a letter to Accuride stating, "The International Union and its Local 2036 hereby disclaim interest in representing hourly employees at Accuride's Henderson, Kentucky facility." Nobody from the International bothered telling the locked-out UAW members of Local 2036 anything, not even so much as "good riddance." Looking back, one has to wonder just what the Fickle Finger meant when he said, "Take 'em out."

In the United States, there are more jobs in the Independent Parts Supply (IPS) sector today than there were in 1979 when membership in the UAW peaked at one and a half million. Profits, as well as jobs, are up in IPS. But wages are down. The problem is de-unionization. And the trend is rolling like a runaway Freightliner.

The dismemberment of the unionized parts sector has enabled the Big Three to drive costs down and profits up. It appears that the survival of an elite corps of highly paid laborers in assembly plants has been secured at the expense of IPS workers. The demise of Local 2036, when seen through the wide-angle lens of historical perspective, is significant to autoworkers everywhere. IPS locals are sacrificed to spare, or postpone, the showdown at the Big Three Cartel.

Accuride is not a small-job shop. Accuride supplies steel truck wheels for GM, Ford, Navistar, Freightliner, Mack, Peterbilt, Volvo—all of them "partners," as they say, with the "new UAW." As Accuride proceeded to

---

* The UAW term for a takeover of a local union.

bust the union, the Rollover Caucus covered their butts with a thong, exerting only the flimsiest of efforts to fulfill the bare minimum of their duty to represent. Local 2036 is not an isolated case.

The Big Three haven't completed their divestment of parts suppliers, but the pattern is clear. Modular assembly is not simply about economy or efficiency, it's about control. Modular assembly divides and isolates unions, whipsaws locals in a tailspinning dive to the bottom of the competitive pile, and backhands the office rats who call themselves International Reps into mild-mannered house pets.

The UAW treats these battles, such as Accuride or the 1998 strikes at [GM's Flint] Metal Fab and Delphi Flint East, as isolated local strikes. The International has failed to develop a unified campaign to combat directly these threats to solidarity, these cracks in the foundation of our united front. While the Rollover Caucus seeks neutrality agreements and partnerships with management, multinationals are picking us off, one at a time.

The office rats at Solidarity House are too far detached from the shop floor to mobilize a broad-ranging solidarity campaign that would threaten the balance of power and send a clear message to union members, community organizers, social activists, politicians, and employers: No Justice = No Production = No Profit.

Solidarity is not negotiable. All unions need to unite behind a single banner and put CEOs on notice that every local dispute against an anti-union company will quickly ignite into a national conflagration: no exceptions, no excuses, no concessions.

The office rats have forgotten that civil disobedience, not meek compliance, built the labor movement. The office rats form partnerships with private corporations at the expense of union members and unorganized workers at Independent Parts Suppliers.

The *New York Times* reported that auto analysts have said: "Mr. Gettelfinger will face pressure to ease contract terms at Delphi Automotive Systems and Visteon, the largest United States parts makers, to keep jobs in the country." The new president "is going to have to do some things that are very unpopular." UAW officials "are going to have to address the question of whether they can sustain the same level of pay and benefits in parts plants."

Ron Gettelfinger, the next president of the UAW, responded with an announcement from Henderson, Kentucky, disclaiming any "interest in representing hourly employees at Accuride."

It's open season on IPS workers. No license required. No restrictions. No limit.

The UAW International has shown a pattern of rolling over at IPS. Will they seek Big Three pattern agreements for Delphi, Visteon, American Axle, Lear, and other IPS plants? Or will they extend the pattern of low wages and de-unionization in IPS that protects autoworkers in the Big Three and postpones the inevitable showdown?

In 1998, GM threatened the UAW with a lawsuit over the strikes at Metal Fab and Delphi in Flint. The dispute was settled in a backroom deal and the lawsuit was dropped. After seven long weeks, the locals gained nothing, not one job. The following week, Delphi was spun off from GM. The following year, Visteon was spun off from Ford. Accuride is a smoking gun.

Why did Gettelfinger roll over?

It's a rhetorical question, just like, Why did the chicken cross the road?

You already know the answer.

33rd UAW Constitutional Convention: Until the Outhouse Blooms Roses

(June 2002)

After reading *Live Bait & Ammo*, a union brother from England wrote to me: *"What, exactly, is a porkchopper? I think we have some of them over here, too."*

The meaning is simple enough to decipher, but the origin of any slang is difficult to pinpoint. I believe the term originated with lumberjacks who survived on grits and gruel and mule droppings while their union agent dined on pork chops. I am sure there are porkchoppers wherever there are workers to *represent*. To paraphrase Tom Paine, a union is a blessing, but a union bureaucracy, even in its best state, is but a necessary evil.

Yokich kicked off the convention with a State of the Union speech. I have my differences with Brother Steve, but I get a kick out of the way he talks. He gives a speech like a pit bull on a short leash. A lot of us had high hopes when he took office that he would walk the talk. But here we are, seven years later, diminished in numbers, expectations, and hope.

Overall membership in the manufacturing sector of the UAW is down. The official President's Report cited "18,000 [new members] in the all-important auto parts industry," but the question that remains unanswered is: how many of those jobs were originally outsourced from higher-paying Big Three plants and then reorganized at lower wages?

He described examples in which Ford exerted pressure on suppliers to be neutral in organizing drives. If a union goes hat in hand to a corporation for help in organizing, what's the payoff? No resistance to outsourcing? New members organized at lower wages?

Yokich talked about the UAW's record of progressive social action. What social movement would be against one member, one vote? He bragged of how the UAW denounced oil drilling in Alaska, but didn't mention the UAW's resistance to fuel efficiency standards that would protect the environment.

Yokich said, "Those bastards in Congress deserve my friend Warren Davis." Well, somebody deserves the bastard, but more on that later. He said we did something "behind the scenes" to help free imprisoned dissidents in Indonesia. He didn't mention that he also worked behind the scenes to repress dissent in the UAW.

Then he remonstrated, "Yet you are going to have members in your plant or work site who speak out against you, if you speak out. Damn, we don't need those kind of members. We don't need them. We need to talk for all of society, not just a small portion of it. We need to be a real union. Talk for brothers and sisters who need our help."

If we don't need members "who speak out against you if you speak out," we could eliminate the entire Rollover Caucus. If we "need to be a real union," we could start by assisting locked-out "brothers and sisters who need our help" at Local 2036 in Henderson, Kentucky.

Yokich said, "Every generation has an obligation. Your obligation is to build a better union."

Amen, brother.

The first resolution opened for debate was organizing. I was one of the first to speak.

If you stood on the roof of Solidarity House and looked out across the city of Detroit, you would see that UAW headquarters is surrounded by nonunion Independent Parts Suppliers. The Big Three have talked partnership while aggressively divesting themselves of parts suppliers in order to whipsaw locals and undermine the UAW's bargaining leverage. In 1999, GM spun off Delphi. Ford followed with Visteon. Do members at Powertrain and stamping plants feel protected? The pattern is clear: You're next. Modular assembly is the organizing challenge of the twenty-first century. We can't put our heads in the sand and say "I don't want to hear that word." [Yokich had instructed company and union officials to stop using the word *modular*.] Modular assembly won't go away and the divestment of parts suppliers, the outsourcing and subcontracting won't go away. We must confront the challenge head-on.

There are more autoworkers in IPS today than there were in 1978, but 80 percent are unorganized. Why have we failed? We need to take an honest look at ourselves and stop making excuses. Was it easier to organize in the thirties? Was it easy when Walter Reuther got his head busted open at the Battle of the Overpass? Was it easy when he took a double-barrel shotgun blast in the back? Was it easy when Victor Reuther was shot in the face and blinded in one eye? Was it easy to organize the occupation of a GM plant in Flint? Was it easy for John L. Lewis to tell the governor of Michigan that if he sent in the National Guard to oust sit-down strikers, "the militia will have the pleasure of shooting me, too"? It has never been easy. It has never been fair. The bosses have never been nice. We can talk partnership until the outhouse blooms roses, but it won't change the stink of the bastards in charge of our livelihoods. [applause]

Samuel Gompers once said that unions need to provide "a practical solution to an urgent need." What do IPS workers need urgently? Fair pay, comprehensive health care, secure pensions, job security. If we want to organize, we must strive to meet those needs. The 33rd Constitutional Convention should set a goal to establish a national pattern contract for IPS.

If we allow the bosses to divide us, isolate us, and treat each local unit as a separate entity, they will continue to chew us up and spit us out. We can't confront a multinational corporation or a supplier to a multinational corporation with small, isolated local strikes.

We need a national pattern agreement and an industrywide strike about basic issues like wages, health care, and pension security that will strike a nerve in a broad cross section of the working class and galvanize public support. An industrywide strike has the potential to place the UAW at the forefront of a social movement to put the health and well-being of the working class ahead of the bossing class.

To that end I propose that we provide a practical solution to an urgent need by establishing a national pattern contract with a national benefits fund pooled industrywide and administered by a joint union and industry committee to cover pensions, health care, and sub-pay* for all of IPS.

Small suppliers like Mexican Industries in Detroit lack the capital accumulation to provide adequate benefits like those enjoyed by workers in the Big Three. A national benefits fund would enable small IPS plants to afford better benefits at reduced premiums and therefore make them more competitive. Furthermore, *pension credits must be portable* and cover all UAW members in separate IPS units under the National Pattern Agreement, thereby ensuring security in a volatile industry. Furthermore, UAW members in IPS should have *preferential hiring and transfer rights* to other companies represented by the UAW, thus meeting the needs of IPS workers for job security and providing a practical incentive to join the UAW...

Yokich cut me off.

"Brother, conclude, your time is up."

"Thirty seconds."

"Nope. Your time is up. Conclude."

"I need ..."

"I know you. You know, I read your e-mails pretty regular. I know you very well. Would you finish your speech? But I'm going to give you about thirty seconds. Conclude quickly."

"Imagine ..."

---

* Supplemental unemployment benefits, paid by the Detroit automakers during plant shutdowns.

"You're done, brother. Shut off the mic. Let me just say one thing, I'm from the IPS. My local is one of the largest IPS locals of a hundred plants; of two hundred it's probably the biggest. We've been fighting this fight for day and night and I can tell you sitting right here why it hurts to see what they've been doing and how they still . . ." His words trailed off into an unintelligible slur. Whatever he said, I felt it was an honor to be on his blacklist.

Yokich didn't counter with one new idea. The Rollover Caucus strategy is to ask their corporate partners to pressure suppliers to whom they have outsourced our jobs to be neutral during organizing drives.

A short time later, Craig Nofnagel, the president of Local 22, got up and said we shouldn't "criticize" the administration, and kizz-azz kizz-azz kizz-azz . . .

If you lobotomize critical intelligence from a social animal, all you have left is an animal whose only conviction is a passionate intensity to follow the herd. A convention without critical opposition would be as reassuring as church. We wouldn't have to think for ourselves. All we would have to do is believe. Trouble for me was, the guy in the pulpit was a sottish, stupid, brutish man with a pug's command of the English language. He spit out words as if they tasted foul.

I swear allegiance to my independence and to the integrity for which it stands, one person, underdog, with liberty, justice, and truth for all.

33rd UAW Con Con, Day Two: Crisis in UAW Solidarity

The second day of the convention opened as usual. We sang songs to the flags of two nations and one occupied territory: Canada, the United States, and Puerto Rico. Then we prayed. Then we heard a bunch of speeches. Then we were read to. A lot of people put their heads down during the readings, an old habit retained from kindergarten. I'm not a gambler but I could hear the coin swallowers calling "ca-ching, ca-ching, ca-ching," an alluring tune for the misbegotten.

The official convention news bulletin declared, "Unionists Right at Home in Vegas." After compiling the rising fortunes of America's most fabulous town, the *UAW News* proposed, "It's good to know that a good chunk of the money UAW members spend in Las Vegas will find its way into the pockets of other hardworking union members."

It's little wonder that Vegas is the fastest-growing union town in America. In a society where industry is irrelevant, workers are dispensable, futures are commodities, options are sold, and the dollar is based on the roulette standard rather than gold, it makes perfect sense that Vegas, a giant mosh pit of low-paying service jobs, would offer deindustrialized workers the illusion that we still have a chance. Win or lose, in Las Vegas we are all players in the sweeping stakes of casino capitalism. Of course, the largest chunk of our money went into the pockets of corpulent thieves.

We proceeded to pass every resolution the Rollover Caucus chose to present. The most surprising was a resolution to transfer seventy-five million dollars from our strike fund to the administration. The Rollover Caucus claimed this proposal was "in keeping with the UAW's tradition of sound financial planning and practices."

The Rollover Caucus is notorious for losing money on bad investments in radio stations, airlines, golf courses, and other nonunion endeavors of questionable merit.

This resolution raised a lot of sticky issues. Did the porkchoppers foresee an impending disaster in the near future? One that might interrupt the steady flow of perks? If there was a protracted strike, shouldn't the families of strikers come first? If there was extra money available in the strike fund, what about other uses like creating a special fund for destitute retirees who lost their pensions because of bankruptcies, or who never had a pension? What about the locked-out members of Local 2036 who had their strike benefits cut off?

There were twenty resolutions submitted by local unions concerning strike funds. I expected a serious debate. Apparently, the porkchoppers did too. They were prepared. Lackeys rolled dollies into the aisles. Whatever the dollies contained was concealed by tarps.

The first delegate rose in support of the resolution. The second delegate called the question, that is, moved to end debate. Yokich didn't object. Hands up, hands down. The band (yes, there was a live band!) kazooed "Happy Days Are Here Again." The dollies were uncovered and picket signs were distributed to delegates who proceeded to form a giant conga line and do a hokey-pokey all around the hall. The signs bore slogans like: "IPS Simply the Best"; "Skilled Work Deserves Skilled Wages"; "UAW Parts Suppliers Deserve Job Security."

I was dumbstruck. We gave them seventy-five million dollars, and we didn't even talk about it. I don't have a very highly developed herd instinct. I sat alone in my chair and watched the lemmings race for the cliff. It's so much fun to lose money in Vegas; that's the magic; that's why it's a great union town.

After the band exhausted "Happy Days," they played "Dixie," and then, of all damn things, "Roll Out the Barrel."

It was hard to calm down after that. The lemmings were breathless, but the show must go on. We were the highest tribunal in the UAW. We had important tribuning to do. After more speeches by politicians who appeared to enjoy licking Yokich's boots and more soporific readings by the Committee for Conventional Conformity, we began debate on the "Crisis in Manufacturing." After my speech on the first day I had a firefly's chance in hell of being called on, but a brother from the writers' union, Lee Sustar, picked up the insurgent banner. He rose in opposition to the resolution:

> I rise in opposition to this motion, not because I disagree with anything that's in it, or with anything that was said by my brothers and sisters who have spoken. I rise to speak against because it doesn't go far enough. The resolution before us takes up the issue of corporate terrorism. I have had the pleasure of meeting some of the best fighters against corporate terrorism that the UAW has seen in recent years. I am speaking about the brothers and sisters of Local 2036 in Henderson, Kentucky, who were locked out by Accuride Corporation four years ago after offering to return to work from a strike authorized by then–Region 3 director Ron Gettelfinger. The corporate terrorism these workers have endured can't be overstated. Marriages have been broken, members have committed suicide, many are dying because of illnesses they contracted working in this dirty and dangerous plant.
>
> These workers are standing up to a corporation which is a key supplier of truck wheels to two of the most profitable plants in the Big Three—the Janesville, Wisconsin, GM plant, and the Louisville, Ken-

tucky, Ford truck plant. This strategic parts supplier local came into existence through a strike eighteen years ago. They didn't inherit their UAW jobs. They went out and organized and fought to get them. I'm sorry to report to this convention, for those who do not know, that in January of this year the members of Local 2036 were cut off for the second time from all strike benefits. This had immediate repercussions in terms of people's medical costs, including one brother who had to go in for major heart surgery just days afterwards. At the same time, their charter was removed by the International. The members were informed by a letter sent to management, not to them. If we are going to organize the parts industry, if we are going to defend the jobs that exist in the parts industry, we have to stand with those who fight for the UAW in the parts industry. That means, I argue, restoring the strike benefits and the charter of Local 2036 in Henderson, Kentucky. I argue, therefore, that this motion, as strong as it is, should be tabled until such time we can have full discussion and a report from the International Executive Board on the decision to remove the benefits and charter of Local 2036 and give us the opportunity to take that position before the convention.

Elizabeth Bunn had been chairing this section of the convention but at this point Yokich pushed her aside. He said: "Well, brother, I can see where your heart is, and ours is, as well. We also have to make decisions as to if you can win or lose. Somewhere along the line, after fourteen million dollars in strike funds for 140 people on strike down to fourteen people." (Yokich seemed stuck on the number fourteen, but these numbers have no relevance to Local 2036, where more than four hundred members went on strike. They maintained a picket for four years even after the International cut off strike benefits. The president of Local 2036, Bill Priest, told a news reporter from *The Gleaner* that about one hundred were still depending on the strike fund for medical insurance when Yokich pulled the charter. Was he thinking about the fourteen million dollars he lost on Pro Air?)

Yokich went on, "Somewhere along the line we had the Big Three UAW VPs go to the corporations that they represent. We have put all the pressure that we could humanly possibly put. We don't like losing, but once in a while you do lose a game, once in a while, and there's a group in this union that has taken that and run it against every damn thing we do good in this union. And I will not sit here and let people talk about this union in the way you do."

In strict adherence to the *Revised Rules of Robert's Disorder* the motion to table was ignored. Elizabeth Bunn asked if anyone wanted to speak in favor of the resolution. A loyal follower responded by calling the question and the debate ended. Brother Yokich didn't ask if anyone was opposed.

Yokich's spin on Local 2036 was revealing. Cutting your losses at the expense of workers' lives is a corporate value, not a union or a human value. Trying to diminish the impact by lying about the cost and the number of people affected is also a corporate value. Unionists believe "An injury to one is an injury to all." But Yokich implied that an injury to some doesn't rate much concern. He asserted that UAW VPs talking to their corporate partners "put all the pressure that we could humanly possibly put."

Tut-tut and possibility punted. Rollover Caucus followers act more like corporate handmaidens than unionists. When Navistar attempted to bust a Canadian Autoworkers (CAW) local, CAW president Buzz Hargrove said, "We are prepared to shut down all of our operations. We are not going to allow them to scab our plants and steal our members' jobs" (*Labor Notes*, August 2002). The CAW kept scabs out and won a fair contract.

The Rollover Caucus did not initiate any solidarity actions on behalf of Local 2036. UAW members were not informed they were mounting scab wheels on trucks. When porkchoppers couldn't get help from their corporate partners, they cut off strike benefits to the locked-out workers. When the International decided to take over Local 2036, Yokich admitted he didn't even know who they supplied (*Local 2036 v. UAW*, Volume 11, Public Review Board, p. 135, 2001). When they pulled the charter, they didn't even inform the members. Instead, Region 3 director Terry Thurman sent a letter to Accuride disclaiming any interest in representing the members. Yokich's accusation that "there's a group in this union that has taken that and run it against every damn thing we do good in this union" is like a drunk blaming a tree for jumping in front of his car.

33rd UAW Con Con, Day Three: The Real Baloney

On the third day of the convention, the auditorium was so full of helium balloons I felt like I was in the bottom of a bubble gum machine. I may have voted wrong a few times. Balloons got in my eyes and several of my industrial brothers were snorting helium and speaking in tongues. The scene reminded me of something former UAW president Owen Bieber once said: "When we get done with them they'll be able to tell the real baloney from the phony baloney." Which is, I believe, a double entendre squared.

There are no surprises in Solidarity Heaven. All Rollover Caucus nominees won by acclamation, and the band played "Happy Days Are Here Again"—again. No one bothered with the formality of asking for other nominations. No one could have been recognized in the babble of balloons anyway.

The official Rollover Caucus promotional booklet cited "our union's vibrant tradition of union democracy" and boasted: "Throughout its history the UAW has produced leaders who have worked their way up through the ranks." For example, three of former president Owen Bieber's sons have International appointments.

Elizabeth Bunn symbolizes the "new" UAW more than anyone else on "Ron's Team." Bunn, an attorney, was appointed in 1985 by Owen Bieber as "an associate general counsel of the UAW assigned to the president's office." She was not a UAW member at the time and didn't become a UAW member until she joined the National Writers Union after they affiliated with the UAW in 1991. She has never filed a grievance, campaigned for elective office, or been told she was lucky to have a job after complaining of sexual harassment. More to the point, she doesn't belong in the writers' union because she doesn't write for a living.

The one-party state is well ordered. The International Rubber Stamp Board was acclaimed, congratulated, and adulated, and nary a balloon went pop. Then we broke off into separate rooms to acclamate our acclaimed Regional Directors.

33rd UAW Con Con, Day Four: Crisis in UAW Democracy

Day four started almost two hours late. Rollover Caucus followers were getting drilled and scripted in separate rooms. It seemed not all had gone well in Solidarity Heaven. Apparently, Region 2 rubber-stamped the wrong guy. Davis was supposed to retire and his assistant director, Rich

Vadovski, was supposed to be acclamated. Both Davis and Vadovski were nominated. Then Vadovski, the loyal follower, declined the nomination.

Under Rollover Caucus rules Warren Davis was supposed to retire. Instead, he pulled a fast one, decided to run again, and won. Suddenly, Steve Yokich's "good friend" and "solid unionist" who was going to take on "those bastards in Congress" was a snake. Judging from the volume of venom there was more than one snake in the pit, and none more vile than Yokich.

Overnight, the Constitution Committee, handpicked by the Rollover Caucus, came up with a new amendment to resolve the problem of the errant rubber stamp: dissolve the whole region. The members of Region 2 would be divvied up among three other regions. The iron fist would not only deprive Warren of his coup, it would exterminate everyone he ever appointed. It was redistricting on a scale that would shame the toupee off a carpetbagger.

Warren Davis poked a hole in the balloon of our "vibrant tradition of union democracy." One lapdog exclaimed, "We didn't have a choice!"

What's the point? We never have a choice in the one-party state. Sorting out the devil in the deal would be much simpler with one member, one vote, but we've settled for a charade.

After Vadovski declined the nomination the delegates were left with no choice but to acclamate a person they had acclamated for years. So what? It wasn't a constitutional crisis. It was a caucus snafu. We should've dissolved the Rollover Caucus, not Region 2. It didn't merit a constitutional amendment to dissolve a whole region. But the caucus rules with an iron fist. The amendment was an impulsive, irresponsible retribution: Yokich's parting kiss.

Erv Heidbrink, a member of the Constitutional Committee, read the amendment, and admonished anyone who dared to say the UAW was undemocratic—as if this amendment was a defense of democracy rather than a political reprisal. Yokich chaired the debate.

A delegate from Region 2 said he'd been attending conventions since 1968 and had never seen anything like it. He had committed to vote for Vadovski, but "Rich decided to give my vote away." After all those years, he finally noticed someone else was controlling his vote?

The next delegate from Region 2 said, "Yesterday our region held a legal election. It was according to our constitution, we had nominations, we had discussion, we had elections. I am outraged at this amendment not because of the politics but because this is America. We have a fundamental right to our vote. And what this amendment does is take away my vote. That's not right."

The next delegate was Willie Hubbard, president of Local 1250, Region 2. "I guess some must think I am crazy for getting up here and opposing this resolution. It's just like running through an open flame with gasoline. . . . I know that trust means a lot. I know once you lose trust you lose a lot. I am just as stunned as anyone in this room by the actions which occurred yesterday. Am I pleased? Am I happy? No. But I ask that you reconsider this resolution . . . for the sake of all the members of Region 2. . . . I myself don't like what transpired as much as you, Steve. I know that you can be a very vindictive person at times [catcalls]. I didn't say vindictive for the catcalls, but I know how Steve can be at times when he wants to clear up a dispute. And it's good to have a person like that because first of all, those of you that are doing the catcalling, you need a person like that [catcalls] when you go into negotiations. Where the company doesn't look at this individual as a weak person [catcalls]. Yes, vindictive sometimes can be an advantage not a disadvantage. For those that are catcalling. But Brother Yokich, I ask you and the delegates here, will you please consider this resolution and restore Region 2 . . . within the UAW."

A delegate from Region 2-B said, "I don't believe that in the history of our union we have ever combined two regions after an election. Is that true or false? [No answer.] If I'd run for election in my region and won, would you then combine regions and overturn my election as well? I ask you this because we have a constitution and those regions are set up prior to the election and after that election, you want to come in here and adjust the constitution? I think it's unfair. I don't agree with it."

Yokich responded. "Brother, let me just say if that was the case I think somebody gave you bad information. I'm not going to debate it with you, but we're going to have a recess this afternoon so the regions can have elections. That's how we've done it in the past. That's how we're going to continue to do it." (Unless the wrong person wins?)

The next delegate, from Region 1-D, said, "Sister and brother delegates, we all know right from wrong. We are all reasonably intelligent people or our membership wouldn't have sent us here. We know what treachery in high places looks like. We know what solidarity is and what it isn't. Brother Yokich, I respectfully call the question."

One may call the question whenever they are recognized by the chair, but it is improper to give a speech and then call the question. He should have been ruled out of order and the debate should have continued.

Yokich responded, "I really wanted to debate this, but. . ."

Hands up. Hands down. Debate done. Amendment passed.

I demanded a Point of Order. I simply stated: "This amendment of Article 10 is untimely and retroactive. It should be rescinded."

Yokich responded, "We'll consider your advice."

Article 8, Section 15, states: "Copies of all resolutions and constitutional amendments to be considered by the Convention must be approved by the Local Union membership and sent to the International Secretary-Treasurer not later than six weeks *prior* to the date set for the Convention" (emphasis added). As I said, the amendment was untimely and retroactive and thereby unconstitutional.

We heard a bunch more speakers. We took a long break so Regions 8, 9, and 2-B could re-rubber-stamp preordained directors. We approved a resolution to give Steve Yokich a cottage at Black Lake. We gave everybody on the executive board raises, plus 3 percent per year, plus cost of living, plus expenses, plus whatever else they wanted.

The Constitution Committee reported that local unions submitted 221 proposed changes to the constitution. Not a single one of those resolutions was discussed. Only resolutions submitted by the Rollover Caucus deserve attention in the one-party state.

We all held hands to sing "Solidarity Forever" but someone forgot to project the words onto the video screen. So we hummed in totalitarian harmony.

2002 UAW Bargaining Con: If Figures Lie and Liars Figure, What's a Gettelfinger?
(June 2002)

A new president doubles the lip service and stretches the limits of jointness.

Back-to-back conventions in Vegas? Sounds like an episode of *Survivor*. The format even included a word from our corporate sponsors. The official explanation for back-to-back conventions was "to save money." But I saw no evidence of frugality.

At the last Bargaining Convention, three years ago in Detroit, a thousand seats were reserved for guests. The atmosphere in '99 was intense. But this year's attitude was, "Oh well, and so what?"

And why not? Traditionally the Bargaining Convention is held a few months prior to negotiations for the Big Three contracts. But the contracts don't expire until next year. The excitement could have been contained in a teapot.

In newly acclaimed President Gettelfinger's opening remarks he cited "accelerating globalization" and unfair trade as the major obstacles to effective bargaining. But there are more autoworkers in the United States today than ever. The market for organizing is fat but the unavoidable fact is: the UAW is a business union, not an organizing union.

"Ron's Team" believes we can improve organizing by bargaining for "neutrality agreements" from our corporate partners in the Big Three. Token neutrality in return for what? The policy reeks of company unionism. What do we give up in negotiations for neutrality agreements? A promise to cooperate with lean production standards and outsourcing? Instead of neutrality we should demand, "No Scab Parts in UAW Shops."

Gettelfinger sent Local 2036 out on strike but apparently without forethought. He had no strategy, no plan to mobilize union members. When the UAW's corporate partners brushed them off, the Rollover Caucus busted the local and washed their hands.

Gettelfinger is a corporatist: that is, he believes our fortunes as union members are tied to the company's apron strings. At the Ford sub-council, where union members convened to devise a bargaining strategy, he invited Lord Ford and his stooges to explain to members how sacrifices would be necessary. Ford's problems are not the fault of union members or union wages. Does Ford invite UAW members to Board of Directors meetings to advise them how they should make sacrifices for the good of the community?

The traditional union goal is to take labor out of the competition by establishing equal pay and humane production standards. When the union accepts the premise of competitiveness, it accepts the inevitability of concessions and job losses and inhumane working conditions.

Gettelfinger's conception of "realistic bargaining" doesn't resolve the conflict of overcapacity and job security by shortening the workweek. His strategy is what Jerry Tucker, the founder of New Directions and a former member of the UAW International Executive Board, coined "democratic concession making." You vote on which concessions you get to make and you debate who gets to make the most.

The Finger made one emphatic point: "The UAW will not, WILL NOT, allow the auto companies to shift the cost of health care onto the backs of our members." (Emphasis *his.*) But then he qualified his line in the sand by saying, "The health care crisis in America cannot be solved at the bargaining table. This is a national political issue." Oh.

We've heard it all before. We have watched our health care coverage erode and our co-pays rise. I expect that we will make more sacrifices, but like last time, they will be concealed until after ratification when the wrapping paper comes off.

The featured speaker at the Bargaining Con was Stephen Girsky, a stock analyst. (In 2009 Girsky became a member of both the GM Board of Directors and the UAW-VEBA, a retiree health care trust.) The UAW has an excellent research department, but Gettelfinger outsourced the job to Wall Street.

Girsky crunched the numbers and graphed the stats, then sagely prophesied that we needed to reduce the cost of health care and pensions and pressure suppliers to cut prices. He said Delphi and Visteon still need "parental guidance," as they aren't ready to promenade in the open market without a chaperone. Not one new thought. We might as well have consulted some fifty-year-old white guy who likes to farm and blow shit up with fertilizer.

After that they read to us for a really long time. Stupefied delegates put their heads down on tables and drooled. At two p.m. we were shuttled onto buses and transported to a picket line for culinary workers on Fremont Street, which is like Old Town in Vegas.

I did not get on the bus. My underdeveloped herd instinct has an aversion to following authority. I went back to my room, dumped my tote, and caught a cab.

The cabbie said, "You want to go the long way? It costs a little more but it's faster."

"Take the fast way, man."

Most cabbies in Vegas drive like they were on the golf course. You'd think they got paid by the hour. But Jake got his training in Chicago. He made a U-turn, cut off an ambulance, tacked across a parking lot like a downhill slalom skier, raced down an alley, and gunned it up an on-ramp to the freeway. It was the most real excitement I'd had in Vegas.

I told him I was with the UAW and I was going to join the culinary workers for a picket. He explained that the rest of the culinary workers at the big casinos on the strip had already settled. They got what they wanted and left their brothers and sisters on the other side of the tracks to fend for themselves. "No way those culinary workers at the old casinos can get the same package now that their brothers and sisters have left them hanging in the wind."

It sounded familiar: settle the Big Three national contracts; leave the locals and second-class IPS members to fight on their own.

"Do you think they settled the big casinos in time for the UAW convention?"

"This is Vegas. It's always showtime. You didn't have to cross a picket line, instead you get to *walk* a picket line, and feel good about it, and go home happy."

"What if the union had said, settle all together, or we picket the UAW Convention?"

"This is Vegas, man. The show must go on. They would have settled."

"That or the porkchoppers would tell us to cross the picket line because it's just an 'informational' picket."

"What's a porkchopper? I think we have some of them here, too."

I joined the picket line. The slogan was: "One Union, One Health Care Plan." We walked around with our signs. There was no trouble. Gettelfinger & Co. Ltd. made speeches. It was a photo op for the same leaders who never made it down to Henderson, Kentucky, once in four years. It was a nice dog and pony show, safe, no one looked into the horse's mouth.

We could have walked, one thousand strong, into the restaurants, sat down, ordered coffee, and sipped for hours, not spending anything but time. What could they do, arrest us? Instead we walked around with picket signs and never bothered anybody.

The show must go on. It was hot. We didn't hang out long. We went back to air-conditioned casinos on the strip, where we could eat and drink and gamble, and nobody had to think too much about culinary workers left in the heat on Fremont Street.

Misreading the Gauge of a Fair Day's Pay
(May 2003)

Working to Rule is a wily craft which utilizes managerial hubris as a fulcrum to tip the scales in a manner Jerry Tucker coined "purposeful misdirection."

One of my tasks as a machine operator is to gauge certain dimensions of the fuel injectors we assemble. One day I saw some measurements that were drastically out of spec. I notified my job setter who in turn notified an engineer. Then a supervisor with extensive experience as an auditor intervened. Before long, two more engineers applied their collegiate wizardry. The B-shift administrator threw his weight onto the equation. Then another supervisor bellied up to the bar to add his expertise to the mix. We set the benchmark for participation.

We examined the parts and checked the gauge, again and again. The positive side of all this strutting and fretting is that for once we were a unified team showing more concern for quality than production counts. Despite the dearth of common sense, that must signify something.

Then Brother Mahoney strolled by and we asked him to look at it. His mind was clear as a blackboard in July. He checked two parts on the gauge and said, "There's nothing wrong with these parts." The lights came on. The depth and breadth of my stupidity was astonishing. I felt like the pied piper of scrap. I had read the gauge wrong. A decimal place can mean the difference between a home run and a bunt. If you're not a baseball fan, try it on your paycheck, you'll see what I mean.

The point is: I misled a whole group of experts. I told them what to see and they saw it. They knew better, they were experienced, but the power of suggestion channeled their perception like blinders. If Pat Mahoney hadn't happened by we might still be spelunking in the murky caverns of Shotwell's mathematically challenged brain, waylaid by a decimal place.

It reminded me of Colin Powell at the UN holding up a vial of white powder. *Fear.* Then he displayed satellite photos of sinister laboratories. *Horror.* He invoked 9-11 and nuclear catastrophe. *Terror.* There could be only one conclusion: we must invade now before it is too late. We did, and Puff! the Magic Weapons disappeared. Now Iraq is safe for US corporations.

When we stop exercising our critical and analytical intelligence we surrender our fate to charlatans. Before the elections we should have debated the recession and White House ties to corporate scandals. Instead, all rhetoric was commandeered by war and questions of patriotism.

We succeeded in defeating a ragtag army that defended itself with pickup trucks and a miscellany of small arms. Now that the techno-spectacle of explosions has subsided, the media buzz is tax cuts tax cuts tax cuts. Shouldn't we question the plunge from trillion-dollar surplus to trillion-dollar deficit? Shouldn't we address unemployment, and the crisis in health care and education, rather than how to subsidize the rich in the vain hope they will trickle down on us?

Real homeland security means full employment, a living wage, Medicare for all, the right to organize and bargain collectively without threats and intimidation, and a public school system that invests more money in our children than the Pentagon squanders supplying ruthless dictators with weapons of mass destruction.

The union vision is prosperity for all, but when we let company men frame the debate we restrict our perceptions and limit our options to pre-arranged concessions. Every time you go to a business update and listen to the litany of lies, you are bound to feel demoralized. They tell us we have to "cut costs to stay competitive." So we cut our own standard of living and call it a victory for free enterprise. Never mind that free discussion was monopolized and the prize was getting entered from behind by the pied piper of crap.

UAW members are getting sucker punched by the crooked bargain of a union organized wage cut in return for *neutrality agreements*. What's neutral about unconditional surrender? What company would resist a union that pledged not to strike and promised to sell out the new hires? Predators don't set agendas, they set traps.

Richard Dauch, CEO and chairman of American Axle, was the highest-compensated CEO in Michigan last year. He collected $27,594,666 in salary and stock options. Bloomberg News reported in January 2003: "As automotive supply contracts go, the agreement that American Axle & Manufacturing Holdings Inc. (AAM) signed with General Motors in 1994 doesn't get much sweeter. Under the seven-year pact, which has been renewed, General Motors is all but prohibited from buying axles, drive shafts, and other critical components used in its sport utilities, pickups, and other light-truck models from any company but American Axle. Hence, the supplier has unusual leverage to maintain and even raise its prices."

Bloomberg News underscored the advantageous position of AAM with the following assessment:

> General Motors today doesn't dare try flexing its muscles against American Axle because sport utilities and pickups are the No. 1 automaker's most profitable vehicles. Should axle or drive shaft deliveries experience any snags, General Motors's assembly lines would shut down. With General Motors over a barrel—and contributing 82 percent of American Axle's sales—the company has been able to post a profit every year since going public in 1999, and now has a market capitalization of $1.24 billion. Dauch's 7.9 million shares, or 14 percent of the company, are worth about $194 million. In terms of total return, American Axle shares have appre-

ciated 41 percent in the past three years, while the S&P 500 lost 28 percent and the S&P's auto parts and equipment index lost 33 percent.

When the International approached Local 2093 in Three Rivers, Michigan, about giving American Axle a third-tier wage, the bargaining committee told them they wanted nothing to do with it. So the International negotiated a concession package without them.

The *new* UAW stands for rollover, not struggle. Instead of hope and justice, the porkchoppers offer fear and despair. The bitter flavor of swallowed pride is sweetened with enhanced retirements for top-tier wage earners. Old-timers who remember what it meant to belong to a union of fighters are offered a sack of silver to sell out new hires.

UAW members at Three Rivers deserve better. They have consistently exceeded all expectations. They should be discussing a raise, not a wage cut. Someone is misreading the gauge of a fair day's pay. They should be talking about a bigger share of the rewards. Instead the Rollover Caucus tells them a wage cut will make the plant profitable and ensure their future survival. The plant is already profitable. Concessions never saved a union. Give in today and all you guarantee is that the bully will be back tomorrow.

American Axle in Three Rivers is providing contract information meetings on company time. Isn't that sweet? I suspect the International isn't acting too heavy-handed about ratification because they want the members to feel responsible for what they get in the end—a diminishing return on the investment of their lives and a legacy of defeat.

Workers Rule When They Work to Rule
(June 2003)

One of my favorite movie scenes is from *Norma Rae*. She asked the union organizer if it was true that Jews were different. He said, "Yes." She inquired, "What makes Jews different?" He replied, "History."

Our history as workers makes us unique. There are people who don't want us to know our history. They want us to believe history is about millionaires and kings, not the struggles of working people against millionaires and kings. There is power in knowing our history.

The history of our struggle for justice is old as Pharaoh's tomb. The ancient Hebrew word for strike is *regiah*, the laying down of tools. You don't think the ancient Jews were trade unionists? The Lord commanded, "Keep holy the Sabbath." Jews interpreted that to mean "No work." You can bet your holiday pay that wasn't management's idea.

African Americans were masters in the art of worker-to-worker communication. Hundreds of years ago, they used songs to instill solidarity, convey messages, and control the pace of the work. The song raised the collective consciousness of workers. The boss couldn't punish someone for falling behind or working too slow because everyone worked at the same methodical pace. They protected the elderly, the injured, the lame, and preserved strength and solidarity with song. The song not only controlled the pace of production, the song also communicated to workers important information. For example, the location of the boss. Such information allowed workers to take breaks, steal supplies, or even escape.

The slogan "work to rule" has a double meaning. Work to rule is a method of slowing production by following every rule to the letter. The aim is to leverage negotiations. Work to rule is also an invocation for workers to govern collectively, to control the conditions of their labor.

Work to rule is an in-plant strategy, a method of influencing negotiations without going on strike. Workers follow the boss's orders but do nothing on their own initiative. They keep their knowledge and experience to themselves, defer all decisions to the straw boss, and let the pieces fall where they may.

Work to rule has roots in the Industrial Workers of the World. Frank Bohn, in an article printed in the IWW newsletter *Solidarity* in 1912, wrote: "Sabotage means strike and stay in the shop. Striking workers thus are enabled to draw pay and keep out scabs while fighting capitalists."

Historically, sabotage did not mean destruction of machinery. The word *sabotage* was first used officially by French labor organizations in 1897. The French word *sabot* means wooden shoe. The term sabotage originates from the French expression *travailler a coups de sabots*, meaning *to work as one wearing wooden shoes*, that is, slow and clumsy. In the 1915 pamphlet *Sabotage*, Elizabeth Gurley Flynn wrote, "Sabotage is not physical violence; sabotage is an internal industrial process."

In the 1930s union members occupied factories. The sit-down strikes were illegal, but there is a higher authority than the bossing class. When workers work to rule, human rights take precedent over property rights. In the 1930s, workers claimed ownership of their jobs and stared down the barrel of a gun to win union recognition.

Why shouldn't we occupy plants? Why should we walk out on the jobs that belong to us? Why should we allow the boss to give our jobs away? Whole communities have been destroyed by ruthless owners. We have a right to defend ourselves. The struggle of the bossing class against the working class is about control of production and corporate manipulation of supply. The name of the game is Monopoly, not Free Enterprise.

Management thinks they control the plant with their clipboards, portable phones, and panties twisted in a knot. But when workers work to rule, the bosses find out who really runs the plant, who keeps machines humming, production flowing, and the money coming in.

Owners have declared an overcapacity in the auto industry. The Big Three, with the support of the Federal Reserve, saturated the market with zero percent financing. In preparation for negotiations, they built up massive inventories. Unemployment escalated as 2.6 million manufacturing jobs were exported. Conditions are ideal for concessions.

Why should workers contribute to the stockpile? Why should we increase productivity when only the least productive, the CEOs, are rewarded? Why should labor sacrifice? There's a solution to overcapacity: a shorter workweek. There's a solution to concession bargaining: work to rule.

In the 1980s, Jerry Tucker, a UAW Servicing Rep in St. Louis, organized a work-to-rule campaign at Moog Industries, an automotive parts supplier. The recession, coupled with Reagan's antagonism toward unions, incited a relentless drive for concessions. Workers needed a new strategy to combat the tactics of heavy-handed union busters.

Moog was profitable, but the company wanted to take advantage of the trend and demand concessions. They hired one of the most expensive union-busting law firms in St. Louis. The legal vultures expected the union to go out on strike, and they prepared. Instead, union members voted the contract down and decided on an in-plant strategy: work to rule.

They continued to work, but without a contract the gloves were off. Workers have a federally protected right to "concerted union activity." They have a right to seek redress for grievances, but without a contract they do not have a *collaborative commitment* with management to resolve the conflict. Instead of following an orderly grievance process, workers confronted the boss *en masse*. Chaos ensued.

Whole departments shut down while workers argued in the boss's office. They "ran the plant backwards." They didn't damage equipment, but they wreaked havoc with production by following all the process control instructions to a T. Without a contract they were free to engage in "concerted union activity" as they saw fit. Everyone refused overtime. It was all for one and one for all. Disciplinary action of an individual crashed into a wall of mass resistance. The in-plant strategy succeeded.

Concessions were rolled back, and all discharged workers were reinstated and made whole. Jerry Tucker helped organize six UAW work-to-rule campaigns in the 1980s. They were all successful. In an era when concessions were the norm and union-busting was in vogue, work to rule empowered workers with the tools to fight back and win.

The bossing class has perverted the traditional meaning of sabotage into "malicious destruction of property." They must have looked into their own souls for this new definition.

When bosses order us to pass along substandard quality, it is, by their own definition, sabotage. When Ford designs vehicles that roll over or blow up on impact, it's sabotage.

When GM sells out, shuts down, spins off, and thereby guts the city of Flint, it's sabotage. When Delphi builds all its new plants outside the United States while closing American factories, it's sabotage. When CEOs lay off thousands of workers and reward themselves with multimillion-dollar perks, it's sabotage. When the president of the United States commits soldiers to war under false pretenses, bankrupts the treasury with lavish rewards to his cronies, and encourages a trade policy that exports American jobs, it's not patriotism, it's sabotage.

Workers are not *saboteurs*. Workers want to build, not destroy. Work to rule simply means: to rigorously adhere to process control instructions and strive to meet the stated goals of high quality, lean inventory, and just-in-time delivery in order to compel *cooperation* from the boss. Working to rule, like keeping kosher, enforces a strict code.

In May 1902, kosher meat prices in New York City jumped 50 percent in one day. Jewish women "entered kosher butcher shops and threw the meat into the streets." They didn't loot, they didn't steal, they didn't destroy property. The owners were free to dust off their product and put it back on the shelves. But the meat was no longer kosher, it was *trayf*, unfit to eat. No one would buy it (Annelise Orleck, *Common Sense and a Little Fire*, p. 28).

Kosher laws, like ISO* Quality Programs, rely on a *collaborative commitment*. Kosher has no meaning outside a working relationship. Kosher, like *quality*, is not a label. It is a living agreement that promotes the highest standards.

By exporting jobs, laying off workers, and passing along shoddy products, management commits a lethal act of sabotage, violates the ethic of work, and betrays the relationship that upholds quality, productivity, delivery, and loyalty.

Labor creates wealth, bosses exploit it. Labor builds community, bosses prey upon it. It's time for labor to let the feces fall where it may and traitors be exposed where they lie.

There is power in knowing our history. There is power in our fingers, power in our knowledge, power in our skill. From the longshoremen to the teamsters, from the mine to the mill, from the warehouse to the clerk, there is power in our work.

Workers will rule when they work to rule.

The Smile Is Wearing Thin
(August 2003)

Speculation about a UAW contract is like religion: everyone has an opinion but only the dead know the outcome.

---

* International Standards Organization

Every player in the Temple of Casino Capitalism has an angle, but only one bet is certain: the House was built on the luck of losers. The big winners never gamble, they make deals.

Speculation is cheap. Let's talk about what we know.

The UAW Rollover Caucus has a history of trading jobs for wages. While wages in Big Three assembly plants remain high, the membership of the UAW has plummeted from 1.5 million in 1979 to less than seven hundred thousand today. Despite the deadly nosedive the bureaucracy of the union has swollen like a zeppelin. Capital accumulation at Solidarity House has increased in inverse proportion to the decline of dues-paying members. The office rats will tell you, "Organizing is the lifeblood of the union," but the books tell another story.

How does a union acquire more capital as the membership declines? By forming a partnership with the company, avoiding strikes, and selling out new hires. The payoff is Joint Funds—a pipeline of cash from the Corps to the porkchoppers at Sold-our-dignity House. On top of that, the International skims 75 percent of the interest from our strike fund for operational expenses. Strikers beware. Solidarity is not forever in the UAW. They'd rather cut their losses than drain the fountain of income.

The stated goal of joint programs is to make the Corps "more competitive." The unstated methods are outsourcing, subcontracting, and speedups. Workers in IPS have been sacrificed on the altar of competitiveness to keep the gods of capital smiling. The smile is wearing thin. A worker eats and is satisfied, but the gods of capital are always hungry.

Work outsourced from assembly factories to lower-paying parts suppliers is organized by the UAW with the aid of neutrality agreements, and brotherly assistance from the Big Three.

Neutrality and partnership aren't free. The settlement at Johnson Controls last year included a neutrality agreement and a "no-strike pledge." Before the ink was dry, Bob King, UAW vice president of organizing, declared a "partnership" with the company.

A Chrysler plant in New Castle, Indiana, was sold to Metaldyne despite a no-sell clause in the national contract. The Rollover Caucus negotiated a wage cut of ten dollars per hour to ice the deal and win *neutrality* at other Metaldyne facilities.

At American Axle in Three Rivers, Michigan, the Rollover Caucus reopened the contract to extend an invitation of a third-tier wage for new hires in exchange for new work. The members said no deal. The Rollover Caucus reshuffled and came back with the same old crap in sparkly shrink wrap: wage cuts for new hires and perks for the privileged voters. The Rollover Caucus had learned their lesson. Instead of giving members adequate time to study the proposal and mount a Vote No campaign, they fast-tracked the sellout of the next generation. It worked. The highest-paid CEO in Michigan, Dick Dauch, just got richer.

The Rollover Caucus colluded with management to outsource seat covers from Visteon to Johnson Controls, where new UAW members are paid twelve dollars per hour. The Rollover Caucus also allowed Visteon, a Ford spinoff, to open five new plants at wages far below the Big Three standard.

At a Lear plant in Grand Rapids, Michigan, the Rollover Caucus reopened the contract to give the company a wage cut. Lear's second quarter profits were up 22 percent from last year.

Bloomberg News reported on the UAW strategy:

> In seeking to gain members at auto parts companies, the UAW also accepts lower wages in factories that make lower-profit items such as wire harnesses, rather than insisting on the same wage scale in every kind of component plant nationwide, said Bob King, the union's organizing director. The UAW had to scrap its strategy of insisting on a single universal wage after Toyota Motor Corp. and other competitors won enough market share to keep the US-based automakers from passing higher wage costs to customers, King said in an interview. "That's reality and we have to deal with it."

No speculation required. The trend is clear. Capitalists don't gamble, they make deals. IPS workers can expect to make sacrifices so that wages and benefits can be maintained at the Big Three and Gettelfinger can claim "historic gains" in 2003 negotiations.

The Die Is Cast: The 2003 GM-Delphi Contract
(October 2003)

The 2003 UAW agreement was indeed historic. Gettelfinger negotiated a contract at Delphi that permitted the company and the union to negotiate a two-tier wage for new hires six months *after* the ratification.

UAW members at GM and Delphi voted together on the contract as if it was one agreement. Since UAW-GM members outnumbered Delphi workers nearly 4–1, UAW–Delphi members were effectively gerrymandered. If all Delphi members had voted no, the contract would still have passed.

I appealed the decision to combine the ratifications. The International argued that the two contracts mirrored one another. There was one fatal crack in the mirror: two-tier. I appealed the decision not to allow affected members of the Delphi plants to vote on the two-tier supplement. The International argued that the only members who would be affected were new hires and that new hires were a "null class," that is, they don't count (PRB Case No. 1504, p. 15, line 2).

Six months after ratification, the International announced an agreement that stuck new hires with a 50 percent wage cut and no pension. UAW members were not allowed to vote on the supplement. In my appeal to the UAW Public Review Board, the International argued that we had already ratified the supplement as part of the national agreement. I argued that it was not possible or rational to ratify a supplement that did not exist at the time of ratification. Furthermore, the UAW Constitution, Article 19, Section 4, states: "National agreements and supplements thereof shall be ratified by the Local Unions involved." I argued that the International could not enter into agreements with employers that overruled the UAW Constitution, a document that is essentially a contract between UAW officers and dues-paying members.

I argued the case for two years. In the end the PRB supported the people who pay them, the International UAW. The distinguished professors decided that the International can combine contracts that affect members unequally and implement supplements without requiring ratification. The die is cast.

Faith-Based Engineering
(November 2004)

Management intends to eliminate one Bodine* operator in Dept. 988. When I read the time study it struck me like a lightning bug—off and on, there and gone. You need a whole jar full of the little buggers to achieve something that resembles illumination. And then they die.

I was puzzled. Like any kid with a curious mind I shook the jar and turned it upside down. I reread the Time Study again and again. Finally, I realized what was wrong. I was looking for something that wasn't there—an improvement, an innovation, a lightning bolt of ingenuity. I expected to learn the reason why an operator could be eliminated without sabotaging efficient production and quality control. There wasn't any reason. The Time Study wasn't based on reality. It was a figment of the Time Study Maven's . . . and then it dawned on me!

What we have here is a case of F.B.E.—Faith-Based Engineering.

"Facts," as John Adams said, "are stubborn things." But a faith-based engineer can outfox facts faster than a half-cocked cracker in a pissing match.

It's no wonder we don't pursue the elimination of scrap or the continuous improvement of mechanical processes. Like President Bush, Delphi's engineers are guided by faith, not logic. Stubborn facts be damned. Delphi's not stuck in a quagmire. We're lean and marching toward freedom and profitability. Before long we'll be throwing flowers at the plant manager and singing "Happy Days Are Here Again."

Ah, but facts are stubborn as scrap. Downtime and continuous containment are more common than car bombs in Iraq. When you have a president who doesn't read and a plant manager who hates the union you can't expect revelation before the world ends.

A few weeks ago my Bodine was making scrap. It went on for weeks. I had to call the union out and threaten to file charges against the company to get it fixed. You know the score. I don't have to tell you how it

---

* Industrial machinery.

works. Each of you has your own tale of mismanagement. Faulty intelligence floats to the top like smoke up a stovepipe because it's what the top dog wants to know. The stovepipe phenomenon isn't an accident, it's engineered to befog, befuddle, and be weird.

If Budget Brown, the plant manager, really wanted to save money he could eliminate half the maintenance supervisors on day shift. No one would miss them. We could replace Booboo Van Whiz with a robot that doubles as a floor duster. We could retire the Human Smog Hog. We could initiate a "Pay for Knowledge" salary rate for supervisors. That should save a bundle. On and on it goes. It's the Scrap Stupid anthem, redundant as the Good Humor ice cream man.

So here we are again, wondering why Delphi is more interested in reducing workers than reducing scrap and downtime. Budget Brown would rather outsource than enforce quality control. But don't underestimate him. He's not faith based. He has his reasons. Mr. Brown isn't here to win the business. He's here to close the business. When you look at it from that point of view, everything falls into place. It's a pattern: make it fail, then blame the union.

Screw it. Don't take the blame. Follow all rules to the letter. Make first-time quality your top priority. Protect your job. Every time we lose a job, we are that much closer to closing the plant. It's not the cost of labor that's hurting the business. What's hurting the business is faulty intelligence and faith-based engineering.

Chapter Two

"Bankruptcy Is a Growth Industry": Delphi and the Rise of Soldiers of Solidarity

When Delphi declared bankruptcy in October 2005, its unionized workforce was 33,100. It became immediately clear that management would follow the example of other bankrupt corporations and try to either extract concessions from workers or ask the bankruptcy court judge to simply tear up the labor contracts.

The bankruptcy filing sparked a revival of activism among rank-and-file workers of Delphi and other auto companies—not just among longtime militants, but among hundreds of workers new to union activity. Members of this new network, known as Soldiers of Solidarity, soon found that they not only had to confront an aggressive new Delphi management, but also had to pressure UAW leaders who were all too ready to agree to still more concessions.

Hone the Guillotines
(March 2005)

The old bard once sang, "There's no success like failure, and failure's no success at all" (Bob Dylan, "Love Minus Zero/No Limit").

Call it a conundrum, or dialectical ambivalence, but sometimes in the world of business, it makes good sense to let the bottom fall out of the bottom line, and reward malfeasance with cash and entitlements.

Let me explain. It's really quite simple.

Workers make all the sacrifices, capitalists make all the gains. Workers lose pensions, capitalists win golden parachutes with dividends and all-expenses-paid vacations.

Workers contract industrial disease, capitalists cancel retirees' insurance.

How can this be legal, you say?

Workers pay taxes, capitalists make campaign contributions.

Alan Dawes, Delphi's Chief Financial Officer, gets caught adding numbers to the wrong column.* Delphi CEO J. T. Battenberg claims ignorance, which makes him doubly fraudulent, that is, both a miscreant and a charlatan. In response to the scandal, the business press gives Delphi the verbal equivalent of a twenty-one-gun salute, and sundry stock analysts with no dirt under their fingernails recommend that the "Troy-based company" file for bankruptcy so as to void its union contract and evade pension obligations. It's the moral equivalent of covering up the dirt with feces.

As the bagpipes of the Fifth Estate blew dirges for Delphi, *Hampton AutoBeat LLC, The Daily Report for Automotive Executives* informed its clientele that "Delphi Corp. has offered nearly $3.9 million in cash to six top executives" plus more than four hundred thousand "restricted shares of stock" to entice the soon-to-be subpoenaed to . . . *stay the course.*

And you thought hard work paid off?

Apparently, Delphi's failure is a success.

To understand this conundrum, we need to go back to the May 1996 issue of *Fortune* magazine, where journalist Alex Taylor, referring to the corporation in question as "a batch of old-line parts operations clumped together," said GM was itching "to get rid of Delphi" and "a slew of retirees and their health and pension benefits."

As an added perk, Taylor explained, GM could shuck off its commitments and buy parts from nonunion suppliers, thereby driving down wages and benefits for organized parts plants.

GM didn't strike a bargain so much as it drove a stake into the heart of the union.

---

* Delphi Vice Chairman and Chief Financial Officer Alan Dawes resigned in 2005 following disclosure of accounting errors dating to 1999, when the company was spun off from GM.

Now the lawyers are lining up like fans for a Metallica concert, because for them too "there's no success like failure." Vulture capitalists will get their share of the booty in due time and lawyers will sprinkle jimmies and skim the cream. It's only that miserable *slew of retirees* from a *batch of old-line parts operations* who think "failure's no success at all."

In May 1999, GM spun off Delphi, and in September 1999 the UAW negotiated to replace the GM pension credits earned by UAW members at the old batch outfits with Delphi pension credits. The deal was unprecedented. We didn't learn of the sleight of hand until after the contract was ratified. Now we're stuck with the luck of the draw and a stacked deck.

Who knew what, and when?

A "not to be published" letter on page 451 of the uncut version of the 1999 GM-Delphi National Agreement states that International reps who came out of Delphi "would nevertheless continue to be employees of General Motors for purposes of accumulating seniority." The porkchoppers were not about to throw their saddlebags over a ringer named after a defunct oracle that spoke gibberish.

As the dust settles and the fingerprints disappear, it becomes clear that Delphi, like most American industry, is run by a bunch of overpaid, incompetent frauds who profit when working people lose. The ethic trickles down and freezes like snot in a snowstorm. You can see the glaze on low-level managers' faces. They are dumbfounded. They have nowhere to go. Union members will recoup, transfer to other plants, take buyouts and early retirement, sell the farm, and revert to ancient rituals like making whiskey in the woods north of Cheboygan. But the clipboards have always relied on the loyalty and largesse of capitalists, only to find that the casino isn't kind to suckers.

Delphi announced in 2007 that it will no longer provide health insurance for salaried retirees who are eligible for Medicare. Someone has to pay for all those lawsuits. Who better than the defenseless?

Ellen E. Schultz revealed in the *Wall Street Journal* ("Retirees Found Varity Untruthful," November 6, 2000) recommendations from a consultant on how to avoid paying retiree benefits:

1) Set up "an offshore company responsible for the retirees but not accountable under United States law and have it go bankrupt and thus terminate the plans."

2) Terminate the plans, go to court, and negotiate a settlement.
3) Set up a company to fail.
4) Initiate "creeping takeaways," whereby the employer reduces benefits in small enough increments that it would not be cost effective for retirees to sue. Over time a precedent of accepting reductions would be established, thereby undercutting legal challenges to more drastic reductions in the future. "Creeping takeaways" include managed care, higher deductibles and co-pays, COLA* diversion, and increased premiums.
5) In the event of legal action, drag the case out, thereby incurring financial hardship for retirees, which would soften their settlement demands.
6) Plead with retirees that the company could not survive without their help, that is, acceptance of benefit reductions.

I'm surprised poison isn't on the list.

America is run by overpaid, incompetent frauds who are served by hacks in the business press. The hacks rely on analysts to do their thinking for them and the analysts always have the same advice: make workers pay.

No matter how deceitful, stupid, ineffective, and criminal executives act, the accepted wisdom in the United States is workers should be more cooperative, work harder, take pay cuts, pension cuts, and benefit cuts . . . and smile.

Delphi was designed to fail. That's why Battenberg and five other top executives have been rewarded $3.9 million in cash. They succeeded.

Hone the guillotines. Battenberg wants our heads to roll, but union members have other ideas.

---

* Cost of living adjustment.

Four-Legged, Long-Tailed Metaphors
(July 2005)

I got laid off for the whole summer. "Come back in September," the straw boss said. I haven't had a summer off in forty years. I was stunned. I felt like a teenager. *Hot town, summer in the city.* Four days later, I got a message on the answering machine from Jack Schmo.

"Come back to work Monday. It's urgent. Please call me as soon as you get this message."

In times of moral dilemma I always ask myself, what would Satchel Paige say?

"Don't look back."

The past is fiction. Facts are in the eye of the beholder. And when there's a Texan in the White House, anything goes.

Sheila and I split town. We were in Chicago for the Blues Festival and didn't come back until late Monday night. That's my story. Delphi paid me for the missed day because it wasn't my fault. I didn't get the message.

High jinks aside, I have twenty-six years, four months, one week, and two days of pension equity in a company that doesn't know what it's doing from one day to the next.

My first night back to work there was nothing to do. Employees were asked to work overtime to help do more nothing. Apparently we were behind. We weren't losing money fast enough. Mike Wittek said, "This is easier than taking money from an ATM. You don't even have to remember your PIN."

We sat in the Containment Area and shot the shit like important people. Everything we said was worth money because we got paid for it. Let me entertain you with some world-class Delphi manufacturing wisdom.

Everything we produce in Coopersville must be contained, that is, thoroughly inspected, because after twenty-five years in the fuel injector business, we can't make it right the first time.

Management thinks the reason Delphi is losing money has something to do with health care, or market share, or insubordination. Like I said, facts are in the eye of the beholder, and the past is fiction.

The local union president and bargaining chair called me into the union office. They looked very serious, or lactose intolerant. They informed me that our personnel director was worried.

"He looked genuinely scared," the pres said.

Mr. Johnson felt threatened by my last *Live Bait & Ammo*, in which I noted that Mr. Johnson reminded me of an opossum when he smiled. It was a metaphor. I wrote, "I couldn't tell if he was smiling or just showing his teeth. An opossum acts like that when cornered. Instinctively I reached for my handgun." It was hyperbole. My weapon is the pen. My bullets are words. Irony may hurt, but it isn't violent. Nevertheless, amends are in order.

I am sorry if I offended any opossums by comparing them to unscrupulous, lazy, lowlife office rats and inferring allegorically that they should be shot.

An opossum never hurt anybody. An opossum never threatened anyone, deprived anyone of income, or robbed anyone of their hard-earned pension. An opossum won't lie to your face or blame his failures on 9–11 like Delphi COO Rodney O'Neal when he tried to convince UAW officials that we should sacrifice for the good of the company that made historic Chevy-in-the-Hole* a scar on the landscape.

Who bombed whom?

Delphi claims they are making money overseas but losing money in the good old USA. In a captive-audience meeting, our plant manager informed us that Delphi is losing money because GM lost market share and consequently we are making fewer parts.

So how come no one is laid off at our plant? Why are we working overtime? Why was the summer shutdown canceled? He couldn't explain any of that. After all, he is only the plant manager.

I can explain. We are building inventory in case of a strike. We make fuel injectors in Coopersville, and we could shut GM down in days.

Mr. Robinson couldn't answer most of our questions. His pat reply was, "I don't know."

But he was certain of one thing: UAW members must take conces-

---

* GM manufacturing complex

sions on health care and pensions if we want to keep our jobs. Workforce demotivation is the full extent of Delphi's business plan. We are about to witness the ultimate capitalist obscenity—the dog will eat itself.

He showed us lots of numbers and charts to prove his point. No one believed him. He may as well have stuck pins in a doll.

Delphi is under investigation by the SEC and the FBI. Chief Financial Officer Alan Dawes resigned and CEO J. T. Battenberg will retire unexpectedly early.

Can you imagine how Mr. Robinson felt when he stood in front of that room full of people, knowing full well he had no credibility with the audience? Does "asinine" come readily to mind?

Of course every scoundrel has a flag to take refuge in. GM and Delphi have the UAW. Two years ago, the *New York Times* stated: "A bill pending in the House of Representatives would allow businesses with union workers to reduce their company pension obligations by billions of dollars, because statistics show that most blue-collar workers do not live as long as other Americans" ("Bill Reduces Blue-Collar Obligations for Pensions," May 6, 2003).

"The United Auto Workers wrote a letter in support of the provision," the *Times* reported.

I passed a copy of the article out at work.

"Get-Fingered can kiss my axe handle," Luis Sanchez said.

"Can I quote you on that?" I asked.

"Sure. Why not? What's he going to do? Not represent me?"

Keep your powder dry and brake for four-legged long-tailed metaphors.

Bury the Hatchet and Raise the Fury
(August 29, 2005)

I ask the straw boss for a week off without pay. I have my reasons but suffice it to say that like an outlaw on the run, I needed time more than money to get ahead.

But Delphi needs me too bad. Can you believe it? A certified slacker like me? "Gotta have them parts," the straw boss said, panting and sputtering like a junkie chasing a fix.

Delphi needs a shot of uncommon sense, but the head dickheads appear immune to verbal inoculations. We may have to resort to old-fashioned, strong-armed persuasion like rolling strikes, wildcats, random epidemics, and work-to-rule disruptions at strategic locations.

[Delphi CEO] Steve Miller, aka "the Hatchet," told the press that even if Delphi files for bankruptcy, it will not interrupt the flow of parts, *especially* to GM.

No shit, it won't interrupt the flow of parts to GM, because GM runs the show. The Hatchet can blow smoke until the cows clean up after themselves before they come home. But in the end, [GM CEO Rick] Wagoner is his daddy, and daddy wants the parts on time.

Just-in-time is our trump card. We can work to rule. If the Hatchet thinks he can take our pension without retaliation, he's inhaling more smoke than he's blowing. Delphi can't expect to steal everything we ever worked for without retaliation, and GM knows it.

Speculators are betting on the power punch of pension extortion via bankruptcy to win concessions. From the docks to the air to the ground-breaking Caterpillar company, corpo-gangsters have taken the gloves off and put the brass knuckles on. They make no bones about intentions to hijack pensions, benefits, and wages. The notion that hard work pays off has been trashed. In conventional capitalist wisdom, workers must pay for management's crimes and failures. This audacious perversion of justice is rarely questioned by the press.

For instance, it appears that the syndicated corporate mouthpiece Rick Haglund spent too much time sucking smoke at the hookah bar with his patrons. He doesn't make sense. He defends lucrative compensation of Delphi executives by comparing them to an even bigger corporate criminal at Kmart. In his column on August 17, 2005, Haglund stated: "Former Kmart Corp. Chairman Chuck Conaway, for instance, received nearly twenty-three million dollars in compensation for just under two years of less-than-stellar work at the retailer, which he ushered into bankruptcy in 2002."

A week later, the *Detroit News* reported: "The US Securities and Exchange Commission on Tuesday charged Kmart's former chairman and

CEO Charles Conaway and its former chief financial officer with misleading investors about the company's financial condition in the months before Kmart's 2002 bankruptcy filing. In a civil case, the SEC is charging Conaway and John McDonald with securities fraud" ("Ex–Kmart CEO Charged with Fraud," *Detroit News*, August 24, 2005).

Haglund's rationalization is as intellectually appetizing as a thick layer of bullshit covered with a frosting of lies. His fallacious analogy doesn't answer the average UAW member's question: Why the hell should we make concessions for criminals? Incompetent criminals at that.

Isn't that the real question analysts and mainstream media parrots should be asking? Not how should we punish workers, but how should we punish the putzes who turned the US auto industry into a demolition derby? Shouldn't their deferred compensation be threatened, not ours?

In the same column, Haglund reported "the cost of an hourly, UAW-represented Delphi worker is one hundred and thirty thousand dollars a year including wages, health insurance and pension benefits." It's an outrageous lie, but it stands uncontested because UAW VP Shoemaker admonishes union officials not to talk to the press. Shoemaker doesn't return calls or make comments to the press himself, and the UAW public relations department doesn't like to relate publicly. Therefore, corporate opinion monopolizes the media. Since UAW officials shirk their duty to defend us in public, truth is reduced to whatever the press will let their sponsors get away with. As a result, distorted facts are mass-marketed by corporate hacks until delusion wears the uniform of conventional wisdom—which is, workers make too much money.

Wall Street front men would have us believe our pension is a welfare program. Our pension and benefits are earned. The real freeloaders are the overpaid, incompetent frauds who are driving the flagship industry of America into the scrapyard. UAW members are too heavily invested to let corporate con artists steal their life savings without a fight.

The Hatchet complains about the cost of contractual responsibility to workers who Delphi deprived of jobs through negligence, dishonesty, and mismanagement. In February 2003 an arbitrator rejected that feeble evasion. "Delphi Corp. would violate an agreement with the International Union of Electronic Workers-Communications Workers of America if it allowed the number of employees at the company's Moraine and Kettering plants to drop below 1,500, an arbitrator ruled." (Shannon Joyce Neal, "Arbitrator Decides in Union's Favor in Dispute," February 19, 2003.)

Delphi claimed the job guarantee was part of a "non-binding memo of understanding." The arbitrator, Anthony Sinicropi, refuted Delphi's distortion of fact. Union members are dealing with executives who have no honor. Their word, their contracts, mean nothing to them. The predominant UAW strategy is cooperation, but cooperation with criminal behavior isn't realistic, it's aiding and abetting.

The Hatchet thinks it is unfair that Delphi should have to compensate four thousand UAW members whose jobs were sold out from under them. If the UAW enforced the Secure Employment Level GM agreed to in the 2003 contract, those employees could transfer to GM, but three out of four new Chevy models are built outside the United States. (The HHR is built in Mexico; the Equinox is built in Canada; the Aveo is built in South Korea. On top of that, the new Buick Regal is made in China.) GM's complaint that the active US workforce cannot support legacy costs is a direct result of their sourcing strategy.

The 2003 UAW contract *Highlights* claimed that "GM agreed to award approximately one billion dollars in new business to UAW-represented Delphi operations." But the minutes of the UAW International Executive Board meeting in November 2004 confirm that the billion-dollar promise was a boondoggle. Shoemaker reported: "Delphi's GM North American content per vehicle in the third quarter was $2,495, a loss of $252 of content per vehicle over third quarter 2003, and a loss of $82 in content per vehicle over second quarter 2004."

Content per vehicle is the most accurate measure of GM's commitment to Delphi. The misrepresentation was intentional. The failure was calculated. GM undermined Delphi's success with one goal in mind: takeaways.

Remember the IPO? Remember when shares of Delphi sold for twenty dollars? Remember the hype? Remember Ed Northern saying, "I don't close plants. I build plants"? Remember when the pension plan was fully funded just a few short years ago?

Where has all the money gone? Overseas. All the profit from Delphi operations was invested outside of the United States.

The Hatchet insists Delphi will only file Chapter 11 for US operations and the court proceedings won't affect Delphi's international business. Leave it to a screw machine operator, Mark Presler, to detect the silver thread in that twisted scheme. Mark said, "If Delphi gets away with selective debt evasion, I'm going to sell everything, buy property in Mexico, and invest all my savings outside the United States. Then come home, max out the credit cards, and declare bankruptcy." Why not? Mark has all the rights of a person, just like a corporation.

At the last sub-council in Chicago, Shoemaker tried to soften the target for concessions by scaring UAW members with the threat of bankruptcy. He says we have to *help* GM and Delphi. Gettelfinger insists there must be an equivalence of sacrifice. I couldn't agree more.

If cuts must be made, they can start at Solidarity House. IRS documents show that in 1994, GM funneled $8.2 million dollars to the International through the conduit of joint funds. We don't know how much that sum may have increased, because the union won't reveal the figures to its members. But nineteen cents for every hour we work cachings into the joint fund kitty to help fluff the featherbeds. Cut the fat, not the meat.

Meanwhile, back in Coopersville, Delphi can't afford to give me a week off without pay because GM needs the parts too bad. In fact, I was forced into work last Saturday. I tried to turn the overtime down, but GM is desperate for parts. UAW members at Delphi still have some power.

Bury the Hatchet and raise the fury.

Demolition Means Progress
(August 2005)

When I see a Roman numeral after a name, I think, "Pope." But the vestments of privilege can be misleading.

When the criminal intent of capital reigns without regulation, discretion, or restraint, wealth passes for wisdom, and piety bows to class until infallibility is exposed as the vanity of an insufferable ass.

J. T. Battenberg III, founding CEO of Delphi, will plead innocent based on ignorance. The final modifier shouldn't be hard to prove, as witnesses have often observed him in the act of ignoring responsibility. Innocence, on the other hand, will require an audacious attorney, a gullible jury, and a truck full of money.

The *Detroit News* reported on July 1, 2005, that an "internal investigation" uncovered what the average shop rat has known for years— management is "inadequate and insufficient" on all counts.

The *Detroit News* reported that the corporate colonoscopy discovered an "ineffective 'tone' within the company that could discourage or prevent personnel from raising concerns with management."

No discernible elevation of eyebrows was detected after the diagnosis, but questions of lineage were overheard. For the record: J. T. the First begat J. T. the Second who begat J. T. the Third who begot the mess that is Delphi. Forsooth, the ineffective "tone" is now entered as a plea—"I didn't know. I'm just a CEO."

According to capitalist canon, workers require threats, intimidation, and financial distress for motivation, while executives may only be retained with oodles of disposable income and deferred compensation.

In March 2005, J. T. the Third pocketed $1,700,000 in cash and 188,550 shares of stock. Nothing less could retain his royal fraudulence. In the canon of casino capitalism the house rules and workers lose their belts, their pants, their shoes, and the chance to choose their preferred method of execution.

Names affixed with Roman numerals weren't the only beneficiaries of crony capitalism at Delphi. Rodney O'Neal, president and COO, was awarded $1.95 million in salary on top of a $724,000 bonus and 77,625 shares of stock he received last March, and . . . in order to retain his ineffective highness . . . O'Neal was promised one million smooches if he didn't get the top squat after hatchet man, Steve Miller, completes his chainsaw massacre.

No, that's not a misprint. O'Neal gets a million bucks if he *doesn't* get the job. His silence is surely golden, at least to the likes of the indicted. Two hundred and six years after the French Revolution, *noblesse oblige*—the elites' version of affirmative action—is alive and well in Troy, Michigan.

Dave Yettaw always used to say, "The UAW is playing checkers, but the corporations are playing chess." You see, the corpo-rats plan every move in advance while the porkchoppers react, one predictable hop at a time. The executives' game plan is to decertify the union: to slowly, methodically strangle it. The scheme is succeeding.

So who neutered the union, and when?

The UAW's balls were embalmed after the 1998 Flint strikes. GM was down for the count and the eyes of the nation were focused on Flint. UAW locals in Michigan, Ohio, Kentucky, Wisconsin, and Tennessee voted to authorize local strikes in support of UAW members in Flint. When GM reopened plants using parts from outside suppliers, workers in Romulus, Michigan, and Bowling Green, Kentucky, disrupted production in protest. At the 1998 UAW Constitutional Convention in June, several delegates proposed a national solidarity action in support of the Flint locals. Delegates saw the confrontation as a national referendum on jobs and outsourcing.

David Sole from Detroit proposed, "Let's take our members, our families and other unions en masse to Flint. We should take our tents and campers with us and be prepared to stay there like we did at Pittston Solidarity Camp."

Suman Bohm from Wilmington, Delaware, said that stealing the dies from the Flint Metal Fab was "an act of aggression against all of us." Sister Bohm asked President Yokich specifically, "What is it that our locals across the nation can do in some sort of massive act of solidarity to support the current strike?"

UAW President Yokich responded, "We are not here to debate a local GM strike." The opportunity for a national confrontation was banished to the back burner, but the pot boiled over.

One GM plant after another shut down. The national economy slowed. The strike was about jobs and outsourcing, but over and above that, it was a struggle for the integrity of the UAW. The world was watching and counting. Fifty-four days. The longest strike against GM since 1970. Then, UAW officials rolled over.

The following year Delphi was spun off. The most sweeping act of outsourcing in GM history was achieved without a whimper, let alone a bang.

The UAW claimed victory but Flint natives know better. The knowledge isn't speculative, it's graphic. Chevy in the Hole is an urban prairie and workers, like buffaloes, are on the nickel.

At the UAW 1999 Bargaining Convention in March, I addressed UAW VP Dick Shoemaker directly. "Stop the Delphi spinoff dead in its tracks or just come out and tell us the truth, now. End the silence. Give us the information we need to make the best decisions for ourselves and our families."

Shoemaker, the hollowest of hollow men, didn't respond. He didn't inform us that UAW members at Delphi would lose their pension credits with GM as a result of the spinoff. Who expects him to tell the truth now?

In October 2004, French journalist Laurent Cibien made a documentary for French television about autoworkers in the United States. He came to Flint because Flint is the heart of industrial conflict in the United States.

GM can demolish the buildings, dismantle the means of production, and undermine the economy of the city, but they can't make people forget that Flint is ground zero. If you're writing about the auto industry in America, and your story needs guts, you go to Flint.

The camera scanned Chevy in the Hole before the demolition was complete. A sign on the property declared, "Demolition Means Progress." The slogan encapsulated the dearth of corporate common sense—sort of like GM downsizing to grow the business, destroying the market to sell more cars, and laying off their most loyal customers.

The filmmakers happened upon two Flint natives in the heart of the city splitting deadwood and loading it onto a rusty red Chevy pickup. The young men were foraging in vacant lots for heating fuel. When asked if they attributed the lack of jobs to GM leaving Flint, they didn't blame GM, they blamed the union.

"We were always sucking on their [GM's] teat," one of the men said, never pausing from his labor. "We became crybabies."

Both men were shirtless in the cool autumn air.

"The union really ruined that kind of industry, being too high paid for very little work. I couldn't help thinking," he said. "They're still crying after all this time when the jobs are going overseas."

He tossed a log onto the truck bed.

"But if they had said something about foreign workers' rights a long time ago, the wages could have gone up there and kept shit down."

He raised the axe over his head and split a log.

"But the unions were only concerned about their own dollar."

Why is common sense so surprising? A union that spends more time and money cooperating with management than organizing workers is an effigy waiting to burn.

The young men personified Flint: strong, energetic, self-reliant, and shirtless. The surrounding buildings were dilapidated, the economy was hooked on chaos and decay, but the woodcutters' spirits were inviolate. They perceived the UAW as wimpy, narrow-minded, and self-centered. The union failed them, but their self-esteem was not diminished by the loss.

GM, Delphi, and the ruling bureaucracy in the UAW are parasites feeding off the carcass of the American Dream. If there is any hope for a new social movement, it will rise up from the ashes of a place like Flint, and cut through the bullshit like an axe. That's the sort of demolition that makes for progress.

"The Future Isn't What It Used to Be"
(September 2005)

A con artist has to win the mark's confidence. So does a salesman, or a politician, or a clown juggling bowling pins. The mark's hope hinges on the con artist's skill. We want him to win, to keep our expectations spinning in the air, defying gravity.

We are all gamblers in the end, hooked on an illusion that we can beat the odds. It's not the occasional windfall that motivates gamblers, it's the suspension of disbelief they crave. The law of reason is as merciless as the wind off Lake Michigan. Not that reason is malicious, it's just cold. Which is why we want to believe the con man when he says, "I'm your best bet." He offers a safe harbor. We want to believe. That's the magic.

Many workers have labored under the promise of a deferred compensation, better known as pensions, for twenty to thirty years. Now, the juggler explains, "Things have changed."

Delphi's new hatchet man, Steve Miller, insists bankruptcy is a last resort. Nevertheless, he keeps bandying the B-word about. It's ludicrous. Delphi stockholders are GM stockholders. The money may be in different pockets, but it's the same pair of pants. A grifter doesn't pick his own pocket. It's union members who are being set up for the shakedown, not inside investors.

Every con begins with a story. Once the illusion is accepted, the *play* bought, and the *confidence* won, all concessions are predictable. The *Detroit Free Press* reported that Miller said, "We can no longer afford to continue to pay all-in wage and benefit costs of approximately one hundred and thirty thousand dollars per year per US hourly worker." ("GM Might Assist Delphi," August 9, 2005.)

Anyone who has ever worked for a living knows this is unadulterated horseshit. But the corporate mouth organs who pass for journalists in the United States accept it without question. How did the Hatchet arrive at this inflated average?

Delphi has 34,000 hourly workers and 14,500 salaried workers in the United States. That's one suit for every 2.4 blue collars (Rick Haglund, "Delphi Filing Could Come by Fall," *Grand Rapids Press*, August 9, 2005). And they accuse laborers of driving Delphi into the ditch? The Hatchet must have averaged production workers with the high rollers in Troy to come up with his one-hundred-and-thirty-thousand-dollar exaggeration. That, or the double bookkeeping confused him.

GM wanted to relieve its legacy costs by outsourcing parts. That paid off, almost. And GM wanted to sweat the parts makers for all they were worth. That paid off, almost, as well. But bankruptcy is not an option when the same swindlers are invested in both companies. Something else has to give, which is where the Finger comes in.

At the 2002 UAW Bargaining Convention in June, UAW president Ron Gettelfinger invited a Wall Street shill, Stephen Girsky, to be the keynote speaker. The gist of his remarks to the delegates was that the UAW needed to make concessions. No surprise there. Girsky is an enemy of working people. He got paid to say that shit, but no one will ever know how much, because joint funds are off the books.

In July 2005, GM hired Girsky to work for the corporation as a consultant. No surprise there, either. Girsky claims he took a pay cut to come to GM. He just wants to help. Apparently his altruism couldn't be satisfied with a Saturday at the soup kitchen.

Now Gettelfinger has hired some other enemies of working people to advise him. "Investment-banking powerhouse Lazard Ltd. of New York will help the union crunch GM's numbers. The New York law firm of Cleary Gottlieb Steen and Hamilton, one of Wall Street's favorite legal advisers, will lend a hand, as will the Washington-based insurance and benefits consultant Milliman Inc." ("UAW Marshals Financial, Legal Help for GM Battle," *Chicago Tribune*, July 23, 2005.)

Wall Street hacks have been saying "Screw the workers" since the first dollar was framed and hung on the wall. If Gettelfinger expects something different, he's insane.

The *Detroit Free Press* explained, "One analyst said the fact the UAW has just hired outside advisers to study GM's finances sounds like what happens at the start of talks, not near the end." (Michael Ellis and Jeffrey McCracken, "GM, UAW Battle over Health Care," July 23, 2005.)

There's a preparation in the works, but it has little to do with number-crunching analysis and much to do with lowering expectations while winning the mark's confidence that "it's the best we could do."

But not all of us are so gullible. Warren Davis, UAW Regional Director in Exile, said, "This is bullshit posturing on Gettelfinger's part. GM might have steered him to these vultures. A decent trade unionist would tell GM to go get bent and to get their best hold."

Billy Robinson, who not only lost his job but had his local union decertified by the International during a strike called by Gettelfinger, said, "The Finger is looking for some place to hide his real intent in letting GM cut benefits for retirees. The workers won't see or feel the real deal until they actually retire. That way, production won't falter."

Gettelfinger hopes we won't notice the sleight of hand, the minor adjustments to the pension plan, incremental concessions, COLA diversions, and co-pay and premium increases until it's too late. The Finger will open the contract, reshuffle the deck, and dare to tell us we won "job security" as if we'd never heard that crap before. As if we didn't understand that winning job security is like handing over your paycheck to a carney in exchange for a stuffed animal.

The whole grift calls to mind Delphi's Suggestion Plan slogan, *The Future Isn't What It Used to Be.*

When you hear an oracle like that you know you are working for extraterrestrials.

What was it the future *used to be?*

Hopeful?

Planned?

Uncertain, of course, but insured in any event?

Well, not any more. *The future isn't what it used to be* and the present is *make believe.*

In a high-stakes version of three-card monte (a short con which requires an inside man, an outside man, and a shill), Delphi, GM, and the UAW want us to believe that concessions are inevitable, that circumstances are beyond their control, and no one is accountable because *the future isn't what it used to be.*

Don't listen to the barker, keep your eyes on his hands. *Money isn't lost, it changes hands.*

Fire the Boss
(October 2005)

Some folks think Steve Miller, Delphi's new CEO, is a straight-shooting, no-nonsense sort of gunslinger. For the most part, these wishful thinkers are hacks writing copy for the corporate press, brokers passing themselves off as "analysts," and assorted brown-nosers who have had their heads stuck up the drainpipe so long their brains have turned into overloaded sump pumps.

The average union member thinks the Hatchet doesn't know his ass from the hole in his head. Hence the confusion between intelligent expression and intestinal effusion.

Miller can't even get his facts straight. He insists the average UAW member at Delphi makes one hundred and thirty thousand dollars per year. If he wants to pay me 130k, I'll take care of my own pension and health care. I'll even donate to the CEO Relief Fund.

The Hatchet is supposed to be a "turnaround specialist." One look at his resume is enough to deduce that's corpo-speak for Pin-the-Tail-on-Employees.

Miller is a corporate carpetbagger with only one tool in his box—bankruptcy. That's not the mark of expertise, it's the tail of a flop. He wants us to believe that stiffing workers and unsecured creditors is the mark of success, but the wreckage left in his wake is off the charts. Any gambler can look successful if they don't tally debt and damage.

Miller's favorite fantasy is how Delphi has been victimized by "legacy costs," that is, the compensation for retirees. But he doesn't admit the total legacy package Delphi inherited tax free: products, patents, machinery, technology, property, and contracts with the largest automotive manufacturer in the world. Delphi was born like a rich man's son—debt free and stocked high with entitlements. And like a prodigal son Miller expects someone else to clean up the mess and pay the price for a squandered legacy.

Do I sound angry? Put yourself in my shoes. A man with no investment of time, energy, or money in Delphi; a man with no ties to the community; a man who won't even be around when the dust settles is threatening to steal my life savings.

The Hatchet thinks Delphi has a legitimate right to renege on its contract with the UAW and its commitment to salaried workers. Why? Because in a capitalist worldview, workers are commodities—products to be bought and sold—not human beings. Allow me a short digression.

Hurricane Katrina ripped the "compassionate conservative" slogan to shreds. Not only is the United States unprepared to protect the working class in New Orleans, the corporate state that passes itself off as a republic is unprepared to protect forty-five million uninsured citizens and countless unemployed or underpaid workers struggling to keep their heads above the waterline. Only the bossing class can expect protection.

The devastation in New Orleans is reminiscent of Flint. One town was drowned by neglect and the other was economically strangled. There are similar pockets of desolation all over this stronghold of "compassionate conservatism." End of digression.

The Hatchet wants to contribute to the body count. And he wants to get it done by October 17, so he can go back to playing with his train set. If Delphi files before the new bankruptcy law takes effect, executives will be able to walk away with fat bonuses.

Delphi wants to close plants in the United States and beg off on its contractual obligation to thousands of workers without any accountability. The company wasn't hoodwinked in negotiations. Delphi understood perfectly well that workers would have to be compensated if and when the company jerked their jobs out from under them. Delphi is not a victim of an unforeseen disaster or free-market catastrophe. GM has been steadily and methodically divesting from Delphi for more than a decade. Likewise, Delphi has been divesting from the United States. It doesn't take a college degree to see the GM-Delphi goal is to undermine the union.

Miller's not a "turnaround specialist," he's a one-trick pony with all the finesse of a Saturday Night Special. A white collar and a tie don't make a thug any less despicable. Miller is loaded with contempt for the working class and drunk on greed.

A company should go into bankruptcy as a last resort, not when it simply wants to nullify a contract with workers and dump the pension. Miller may call it Chapter 11, but if it acts like extortion and it smells like extortion, it is extortion.

If Delphi can restrict the repercussions of bankruptcy to holdings in the United States, what will deter GM from following suit? And every other multinational corporation thereafter?

GM lost money in European, South American, and Asian markets for years. North American operations subsidized those lackluster investments. Likewise, Delphi since its inception has taken profits out of the United States and invested them overseas. The pirates of industry have stolen our legacy. Now the Hatchet wants to drown the survivors by claiming bankruptcy in the United States. If this bankruptcy scheme is pulled off, it will tear the veil from our legal system just as violently as Hurricane Katrina tore the thin veneer of civility off the face of capitalism. We're lost in the reign of a predatory corporate state where, as the old bard once sang, "The cops don't need you and man they expect the same" (Bob Dylan, "Tom Thumb's Blues").

The choice is clear: arm yourself to the teeth and wade into battle or hang from the rafters and wait for a rescue.

Delphi can't reasonably expect workers to sacrifice everything they ever worked for without retaliation. Delphi can't reasonably expect a union to sacrifice its members for a limited truce with an unscrupulous adversary. Likewise, the UAW can't expect to survive if they divide the solidarity of active, retired, and newly hired members into descending tiers of irrelevance. The UAW wants to negotiate opportunities for UAW members to flow back from Delphi to GM, but the deck chairs are blowing overboard faster then they can arrange seating. If we make concessions today, thugs in suits and ties will be back for more tomorrow.

But the company needs to cut expenses, you say?

Fire the boss.

No Holds Barred
(October 17, 2005)

If Delphi UAW members go on strike, they will play into Miller's hands. He will lock us out and shut us down with a chuckle and a grin. A lockout is as good as a quit. Besides, we can't trust the International. We have seen what happens to striking UAW members who get locked out. They lose their jobs, their strike pay, and their local union charters.

Workers concerned about losing homes are anxious about income. It's unreasonable to ask Delphi members to go on strike. If GM-UAW members who voted on our contract want to strike, we welcome the support. But Delphi-UAW members need a radically different strategy.

We should work to rule. We need to stay inside to preserve income, save jobs, and fight back. If we follow every rule in the book, production will slow to a crawl. We can control the flow of parts by ensuring quality and following rules. It's perfectly legitimate.

Work-to-rule creates overtime—something workers faced with a pay cut and loss of pension and health care desperately want and need. Work-to-rule is safe. You can't be fired for following rules. I am not suggesting sabotage or anything illegal. Make no mistake, I am stating clearly and unambiguously, control the shop floor by following all the rules. Workers rule when they work to rule.

Make Health and Safety reps put their donuts down and do some real work for a change. Call out your committee person every day. Of course you have questions. It's only natural. Delphi is in turmoil. It's not our fault. We didn't break the contract. Delphi broke the contract. When there is no trust, there can be no peace.

Miller is the perpetrator here, not us. We aren't the ones who kicked the hornet's nest. Delphi-UAW members have everything to lose. If we roll over without a fight, no amount of concessions will be enough. Concessions only serve to cover closing costs and plump pillows for executives. Why should we pay for their bonuses? There is no empirical evidence that Delphi will stay in the United States. None. Court documents make no bones about Delphi's plans to exit the United States.

Since a lockout is as good as a quit, the International may encourage strikes at Delphi to help GM out of its problems. A lockout would get rid of us. My statement isn't mere cynicism, it's a history lesson. For two decades the UAW has methodically sacrificed members in the auto parts sector to help the Big Three look competitive. Here's how it works.

The International goes along with outsourcing in exchange for organizing workers with the blessing of the new employer. It's called a "neutrality agreement." The process of organizing work formerly done by UAW members in the Big Three for lower wages at a new location is a sleight-of-hand wage cut—less painful but no less insidious.

In 1997, Ford helped the UAW win a strike at a newly organized Johnson Controls plant. Ford refused to install seats it had ordered until JC settled with the UAW. The deal Ford made with the devil-in-disguise was cut out of the same cloth as UAW cooperation with outsourcing. Ford was complicit in organizing and the International was complicit in cutting wages for work outsourced from Ford.

Likewise, a GM-Delphi plant in Grand Rapids, Michigan, was sold to Lear in 1998. Their work was outsourced to newly organized Lear plants with lower wages. Despite concessions, the old plant will close in December. The International was complicit in the scheme to cut wages in order to benefit General Motors. Neutrality agreements aren't free. Someone has to pay.

I believe the UAW PR Department has consistently failed to publicly defend Delphi members for a reason. The International is eager to help its cash cow—GM—by tacitly justifying the purge at Delphi. For example, when Miller says Delphi workers average one hundred and thirty thousand dollars per year, the UAW doesn't correct the record because it wants the public to believe that we are overpaid. I'm not cynical, I'm knowledgeable.

IRS documents show that GM funnels millions of dollars to the International UAW through the conduit of joint funds, which are controlled by the UAW-GM Center for Human Resources (CHR), an independent nonprofit corporation chaired by union and management personnel including UAW VP Dick Shoemaker. The stated purpose of CHR is "to enable the employer to compete in a global marketplace" (UAW-GM Center for Human Resources By-Laws, Article II). How do they achieve competitiveness? By reducing jobs and cutting wages.

The GM-UAW Team planned a wage reduction at Delphi, but hoped to control the process and manage the upheaval through attrition and transfer. The pop of the stock market bubble and concomitant fraud blew the cover. As the urge to dump legacy costs accelerated, the slow train of wage reduction jumped the tracks and ran smack into an immovable object—the contract. The company-union team decided there was only one solution: the cremation of the National Agreement.

Now Miller has the chutzpah to tell us he will preserve pensions if we agree to wage cuts. Does he really imagine that anyone trusts him?

There is much uncertainty these days, but there are three things we know for sure:

1) No Delphi executive can be trusted. They are crooks.
2) Miller is determined to hijack our pension fund, gut our benefits, and cut our wages.
3) The UAW will present a concession agreement which they will claim wins *job security*.

I am not making a prediction, I am reiterating history. Every time the International presents a concession contract they claim they won job security. There is no historical evidence to support that spurious job-saving claim, but Shoemaker will act like he saved us from the jaws of death. It's a lie. He wants us to make sacrifices so he can help his business partner, General Motors.

The concessions Shoemaker will try to sell us will further divide the UAW. There may be a deal to let some of us retire early rather than face wage cuts. Such deals cannot be trusted. They will pit member against member. This is not conjecture, it's UAW history. A contract that divides workers is anti-union and destined to self-destruct. Retirees can't screw the people they leave behind and expect to live happily ever after.

The UAW was well aware of GM's long-term plan to shuck pension liability and cut costs. They cooperated behind a curtain of job security clauses. The curtain caught fire and the guarantees went up in smoke. International office rats are negotiating for their own survival now, not ours.

The only thing that can move an inert object—UAW International—is an unstoppable force—rank-and-file militancy. To that end, we should organize rank-and-file meetings at various locations to demand answers and take action. We don't want lawyers. We want action.

We should hold rank-and-file meetings so we can brainstorm how to fight back and win. I don't believe we will be able to live in peace if we shrug our collective shoulders and say, "There's nothing we can do about it." The serenity of spiritual surrender is not achieved without struggle. Like an elderly woman said during the bus boycott in Montgomery, Alabama, "My feets is tired, but my soul is at rest." Peace of mind does not come from avoiding conflict, it comes from the right action.

Perhaps the inertia of the International Union is immovable, but that doesn't mean the momentum of the rank and file is stoppable. We just may have to run them over.

Miller has backed us into a corner. He expects us to give up without a fight. He said, "No one will like it, but in the end they will do it, and they will do it the right way." He plays a good game, but for us this isn't a game, it's our life, and we must fight for all it's worth.

Realistically, I don't believe we can succeed alone. GM-UAW members and the International will probably not stand in solidarity with us. If, in the end, it comes to that, we may as well bring the house down with us. When the judge nullifies the contract, it's no holds barred. Welcome the wildcat and say hello to chaos. If we are forced to lose our life savings—pension, health care, wages—why should we heed Miller's advice? "The best thing they can do is stay on the job," he said. Screw that. We may as well go for broke.

Why should Miller and his band of thieves profit from our demise? Shut them down. Delphi wants out of the United States? Get out now. GM wants our products but not our retirees? Cut them off cold. Solidarity House wants to be partners in the business? Charge them with collusion. Miller wants a controlled bloodbath? Let it flow. There is no reason why the bloodbath should be restricted to Delphi workers and retirees. Bring the whole rotten edifice—GM, Delphi, and the UAW—down.

How's that for a legacy, Mr. Miller?

Promises Are Like Deer Prints
(October 30, 2005)

On October 27, the Bobble Heads distributed a petition from our regional office. The attached letter requested that UAW members enjoin their friends and family to sign this petition requesting the bankruptcy judge to be nice to us and uphold our contract. The last sentence actually read, "We pray you use your power wisely."

Pray? Does the UAW Regional Director want us to believe we are talking to God? What next? Will the International organize a caravan of buses to the courthouse in New York where UAW members will hold hands, and on the count of three . . . start crying?

The headline would read: "United Auto Whiners Speak Tears to Power" . . . until Miller pulls up in his stretch Hummer and scolds, "Dry your eyes, blow your noses, quit whining and sniveling, and get back to making car parts."

The petition doesn't have one legal leg to stand on. The judge will never read it. His secretary will file it under *Useless And Worthless*. UAW Region 1-D director Don Oetman knows the petition is pointless. Oetman is trying to pretend he had a brainstorm and the Bobble Heads are going along because it's so much fun to pretend.

I appreciate the rank-and-file members who in all sincerity have written and circulated petitions seeking public support for Delphi autoworkers. They are genuine, but for Oetman this is a sideshow, a diversion from the fact that he is holed up. A real leader would've been on the shop floor when the shit hit the fan, not crouching in his bunker with a bag of donuts and a cocoa.

The rank-and-file meeting in Grand Rapids is attracting interest from UAW members all over the Midwest and even New York. Many who plan to attend are not Delphi workers. They see Delphi as the lead domino and the GM health care concessions for retirees as the breach of a sacred trust. The broad response to what was intended to be a local meeting is an indication of a vacuum of leadership at the top. Reporters aren't the only ones who get "no comment." The silence out of Solidarity House is ominous.

GM-UAW retirees feel betrayed, for good reason. They've campaigned for COLA on pension since 1976 when International reps gave themselves COLA on pension. The International's response was always, "Don't worry. We will always take care of you." It is unethical to take contractual benefits from retirees. The UAW does not have the legal right to bargain for people who are not working, who don't pay dues, and who can't vote on the rotten deal.

Meanwhile, Delphi UAW members are feeling the heat from Commando Miller's flamethrower. He verbally backhands us every day in the press. Delphi workers don't know if they will be able to make the mortgage payment or retire with their shirts on, but they keep paying union dues and waiting patiently for the cavalry. As my union brother Dean Braid likes to say, "Is it time to put down the golf club and grab hold of the picket sign yet?"

Where have all the International reps gone? Are they still singing "Kumbaya" with their corporate partners at the Center for Human Resources? Has anyone seen a Regional Director anywhere? Oh that's right, the local union leadership was invited to the regional office to shake hands with the governor of Michigan, Jennifer Granholm. Maybe she will fight for us? Is that what unionism is based on? Pretty blondes and wishful thinking? Golf lessons and campaign contributions?

Wishful thinking is the notion that someone else will take care of your business and fight your battles for you. Hope is fighting like hell against all odds. I don't believe in wishful thinking, but like many other UAW members, I am full to bursting with hope.

Union bureaucrats have operated under the competitive-partnership model for so long, they don't have a clue how to respond. They've lost the ability to mobilize members and fight to win. Perhaps we should be more understanding; their partners just kicked them out of bed and they have sore tushes and wounded feelings to nurse.

Office rats don't have answers. We, the members, are the answer.

We have nothing to lose and everything to gain by fighting to win. Members demoralized by years of company unionism and teamwork slogans are looking at their hands and listening to their hearts. We can build, repair, produce, and deliver for Commandant Miller, or we can bring GM-Delphi to their knees by simply doing what we are told by the bosses—nothing more and nothing less. We can turn up the volume and let the silence humming out of Solidarity House numb our brains, or we can listen to our hearts and trump company-union defeatism with the courage of a single conviction: we are worth fighting for.

Delphi deserves what it pays for: a half-day's work for a half-day's pay. Or was that a third?

The corporations sense the labor movement's weakness. They are determined to decimate and throttle the working class while we are down and in disarray. We must connect the Delphi plants so that our efforts are coordinated and strategic rather than random. We must also connect with other union members who may rise to our defense. Strikes are a valuable tool, but Delphi is eager to shut down a lot of sites. Those plants at risk of closure must continue to operate and/or be occupied if idled by strikes in other locations. Miller ignited the fire; it is up to us to bank the fire and spread the resistance.

Furthermore, we deserve to be treated like dues-paying members. When we ask to see a legally binding copy of the GM-UAW Benefit Guarantee alluded to in the 1999 Delphi-UAW contract *Highlights*, the Bobble Heads tell us we have to trust the International. If it exists, why can't we see it? Why shouldn't our brothers and sisters with thirty-plus years of service be allowed to make decisions based on verifiable documents? "Promises," as my friend and coworker Jimmy Jean says, "are like deer prints. They're exciting, but when you fry them up they don't amount to a forkful."

Reporters insist there is a Benefit Guarantee because the corpos told them so. They still don't get it. Their primary sources are frauds and the annual report is a deer trail. Sure, where there's hoof prints there's deer, and GM may be responsible for a bunch of children it can't afford, which, like the old song says, "is what you get for making whoopee." But the point is, the Benefit Guarantee is not laid out in the UAW-GM-Delphi contracts. Custody will get worked out in court. The honeymoon is over, children, and stepdaddy is all stick and no carrot.

Our series of rank-and-file meetings, beginning November 6 in Grand Rapids, Michigan, and the following week in Kokomo, Indiana, have a straightforward agenda. It's an enlistment drive. We need what Brother Miguel Chavarria calls "Soldiers of Solidarity." Our object is to unleash our unruliness on the system of production and strike down the Finger's betrayal of our sacred trust with retirees. The Soldier of Solidarity code pledges to protect retirees as they protected us and to protect new hires as we expect to be protected. Soldiers of Solidarity represent hope for a new direction in the future of the union, because we're willing to fight like hell against all odds and never give up.

Where Cost and Profit Punch It Out
(November 22, 2005)

The UAW is in the midst of its worst catastrophe since Caterpillar, and the November issue of *Solidarity* magazine features stories about Hurricane

Katrina. Not one word about Delphi. Must have bad reception at the country club. No one on the mag seems to have noticed that Miller shot jointness right between the eyes.

On November 2, Gettelfinger saddled up and joined the fightback posse, too late and a bottle short, but laggards are always welcome at the Lost Cause Bar. At the UAW's corporate offices in Detroit (Center for Human Resources) Gettelfinger told local union leaders that it was time to "work to rule."

I am not sure if he knows what that means, because the International hasn't followed up with an education program or an organizational strategy, but fish are in the barrel and we Michiganian rednecks are always well armed and ready to shoot.

Shoemaker concurred with Gettelfinger that the UAW is on a collision course with Delphi. It appears a strike is inevitable, not because the International doesn't want concessions, but because Miller doesn't respect them enough to sleep with them.

For rank-and-file members the choice is clear: strike on the outside or strike on the inside. Frankly, I prefer the inside. Michigan is getting colder than a witch's tear.

Most of us saw the train crash coming a mile off, but then we have our ears to the rail every day. I hope the Shoe-Finger duet doesn't get the pasta syndrome because the temperature is only going up. High-ranking office rats are famous for going limp at high temps, but hot water tends to make the rank and file mean. Brother Pat Ladwig, for example, took offense to a statement by Dean Braid in the last *Live Bait & Ammo*. Dean said, "Is it time to put the golf club down and grab hold of the picket sign yet?" Ladwig argued that he can carry both.

Scabs beware. Ladwig is wielding a nine-iron.

In a very short time, we will either be on strike or working without a contract at drastically reduced wages. When there is no contract, there are no rules, and members must rely solely on their solidarity, creativity, and collective action for protection. We can't beat the company at the legal game. They own the courts and the politicians. As Brother Mike Wittek said, "The only thing the company fears is workers sticking together because they know we control production."

Working to rule is simple. The machine stops. The boss says, "What's wrong?" I say, *I don't know*. He asks the job setter, who replies, *I don't know*. He asks another coworker, who replies, *I don't know*. Then we all look at the boss and he starts sweating because he knows that we know—he's the one who *really* doesn't know.

Bosses like to boss, so do them all a favor and give them lots of bossing to do. The boss will like you for it and everyone will be happy keeping labor costs down by *outsourcing all decisions to the boss*.

In a concerted effort to uphold lean inventories we should pay meticulous attention to details in the process control instructions and concentrate on safe practices like *lockout*.

Working to rule is not complicated. Just follow orders: nothing more, nothing less. If you do what the boss says, you can't get in trouble, but rest assured, it will be something stupid. Don't question it, just do it. For example, if the boss says, "We need parts really bad," give him what he asked for—"really bad" parts.

I'm joking. Our customers are more important than the numbers. We don't want one of our brothers or sisters who buys a GM vehicle—oh, that's right, no one in our families will ever buy a GM vehicle again. Well, we don't want to hurt any poor schmuck who is foolish enough to buy a GM product. So please, maintain quality *at all costs*.

Furthermore, remind fellow union members at GM to inspect all Delphi components carefully and if they find any defects, *send them back*. Never forget, we want to *exceed our customers' expectations*.

And why not refuse voluntary overtime, knowing full well that Delphi will have to make up for it? Delphi is geared to run overtime all the time. Turn it down now, or strike for it later. The overtime you work today will extend the picket line you walk tomorrow.

Now, don't get me wrong. We all want to "take the money and run," as Steve Miller sang while his cloven-footed cronies waddled up to the trough before claiming bankruptcy. But we must look at the proposition like reasonable businessmen. If we can't raise the price of our product, which is our labor, the only way we can make a profit is by reducing our cost. What is our cost? Our cost is the effort we put into our labor. So work smart. The less effort one expends, the higher the profit margin. We should all follow Mr. Miller's ethic and reduce the cost of the product we sell in order to be more profitable. What capitalist can argue with that? We are on the same page of the same hymnbook when we reduce costs in order to make bigger profits for ourselves.

Bolster the movement, member to member, and remind each other, over and over, you can't rush quality any more than you can make a fish bite a bare hook. And please, be kind to union officials—they need us more than we need them. Without the collective strength of members on the shop floor, officials have no gunpowder. If the rank and file walk out the door, it's a strike. But if the bargaining chair walks out the door alone, he's fired.

Having said that, I want to reiterate: I am not a union official, I am a wordsmith. I don't call the shots, I just fire them straight to the heart of the matter—UAW officials are AWOL. They claim to have a plan, but they don't want to tell anybody what it is. That's the same thing Yokich told Accuride workers from Local 2036 before he threw in the towel and decertified the Local. Secrecy kindles suspicion.

At Local 2151, we still have appointees lounging in the front office with management and sipping tea as if everything was cozy. Our local union vice president actually doubles in an appointed position called "Win the Business." We have another appointee taking "suggestions." And one whose sole purpose is to promote "teamwork."

The honeymoon is over, folks. We have an openly adversarial relationship with management and appointees are literally collaborating with the enemy. What's more, they accuse rank-and-file members of "dividing the union." They are so indoctrinated the irony escapes them.

When the bear comes for your lunch you don't have to unwrap it for him, heat it up, put it in a clean bowl, and spoon-feed him with a smile. If you feed the bear, he will be back for more tomorrow and every day thereafter. Don't feed the bear. Don't fraternize with the enemy and don't expect office rats to fight for workers.

The UAW International, organized like a totem pole—one empty wooden head on top of another—recently banded together with five other totem poles (Mobilizing@Delphi—a union coalition organizing program) for a bureaucratic slowdown. They chewed each bite of pork chop twenty-five times and the walls of CHR trembled like Jell-O. Bureaucrats often confuse hyperventilating with mobilizing.

Did anyone imagine they would actually hurl their bodies onto the greasy gears of commerce? Heck no. They went out to eat. They binged and merged in an orgiastic confabulation to make themselves feel bigger. Too bad fatter doesn't equal stronger. Nevertheless, we should take heart in the development. As Dean Braid said, "That's great. Now we'll get double lip service."

The rank and file have a plan, and we don't mind telling everyone it is based on inflicting economic hardship on GM-Delphi until management understands that a fair contract is cheaper than industrial combat. We have no intention of sheepishly walking off the cliff of economic self-destruction. We have no intention of being replaced. We have no intention of handing our union to Miller on a silver plate. Delphi's failure is the result of mismanagement, racketeering, and fraud. We refuse to bear the punishment for their crimes and incompetence.

Rank-and-file members are organizing horizontally at the make-or-break point of production where cost and profit punch it out. Miller can blow smoke up the stack until the sky turns black and analysts pass out from lack of oxygen. But when workers run production backwards, cost exceeds profit and the consequences fit the criminals like handcuffs.

Until Their Ears Bleed and Their Wallets Weep
(November 29, 2005)

The UAW gave GM the biggest concession package in history (the initial Voluntary Employees Beneficiary Association plan, or VEBA, which included cuts to both active and retired members) and GM responded by spitting in our collective faces. The announcement of plant closures and the elimination of thirty thousand jobs underscores what UAW dissidents have asserted all along: Concessions Don't Save Jobs.

For Delphi workers, the plant closures mean No Exit. The news strikes them like a door slammed in their faces. We aren't alone. Thousands of supplier jobs will be lost in the wake of GM plans to idle production. There's nowhere to run, nowhere to hide, and everything to fight for.

Since the announcement of bankruptcy at Delphi the UAW International has gone into the bunker crouch: hands over head, head between knees. What little information we do get is delivered to local officials unsigned. Local leaders are expected to bear responsibility with their own signatures. When reps don't want to leave tracks, you know you're about to get stabbed in the back.

The latest unsigned information sheet described the "Benefit Guarantee Letter." Already the language is changing. Formerly, it read, "GM will *provide* up to seven years of pension credits." Now it reads, "up to seven years of additional pension credits *can be earned* by a Covered Employee who continues to work at Delphi or a successor employer" (emphasis added).

In other words, if an employee wants to salvage a pension, he or she must continue to work for Delphi at reduced wages. The need to *earn* additional pension credits, coupled with the lack of transfer opportunities, handcuffs us to the pay cut. There's no exit. Fighting back is the only option.

This latest bit of untraceable information states, "There is no contractual or legal advantage to retiring at any time now or in the near future if one is currently retirement eligible." If now or later makes no difference, should we deduce that the screwing is complete? Countersunk, so to speak?

The letter concludes, "This summary is based on current understandings of contractual obligations and pension laws. This is neither a Summary Plan Description nor the Plan Document."

"Current understandings?" Why the plural? Is there more than one understanding? Does the modifier "current" imply that "understandings" are temporary and thus subject to change?

There are many questions, but no International rep has stepped forward to answer those questions. If there was a legitimate contract or supplement that enumerated the terms of the GM Benefit Guarantee, all our questions could be answered by Local Benefit Reps.

But no such document exists.

Shoemaker said the Benefit Guarantee was part of our contract. If US Bankruptcy Court judge Robert Drain voids the contract, will the Benefit

Guarantee be drained as well? Does anyone else find it suspicious that we can't see a Summary Plan Description or the actual Plan Document?

GM insists its liability ranges from zero to twelve billion dollars. The wide range of the estimate indicates that the guarantee is in negotiation and the outcome is uncertain. The UAW's reluctance to produce a legally binding document indicates the exact language is uncertain. The UAW's unwillingness to sign letters of information concerning the Benefit Guarantee indicates that UAW reps themselves are uncertain. The International insists we must trust them without question, but their history renders their credibility uncertain. The only thing we can be sure of at this point is uncertainty.

The UAW is dominated by the Administration Caucus. After twenty-five years of collaboration with the companies, the Ad Caucus may as well change its name to the Concession Caucus. Different names, same difference, like two sides of a coin called company union.

We must prepare to mount a Vote No campaign because the Concession Caucus will try to sell us out. This is not speculation, it's historical perspective. The Con Caucus has the same worldview as the bosses: that is, workers must sacrifice for the good of the company. As a result, the Con Caucus feels duty-bound to deliver concessions to its "partners in the business."

The Con Caucus slogan is "Buy American," because they believe the union's mission is to promote the company by selling cars rather than organizing workers. It's a falsehood. If the Con Caucus had organized America rather than sold America you could buy any nameplate you wanted and rest assured it was union. Furthermore, the transplants and nonunion suppliers wouldn't have a competitive advantage, because the Con Caucus would have taken workers out of the competition rather than throwing them to the dogs.

Let's quit speculating and rely on what we know for a fact. The Con Caucus already agreed with Delphi on benchmark "competitive wage and benefit levels."

In the Delphi-UAW Supplement signed on April 29, 2004, the Con Caucus determined that fourteen dollars per hour was "competitive." How can they argue differently now? Furthermore, the Supplement eliminated COLA for the first four years, and granted only 70 percent of COLA until the third quarter of the sixth year of the agreement. On top of that, the Con Caucus agreed to reduce health care benefits and eliminate pensions.

Miller wants even deeper pay and benefit cuts. There is a pattern here.

At the Lear plant in Comstock, Michigan (which was formerly GM, then Delphi before it was sold to Lear), UAW Local 1231 members were coerced into accepting a wage cut in order to "save jobs." The plant is now closed. The work was disbursed to other Lear plants that *won* the whipsawing competition. At an IPS conference in May 2005, UAW vice president Bob King gave Lear an award for being "union friendly" because they let him "organize" new Lear plants that took work from previously organized Lear plants. The Con Caucus sanctions outsourcing, then calls it a victory when they organize the old work at reduced wages.

Based on historical evidence we can reasonably expect the Con Caucus to deliver a concession package that includes a promise of "job security." That's right, "job security." Every concession contract and tax abatement comes with the promise to "save jobs." The promises never materialize, but hustlers never let honesty get in the way of a deal. The Con Caucus is determined to come to the aid of GM by sacrificing members in the parts supply sector again. That's not speculation, it's their MO.

We must prepare to fight the war on two fronts. First against GM-Delphi, and second with a Vote No campaign against the concessions the Con Caucus is sure to deliver wrapped in buyouts and bonuses and sparkly promises.

Liberals fight for a cause, radicals fight for their lives. Our lives are on the line. How well we organize on the shop floor will seal our fate. This is not a battle one can retire from. There's nowhere to run and nowhere to hide. GM-Delphi is determined to take away everything we ever earned: wages, pension, benefits, seniority, and humane working conditions.

We don't need to hear any more crap from International reps about how we need to get more involved. We are involved. We are involved in a battle every day with a company that treats us like scrap. In fact, we can't escape. We are on the front lines of the class war, and we don't need to hear another dumb-ass speech promoting campaign contributions to Democrats as the hallmark of unionism.

The barn is burning. The Big Three and their Two Ugly stepsisters, Delphi and Visteon, have been talking about partnership, teamwork, and "growing the business" since 1984. The real goal was always *soften the target and move in for the kill.* The kill is here. No politician is coming to the rescue.

What we need are tools and direct-action tactics, not bureaucratic bullshit and informational pickets organized by the Con Caucus and condoned by Miller because, as he related in a voicemail to managers, the pickets "won't disrupt production." That's what counts—production.*

Miller is the master ringleader of sideshow distractions. The real issue is the looting of our pensions and the destruction of our standard of living. We need to exert pressure at the point of production, the true fulcrum of worker leverage. If we take the battle to the shop floor, the intersection of Cost and Profit, we can turn the cutting edge of the axe against Miller and his band of incompetent frauds. We can force them to exit by grinding the gears of production until their ears bleed and their wallets weep.

"Three Choices: Strike, Work to Rule, or Lie Down"
(December 17, 2005)

In 2003, UAW members at GM and Delphi negotiated together and ratified the National Contract together as if they were one bargaining unit. The International Union justified the combined ratification by asserting that our contracts were "mirror agreements" and that our mutual interests were inextricably bound together. I appealed that decision to the Public Review Board. I argued that the companies were separate and independent and thus we should have held separate ratifications (PRB Case No. 1504).

---

*The UAW organized informational pickets with the permission of Steve Miller.

I lost. The Public Review Board upheld the International Union's decision. Who am I to question the distinguished judgment of the Public Review Board? I humbly concur.

The UAW bargained with GM and Delphi as if they were one company in 2003. UAW members at GM and Delphi ratified the contracts together as if they were one and the same agreement. If that was a wise strategy in 2003, then striking GM and Delphi as one union should be the logical outcome of that strategy in 2005. As Walter Reuther said, "If you close one plant, we will close all the plants."

The contract we ratified together is under attack. The International Union cannot in good conscience let Delphi UAW members get cut from the herd and led to the slaughter alone. If we were one union in 2003, then we damn well better act like one union now.

GM and Delphi are not separate, independent companies. The machines in Delphi plants are tagged "Property of General Motors." GM didn't spin off the means of production, it simply spun off its responsibility to workers.

If GM breaks the union at Delphi, where will the reign of economic terror end? In retirement? Our retirement is only as secure as the members we leave behind. Real social security is solidarity. If we abandon our brothers and sisters, leave them to fight alone, or stick them with a disastrous wage cut, we are writing our own epitaph. To cut and run is not a union option.

In 1970, the UAW struck GM for Thirty-and-Out* and COLA. We all benefited from that battle. Now, it is our generation's turn to engage in the struggle for economic justice. This is our historical moment. The course we set today will determine the future of the union.

GM set up Delphi to dump our pensions, cut our wages, and bust our union. It's not just about the money, it's about power and control—power to dictate the conditions of our labor, and power to control production without restraint.

According to the dictates of this proposed contract, GM-Delphi will close or sell plants at will. Whoever buys a GM-Delphi plant will not be required to honor the existing contract. Delphi will hire a large number

---

* Retirement after thirty years.

of temps. Lines of demarcation will dissolve, as will job preference. Seniority will count for nothing. The only clause in the contract that GM-Delphi wants to preserve untouched is the "no-strike" clause.

This proposal isn't just about the money, it's about union busting. And it's not going to stop at Delphi or Visteon. It's coming to the Big Three in 2007.

When sit-down strikers in Flint won recognition for the UAW in 1937, they didn't win it by writing letters to the editor. They didn't win it by donating to union-controlled political pots and voting Democrat. They won by taking power into their own hands. When we turn control over to politicians, or International reps who claim to have a plan but won't tell us what it is, we don't empower ourselves, we only reinforce the pattern of learned helplessness.

We have been indoctrinated with the policy of helplessness. It's a lie. We are not defenseless victims. We have power. We control production. We can bring General Motors to its knees. The sit-downers won because they seized control of the shop floor. They won because they shut down GM. Our challenge is no less. As Marty Shawl from Local 699 said at the Soldiers of Solidarity meeting in Flint, "We have three choices: strike, work to rule, or lie down."

We must shut down General Motors or we will all—GM, Delphi, Ford, Chrysler, Visteon, American Axle, Lear, Caterpillar—lose everything we ever earned. GM is leading the assault on the working class. And the rank and file is leading the resistance because there is so little leadership coming out of Solidarity House.

Shoemaker reported from the UAW's corporate offices, the CHR, in Detroit on December 1, 2005, "The *most* we can expect is a soft landing." In other words, a crash landing is more likely. Shoemaker said it "might" be possible to get assistance from GM "through the end of this contract." What contract? The one UAW members from GM and Delphi voted on together? Or the one Judge Drain is about to flush?

Shoemaker claimed the UAW gave Delphi a two-tier supplement in order to "help Delphi compete." That's not a bargaining strategy, it's collusion. Gross mismanagement, fraud, and racketeering, not workers, are responsible for GM-Delphi's failure.

The Concession Caucus has the same worldview as the corporations: that is, workers must sacrifice for the company and compete with other workers. Whereas Walter Reuther said, "We must take labor out of the competition," the Concession Caucus forces workers into competition. When the Con Caucus adopted the corporate view of the world, they bound our wrists and instructed us to work with our hands. The Con Caucus won't tell us what the plan is, because the plan is to sacrifice Delphi workers for the benefit of GM. That is not speculation, it's their pattern, their MO. The Con Caucus has consistently sold out members in the parts sector of the industry to prop up the Big Three. Why should Delphi or Visteon members expect anything different?

Shoemaker said we must "try to save jobs," presumably with concessions since that is all he knows how to do. The fact that concessions have never saved jobs doesn't faze Shoemaker. He said, "the best we will probably be able to do is to buy time for retirements and save some plants." Shoemaker is waving the white flag before the fight begins. And why not? His retirement is not in jeopardy. He will walk away with a gold-plated pension, free health care, and . . . a facelift, courtesy of the corporate media.

SOS members have been accused of dividing the union, but we aren't the ones who collaborate with management. We aren't the ones who enjoy the perks of partnership. We are the ones who, as Dave Yettaw said, "have dedicated the best part of their lives working on the relentless assembly line, day after day, to provide a dignified life and decent standard of living for their families."

Get It in Writing
(January 2006)

Delphi has scaled the pinnacle of incompetence. I asked for the verification of nothing, and management could not deliver. I was floored. I thought surely they could expeditiously confirm nothing. Who could ask for less? I felt like the bottom fell out of the bottom.

My query was not an existential dilemma. I simply asked management to confirm that I did not have a locker in the plant. I requested in writing the verification of nothing. How hard could that be? Security checked the roster and indeed my name had been removed from the infamous locker list long ago. But management refused to give me written confirmation that I did not in fact own a locker.

The security head acted as if I was trying to trick him. He got all Nancy Drewish and sly about it. He wasn't going to let a non-knowledge worker con him into falsifying documentation. He was convinced it was a scam.

I'm the one who deserves to be suspicious. I know they want to fire me. I can see the bile dripping from their lips. When I punch the time clock I feel like Pavlov's bell ringing for the dogs at the gates of hell.

Recently, management brought cops with drug-sniffing dogs into the plant. They didn't find anything. No one was surprised. Once through the doors, the poor dogs' nostrils were choked with the acrid scent of calibration fluid. No one's nostrils, not even a dog's, can smell anything after a whiff of that shit.

I got rid of my crappy company locker long ago. I know the game. No matter whose name is attached, if it's on company property, the company owns it and retains the right to invade it. I wasn't going to let them set me up that easy. I relinquished ownership and became a man without a locker the day before I distributed *Live Bait & Ammo* #1.

Now, since the drug-sniffing-dog incident, I wanted written confirmation from management that I did indeed *not* have a locker for them to stash dope in. I wanted written verification of nothing, but management couldn't deliver.

I am used to fighting with management. I have accepted that it is part of my job to force management to do their jobs. Every day, union members have to fight with management to provide us with the tools and the resources we need to manufacture quality products. It's nonsense, but it's the Delphi system. I am accustomed to calling out the union to enforce quality standards, safe work practices, and strict adherence to process control instructions.

We actually have a formal procedure for this chronic altercation. If union members have a quality concern they are instructed to follow the

Quality Network process up and down the Himalayas of corporate hierarchy. A salmon could swim upstream, spawn, fool around, outwit death, haggle a fisherman out of his hat, and escape to the high seas faster than a worker could navigate the Quality Network rapids. If you want results, stop production and demand an AVO (Avoid Verbal Orders). In other words, my Standard Operating Procedure is "Get It in Writing."

Here's the drill: under normal conditions union members work to the rule and management works against the rule. That's the rule at Delphi.

If Delphi abolished all the rules, it would be less chaotic, but then no one would want to purchase products from them, so they abide by all the standards and procedures of a world class manufacturer . . . on paper.

In the mind of Delphi, if such a thing may be said to exist, anything on paper is real and anything with material substance is questionable. Thus, my demand for written confirmation of nothing turned a mirror on the poor foreman's origami mentality. I was in essence asking him to make nothing real. I thought he was going to have a nervous breakdown or a Zen breakthrough.

"Get It in Writing" is my motto. I have a file chock full of AVOs giving me orders to run scrap. It is standard operating procedure at Delphi to violate the rule against making scrap. A worker can be fired for making scrap, but Delphi has to have those numbers and they can't wait for the fix. Quotas take precedence over quality standards and error-proofing. Which is not to say that we deliver poor-quality parts to our customers. We don't. We just have to sort a lot of crap. We don't build quality, we inspect for quality. Or as Mike Wittek says, "We don't have time to do it right the first time, but we have time to do it over and over and over."

It doesn't have to be that way, but management insists on working against the rule. Anything Edward Deming, the master of quality control, ever said is taboo at Delphi. Continuous paperwork, not improvement, is the practice. In fact, Delphi is so adamant about working against the rule that they are offended by workers who wear "Work to Rule" buttons. Some supervisors act insulted by the insinuation that anyone would even want to work to rule.

USA Today reported, "In one instance, Delphi sold one hundred and forty-five million dollars, worth of scrap inventory to Murfreesboro,

Tenn.–based Setech Inc., an inventory management firm, and booked the sale as income even though its agreement with Setech required Delphi to buy the inventory back. The suit claims Delphi executives arranged a total of four hundred and forty million dollars' worth of similar deals." ("Pension Funds Sue Delphi over Accounting Practices," *USA Today*, October 6, 2005). In other words, Delphi sold scrap and recorded it as profit. Bought it back and recorded it as an asset.

Such actions may seem confusing, even fraudulent, unless you view them through the lens of the Delphi Ultimate Management Action Strategy System (DUMASS).

The key to a balanced budget is *eliminate scrap*. The key to higher productivity is *eliminate scrap*. The key to first-time quality is *eliminate scrap*. The key to on-time delivery is *eliminate scrap*. The key to higher efficiency is *eliminate scrap*. The key to profitability is *eliminate scrap*. The key to success is *eliminate scrap*. DUMASS #1: Ignore the obvious.

If Delphi really wanted to save money the Board of Derelicts could replace Miller with a smoke machine. They could replace half the supervisors with robots that doubled as floor dusters. They could initiate a *pay for knowledge rate* for executives. They could reward success instead of failure and fraudulence. DUMASS #2: All feedback must affirm that the boss is right.

The guiding principle of the Delphi system is simple: tell workers we are family, then advise them in the most unctuous paternal voice that the only solution is human sacrifice. If this was Japan, Delphi executives would kill themselves, but in America it is conventional wisdom that workers must sacrifice themselves for the incompetent cronies of the corporate class. DUMASS #3: Regard workers as waste to be eliminated. Disregard scrap as the cost of doing business.

If success depended on juggling jargon, flipping flow charts, or a business plan based on acronyms such as LEAN (Layoff Every American Now), Delphi would be leading us into a new era of Industrial Revolution. Alas, there's nothing virtual about car parts. They're as real as rust and harder than Chinese arithmetic. DUMASS #4: Cover up the bullshit with crap—PowerPoints and graphs.

Delphi's reorganization plan hinges on cutting wages below the poverty line, depriving people of health care, and draining the pension fund. Our children won't be left behind in school because they aren't tested. Our children will be left behind because they are hungry, because they need health care, because their parents can't find work, because we can't afford teachers, because in Miller's world no one counts but him. DUMASS #5: People are the least important resource. Screw them all.

The other day I pointed out to my supervisor that 25 percent of the fixtures on my Bodine were turned off. (A Bodine is a complicated piece of machinery with multiple functions running simultaneously off several different cams. The Bodine synchronizes pneumatics, lasers, cameras, various mechanical apparatuses, and an automatic welder. It assembles a fuel injector and probably replaced a dozen workers.) Twenty-five percent of the fixtures were turned off because they were broken or malfunctioning. I showed him this material fact and revealed the computer graphics to support my assertion.

"What should we do?" I asked. "You're the knowledge worker."

He just looked at me. I thought to myself, "I better get it in writing."

But the look on his face was completely blank. He didn't understand that I was asking him to produce the knowledge and direction for which he is paid. He was dumbfounded.

Finally, he muttered something unintelligible. I asked him to repeat it.

"We've been having some problems with those inserts," he said.

"We don't make excuses here, we make car parts," I replied.

And then it dawned on me how absurd I was acting. I apologized.

"I'm sorry, sir. I forgot where I was. This is the Delphi Ultimate Management Action Strategy System. Twenty-five percent inefficiency is built in. But for the record, could you put that in writing, so no one thinks that by working to rule I am obstructing production?" DUMASS #6: If you get caught covering up incompetence with double bookkeeping, create a distraction and blame the union.

A Rat's Fur

(January 3, 2006)

GM-Delphi's hired gun, Steve "The Hatchet" Miller, is playing coy. He copped a new attitude, pulled his death threat off the table, and vowed silence until GM, Delphi, and the UAW can work out a "consensual" agreement.

He must think we don't know a whisper from a snake in the grass.

Rope-a-dope worked for Muhammad Ali but Miller is not the King of the Ring, he's a sociopathic schemer, a con man, a creep. Soldiers of Solidarity (SOS) won't drop their guard or stand down. We know his history. We know his character. Miller doesn't negotiate. He breaks contracts, bankrupts companies, dumps pension and health care responsibilities onto taxpayers, and rips off investors. The only way to repel brute force is with greater force.

Miller isn't backing down, he's maneuvering. Anyone who believes otherwise is ignoring the fact that GM-Delphi is building an inventory and preparing for a long strike, a strike GM-Delphi will provoke when they are good and ready.

GM-Delphi is damn good and ready. The showdown has been a long time coming. The only one who doesn't appear ready is Gettelfinger. The Concession Caucus has done nothing to prepare the rank and file for a confrontation that appears inevitable. Maybe that's the plan the Con Caucus has been alluding to: the we-were-caught-by-surprise plan. Remember how Shoemaker was surprised by the spinoff, and surprised by the bankruptcy. What will surprise him next?

I don't believe in speculation. I study history, patterns of behavior, and the facts on the ground, such as vehicles on lots and parts stashed in filing cabinets. That's right, in Coopersville, screw machine operators discovered filing cabinets stripped of their paper and jam-packed with components. Apparently, there was nowhere else left to stash the oversupply. Union members working overtime are extending their days on the picket line.

Production isn't exceeding demand because GM-Delphi wants to drive down prices. Management wants to drive down wages. The strategy isn't complicated. A controlled strike is needed to appease irate union members.

The fix is in.

The Concession Caucus has a long history of appeasement and compromise. Contrary to Doug Fraser's comments in the *Automotive News*, concessions in the 1980s were not "pragmatic." We have proof.

The UAW lost more than half its membership while the Canadian Autoworkers doubled in size after splitting with the UAW because the CAW refused to compromise. Only a company-union man could call that result "pragmatic." The UAW membership never won an iota of job security from concessions. To the contrary, we lost eight hundred thousand jobs while the Big Three churned out more vehicles than ever. Market share went down, but productivity went up. We produce more vehicles with half the number of workers. Now the final payoff for that compromise is due.

Both GM and Delphi have more plants overseas than they do in the United States. While we were busy buying American, GM-Delphi transferred all the money they saved on concessions overseas. And you wonder why they advocate free trade? The plan to evade legacy costs and become an importer to America has been in the shuffle for a long time.

Shitcan the rhetoric and study the action. The Con Caucus chose not to enforce the Secure Employment Level in the National Agreement. They chose to side with their corporate partners year after year. As a result, UAW membership declined. That's not pragmatism, it's collusion.

Last spring, syndicated columnist Rick Haglund, reported that Dale Buss, writing for the anti-union Mackinac Center for Public Policy, "gushes that the cooperative attitude of Fraser and Bieber pales in comparison to the UAW's newest strategy under President Ron Gettelfinger."

How should we assess a union leader who makes our enemies gush with praise?

Miller may be the King of Crap but Gettelfinger is the King of Concessions. In the Delphi-UAW Supplement signed on April 29, 2004, the Concession Caucus agreed that fourteen dollars per hour was fair pay. After four years at that rate with no COLA, no defined pension, and increased co-pays on health care, any autoworker with a family would be on food stamps.

What can Delphi-UAW members expect now?

More of the same.

Disregard opinion. Look at the facts.

In 2003, Gettelfinger promised to hold the line on health care. In 2005, he promised not to open the GM contract. He hasn't made any promises to Delphi-UAW members. It's just as well. His word isn't worth a rat's fur.

Quotations from Chairman Shoe
(January 2006)

How do you negotiate with a hostile employer without taking a strike vote?

"You approach the bargaining table waving a white flag."

How do you get the members to ratify concessions?

"Keep them in the dark, rush the vote, and echo the employer's threats."

How can a company legally pay for union expenses in contract negotiations?

"Funnel the money through a dummy corporation like the Center for Human Resources."

Make Them or Break Them at the Point of Production
(January 19, 2006)

Miller changed his tune. He says he wants a "consensual" agreement with the UAW. Consensual is an interesting choice of words. Consensual is the word defense attorneys use in date rape cases. Your consent will not make the "date" less painful.

Miller's stall-and-delay tactic is rope-a-dope. He wants to lull us into complacency and knock our lights out. GM didn't spin us off to take us back and Delphi didn't hire Miller for his *consensual* personality.

As one analyst told me, "Miller pulled the suicide defense." He put a gun to his head and said, "Give me concessions, or I'll pull the trigger."

My committeeman, Dennis Krontz, said, "Oh, no! That's not necessary! He doesn't have to do that! I'll pull the trigger for him."

If you are fed up with threats and intimidation, you have two choices:

call the bluff or fold; strike back or roll over; consent or fight back.

We may be the small dogs in this fight, but we have more fight in us than any other animal on the block and nothing to lose but our wages, pensions, benefits, seniority rights, job preference, vacations: in short, our fur. There are thousands of us willing to fight back for all we are worth. We made GM, and we can break GM.

Some people believe they can retire and glide off into the sunset without a care. Some people imagine that if they just sit there and stare, all their dreams will come true. Some people think television is reality and the couch is a safe place. But when the wolf is at the door, the remote control won't save you. The wolf will not go away when you pretend no one's home.

Who will take care of your interests when you are retired and can't vote on the contract? The members you left behind with a broken union and poverty wages? The Concession Caucus opened a new door in negotiations—takeaways from retirees. Where will that end? Do you think GM won't be back for more? The Concession Caucus sent a clear message: retiree benefits are up for grabs.

Real hope is fighting like hell against all odds. Likewise, optimism isn't the dopey notion that everything will turn out right in the end be-cause we are nice people. Real optimism is confidence in one's ability to prevail. If we aren't willing to stop production and drag GM kicking and screaming to the bargaining table, we have no right to cry foul after the fact. No resistance means consent.

A reporter asked me, "If you strike and shut down GM, won't you be biting the hand that feeds you?" We aren't biting the hand that feeds us. We are biting the hand that slapped us, cheated us, and robbed us. First, we'll bite the hand. Then, we'll go for the throat. What have we got to lose?

The leaders of the Concession Caucus are already waving the white flag. They're talking about concessions and compromise and "equality of sacrifice" as if the big cheeses didn't have golden parachutes strapped to their asses.

Why should we make sacrifices? We're not responsible for misman-agement and fraud. They're not bankrupt. GM-Delphi drained profits from the United States and sheltered the assets overseas. They act like extortion is a business plan. GM-Delphi's intent is to break the union in half. The Con Caucus can wave the white flag over their own graves. Soldiers of Solidarity will not stand down.

The Concession Caucus accuse SOS of dividing the union, but they are the ones who brag about their partnership with GM-Delphi and stick us with a two-tier wage that condemns new hires to a life of poverty. What could possibly be more divisive than two-tier?

The company-union partnership never won us job security. Now the Con's partner is threatening to close plants and throw UAW members out into the street. In return, they expect our consent for a deal that will *temporarily* protect pensions by sticking younger workers with a pay cut and closing plants.

We go face first into a cow pad and they call it a "soft landing?" If we consent to that plan, active workers will one day do the company's dirty work and decertify the union. Once we start cutting each other's throats, no one is safe. The only real social security is solidarity.

Your silence will not protect you. If we are silent, GM-Delphi will steamroll us. Do you recall what happened to the steelworkers? Do you recall what the president of the steelworkers' union, Leo Gerard, said when Steve Miller and Wilbur Ross conspired to deprive ninety-five thousand retirees of their pensions and health insurance?

There's a very good reason that you do not recall what Gerard said. He didn't say anything. There is a very good reason that you do not recall the outrage and the resistance. There wasn't any. Miller expected the same consensuality from the UAW, but SOS crashed the party.

On December 13, 2005, the *Automotive News* reported that Tower, a major supplier for Ford, expected to get a "consensual" agreement from the UAW. On January 6, 2006, Tower petitioned the court to revoke the UAW contract, cut wages, slash benefits, and dump pensions.

Did anyone hear a squeak out of the Concession Caucus? Cooperation will not protect you. The first indication that you are about to be date-raped is an appeal for cooperation. Do you recall what Miller said last fall? "No one will like it, but in the end they will do it, and they will do it the right way."

We will indeed do it the right way, but it won't be Miller's way and he will not like it when we pull the trigger. One wrong move on his part could incite a wildcat strike, and one wildcat could incite a stampede. If Miller's buddy, Judge Drain, strips us of our contract, workers who have been sitting on the fence will make the leap.

Our survival depends on our willingness to take the fight to the enemy and attack where it hurts most—at the point of production. We need to exert our power where we have the most leverage—the shop floor. We can make them or break them at the point of production.

A strike, even if you win, comes to an end. But once workers understand that they control the shop floor, we will win day in and day out. The shop floor, not the bargaining table, is the battleground.

Miller is an economic terrorist. He doesn't negotiate. He extorts. Playing it safe is more dangerous than the risk of fighting back.

I heard a supervisor tell a worker that the situation is out of our control. He said, "I don't like it either, but we have a job to do and we have to do the best we can."

The supervisor's thinking is irrational, because it does not acknowledge that the relationship is abusive. To act as if everything is normal when it is obviously not normal is insane.

Yes, we have a job to do. We have to defend ourselves and our families. Cooperation will not protect us. It will only legalize the assault.

Put the Backbone Back in the UAW
(January 31, 2006)

Whenever someone tells me that Miller has toned down his rhetoric and softened his approach, I recall what Vietnam veterans told me about the jungle when it got real quiet.

Wagoner said it would take GM six months to switch suppliers if the UAW struck Delphi.

Miller called for a cease-fire.

Delphi workers from Athens, Alabama, to Lockport, New York, report that management is stockpiling. Workers at plants that supply Delphi report a jump in orders as well. Looks like Miller took a page from Ho Chi Minh.

The facts on the ground lead me to believe that Miller's idea of labor peace is Shoemaker holding his coat while he beats the snot out of a line worker.

Coincidentally, "soft landing" is street lingo for a quiet fleecing where the mark is too frightened to squeal.

Corporate mouthpieces talk about restructuring in the same tone of voice that chicken hawks talk about collateral damage.

The wheels are greased. Union officials police the peace. No one has heard anything in weeks. Mobilizing@Delphi, the six-union coalition that includes the UAW, makes the sound of one hand clapping. I don't need to speculate. I got eyes, man.

I know when the leopard lies down in the grass, he's prepared to attack.

In Coopersville, Delphi hired twenty new workers. One was a former contract engineer. He came in as an electrician. He doesn't even own tools. A few of the new hires were former supervisors.

One man's hunger is another man's weapon.

Gettelfinger gave GM the largest health care concessions in UAW history. Look what it got us: plant closings, job cuts, more threats.

No sooner is one concession made than another one appears. Dick Shoemaker with one hand over his heart and the other in his pants.

Contract negotiations have already begun, but UAW officials haven't held a strike vote or asked the rank and file for resolutions. The Concession Caucus says, "We have a plan," but all we have seen so far is an orderly retreat turned into a rout.

If Delphi members had a benefit guarantee from GM, it wouldn't be on the table. But apparently, it's in negotiation. GM is dictating the terms, and Shoemaker is taking shorthand.

The Concession Caucus accuses SOS of being divisive. My favorite accusation is "socialist." The capitalists are eating our lunch every day and we are supposed to be afraid of socialists? GM is partners with China and the Concession Caucus tries to red-bait *me*?

The SOS goal is straightforward: save jobs, pensions, benefits, wages. Where's the wedge?

If UAW officials don't agree with those goals, they should stand up and state their case for concessions publicly. If UAW officials don't agree that workers are worth fighting for, than we should elect delegates to the national convention who will demand "equality of sacrifice" from the International. Cancel *their* pensions, cut *their* wages, slash *their* health care, and eliminate *their* jobs.

It's time to ratchet the jack another notch.

Put the backbone back into the UAW.

Delphi workers are facing the bayonet today, but the impact of the attack will be broad and deep. Workers at the Big Three and every supplier in between are staring down the barrel of a long-range cannon.

Management likes to throw money at problems. We need to create a problem for management to throw money at. A big problem. Namely, production.

Put the backbone back into the UAW. No Concessions = No Remorse.

The Answering Machine
(February 2, 2006)

Paul Krell, UAW spokesperson, is not a person. Paul is an answering machine. Which explains why he can't return calls and always says the same thing: "No comment." Since the UAW does not have a spokesperson per se, I don't have to be concerned about stepping on anyone's toes. Thus, I have taken it upon myself to answer some commonly asked questions.

How can Delphi continue to pay wages higher than the competition?
I agree. It doesn't make any sense to me that GM-Delphi should continue to pay executive wages twice as high as their German and Japanese counterparts. Especially since GM-Delphi executives can't measure up to the competition.

Productivity increases more than justify the cost of labor. We make more car parts today than we did twenty-five years ago with half as many workers. But where is the evidence of management's productivity? GM-Delphi have three times as many supervisors as German or Japanese companies.* The only way they can justify this excess burden is by deflecting attention and blaming workers who actually produce something of value. Take Steve Miller, Delphi's CEO, for example; what he calls work, most workers call "shooting the shit."

Japanese executives not only achieve better results for less pay, they don't wear out their welcomes, and when they fail they don't expect cash bonuses and stock options, they kill themselves. We simply can't compete when we have this built-in disadvantage. Mandatory euthanasia for executives who run companies into the ground should be institutionalized.

To be truly competitive, we should cut executive compensation by 63 percent, donate their golden parachutes to soldiers in Iraq, and make them wait in line at the emergency room when they get sick. It's a prime example of the Theory of Moral Hazard. If you reward people for failure, they will fail.

But don't UAW members make more money than nonunion members?

Of course we make more money. We're organized.

The disparity of wages between UAW members and nonunion workers is a result of inflation, not exorbitant raises. We aren't congressmen. We've never received an annual improvement over 3 percent, and many years we went without any raise at all despite productivity gains. But we did receive cost of living adjustments just as retirees do on their Social Security. COLA merely keeps a worker's nose above water. The trouble is, nonunion workers are drowning and the corporate state is throwing luxurious life rafts to lazy, undeserving executives.

Nonunion workers deprived of COLA watched their standard of living sink like a house built on swampland. They suffered a wage cut, not from the boss, but from the system that undermined them.

When a worker loses purchasing power because of inflation, the robber has no face. It's humiliating to work harder and longer and still fall

---

* David M. Gordon, *Fat and Mean: The Corporate Squeeze of Working Americans and the Myth of Managerial "Downsizing"* (New York: Free Press, 1996).

behind. Underpaid workers resent union members, when in fact it is management dealing from the bottom of the deck who have deprived them of COLA. The real injustice is that nonunion workers are used like sandbags to dam the rising tide of inflation while non-productive executives float off into the sunset like bloated whales.

What good will it do to strike Delphi? Aren't they bankrupt?

Delphi isn't bankrupt. They are sitting on five billion dollars in cash, and they own one of the most valuable patent portfolios in the United States. They pay their bills and continue to manufacture. They brag about their lucrative assets overseas—assets purchased from the legacy of profits American workers produced. Delphi never comes up short in regard to executive compensation. The money is there. JPMorgan Chase offered to loan Delphi two billion dollars to buy Motorola. Delphi is not broke. They are just trying to bargain us down.

GM-Delphi want to dump pension and health care responsibilities onto the government, which amounts to corporate welfare. They demand handouts from the government in the form of tax relief to compensate for mismanagement. Miller attempts to deflect attention from high-level fraud by blaming workers while he stuffs his pockets. He wants to pay poverty wages for expensive products. Miller is a corporate carpetbagger—all swagger and swindle, but no enduring value.

What good will it do to strike Delphi, you say? A strike will shut down GM, the company that is ultimately responsible for Delphi, and force them to the bargaining table. Miller threatens to kill the goose if workers don't give him concessions. We intend to call his bluff. Why should workers sacrifice their lives so Miller and his band of incompetent cronies can profit from failure and fraud? It's morally hazardous to reward criminal negligence and penalize honest labor.

Won't a strike at Delphi threaten GM with bankruptcy? In which case no one wins?

Yes, a strike at Delphi would threaten GM. That's precisely the point. If we go down, they go down. GM-Delphi will not be permitted to profit from the destruction of the middle class. The Reservoir Dogs are all on point.

Won't executive bonuses only be paid if Delphi emerges from bankruptcy successfully?

According to the current plan, executives will be rewarded even if they fail. In fact, executives have already been rewarded for failure, and they think it's better than working for a living.

Don't union rules impede production?

Unionized plants have higher productivity, because union rules prevent management from whipping the horses to make the buggy go faster. Instead of whipping the horses, management is compelled by the union to improve the buggy, a more innovative and humane approach to productivity. As a result, work is safer and more efficient because unions enforce safety and quality standards, which in turn motivates companies to utilize more advanced technologies.

Three Delphi plants in the United States—Kokomo, Grand Rapids, and Coopersville—together made nine hundred and fifty million dollars last year in a depressed market. Why? Because GM-Delphi invested in technology and products at those sites. At other US operations, GM-Delphi made calculated decisions to divest and thereby undermine the competitiveness of US operations.

How can companies afford to pay workers in the Jobs Bank* for not working?

I don't know. It doesn't make sense. The question should be, why aren't they working? If we focus on unemployment compensation we lose focus on the real problem, which is irrational management and underutilization of human resources. GM-Delphi wants to eliminate unemployment compensation so they can reward themselves more money for underachievement.

We have a better idea. Put unemployed people to work making products that customers want and outsource management. Reducing the cost

---

* Formally called the Job Opportunity Bank-Security (JOBS) program, the Jobs Bank pays workers who are awaiting reassignment rather than laying them off.

of downsizing isn't the path to success, it's another incentive to lose market share and bankrupt North American operations. Evasion of responsibility to laid-off workers is not the solution to chronically incompetent product development and irrational management.

Why would GM-Delphi create incentives to fail rather than succeed?

Because bankruptcy is easier than working for a living. It's easier to profit by evading debt and responsibility to workers and retirees than by practicing innovative design, production, and marketing techniques.

Delphi is the test case. If the court allows Delphi to bankrupt US operations while sheltering assets overseas, other multinationals will follow suit. When the smoke clears, they will return under another name.

I worked twenty-seven years for the same company. First it was called GM, then Delco, then AC Rochester, then Delphi. Management never changed. I may have forgotten a few of the aliases, but you get the picture; this isn't a shakeout, it's a shakedown.

GM pays one thousand five hundred dollars per vehicle for health care expenses and an additional thousand dollars for pensions. How can they compete against rivals who do not share that burden?

Simple. It's a lie.

GM does not pay one thousand five hundred dollars per vehicle for health care and a thousand per vehicle for pensions. It's a false analogy perpetuated by parrots in the corporate press. Five-sixths of the one thousand five hundred dollars figure is for retirees. (Retirees outnumber active workers five to one.) Thus the real cost of health care for active workers is two hundred fifty dollars per car.

The money for retirees' health care should have been set aside while they were actually working. Last spring, GM bragged that it had twenty billion dollars in a VEBA (Voluntary Employee Benefits Association), which is a trust fund for benefits. The expense for retiree health care comes from the trust fund, and should not be added to the burden of active workers. Likewise, pensions are earned while employees are actually working, not after they retire. Executives who mismanage fiduciary responsibilities and commit fraud should go to prison.

When Steve Miller claims that Delphi workers earn seventy-six dollars per hour he is perpetuating the fraud. *Crain's Business* reported: "The seventy-six dollar figure includes $22.63 in legacy costs. The remainder is for employee wages and benefits."* The remainder also includes Social Security, which is a federal tax, not employee compensation.

Management, not active workers, is responsible for legacy costs, which are deferred compensation owed to retirees. Legacy was earned in the past. Adding the legacy cost and Social Security tax to current workers' hourly wages is the same as putting numbers in the wrong column in order to deceive investors. If the company is allowed to include Social Security taxes as a part of total compensation for employees, then employees should likewise be allowed to deduct the taxes they pay from the total compensation. It doesn't work that way. Only Miller is allowed in the kitchen when he's cooking the books.

Why doesn't the International UAW make this information public? Do they want UAW members and the general public to believe that workers are overpaid and GM-Delphi needs concessions?
I'm sorry. I think I'll have to pull a Paul Krell on that one. "No Comment."

And All of Them Wild
(February 21, 2006)

GM CEO Rick Wagoner winked. Miller bit his tongue. Gettelfinger whispered out the side of his mouth to UAW PR man Paul Krell, "How should I know? Tell them, no comment."

Then the trio filed out of Judge Drain's chamber and disappeared like humor in a paternity suit. Nobody wants this baby.

Meanwhile, Russ Reynolds, president of UAW Local 651 Delphi Flint East, is praying for more rain because he's running out of excuses

---

* James B. Treece, "Delphi's Miller Expects UAW Pact 'In Principle' in 1Q 2006," *Crain's Business*, December 13, 2005.

not to fight. Mobilizing@Delphi is in "raging defense of the status quo," as Jerry Tucker would say with a face as stone-blank as a pitcher who just dusted off the batter.

There's a persistent sound of drilling in the background. Someone keeps whistling the refrain from "Working to Rule" with the mindless repetition of a chain gang. And I just sit here humming "Stuck Inside of Delphi with the Whipsaw Blues Again."

All this waiting makes me feel like I have a hole where my brain used to be. A delay is not a reprieve when you're standing in front of the firing squad. When two-thirds of the workforce is scheduled for execution the remainder don't feel safe, they feel terrorized. When progress by Miller's definition means demolition, the partisans go underground and resistance spreads like a vicious rumor—without discretion or restraint.

It appears Wagoner wants to squeeze the last drop of sweat from Shoemaker. Miller isn't amused. He has better things to do than watch a patsy squirm.

Miller has good reason to be antsy. He needs to accelerate the bankruptcy, because Delphi has really become a sinking ship, losing $1.1 billion in the last quarter. Work-to-rule is drilling holes in the boat and it won't get better when the Hatchet cuts wages, benefits, and pensions and bends the work rules to suit His Highness.

Delphi's losses up to now could be attributed to the "business plan," but the losses are spinning out of control. GM-Delphi engineered the bankruptcy through fraud, racketeering, and investing profits overseas while undermining factories in the United States. For example, Delphi Coopersville is selling parts to China below cost. The transfer of profits to China delights workers. Especially the Vietnam vets who know from experience you never bet a man at his own game. You take him off his square and break his marbles.

Miller's train is derailed. Workers are exerting pain the only way they know how, by raising production costs for Delphi. Miller isn't used to street hockey—players who won't play by the rules. He wants to take his puck and go home, but nobody will give it back to him.

Miller's game is in the courtroom, but apparently we've taken him off his game, because he has postponed three times. He's not known to equivocate, but he's having second and third thoughts now.

If Miller were left to his own devices, he would hold a fire sale and pass the patent portfolio to his crony Wilbur Ross.

Ross isn't in the game for money. He already has all the money. He wants power. If he gets his mitts on the patents, he can control the industry, and that will be Miller's revenge. We may have to give the Hatchet a golden parachute without a ripcord, but I expect Wagoner will do the dirty work when the resistance begins to deconstruct GM.

Miller's game is bankruptcy. We can't beat him on his own turf, which is why we had to lead him astray. He thinks we will settle for half a share like we're ignorant palookas fresh off the boat. What he didn't count on is that, in a game of Mutually Assured Destruction, the party with little or nothing to lose grows more murderous by the hour. "Let's just get it over with," is the phrase I hear every day. My fellow workers aren't talking about the job. They're talking about "The Job."

I mean to say that working to rule is almost as hard as running a Fortune 500 company—with no debt, a fully-funded pension, a patent portfolio with more jewels than the Queen of England's crown, and a guaranteed market with the world's largest automaker—into the dirt. Working to rule isn't easy, but given the right incentive—say, revenge, or survival—it can be invigorating. Once you get the knack of it, losing someone else's money is easier than punching holes in an inner tube.

GM picked up the tab for the UAW's legal fees in the phony lawsuit over retiree benefits. We saw how that played out. Now it's Delphi's turn to date the escort and pay the fancy man. What the trio didn't count on was the fourth stakeholder, Soldiers of Solidarity, with a fist full of cards and all of them wild.

First rule of the street: never fight a man who has nothing to lose but his anger. SOS is like a phantom at the table, because the honchos can't put a collar on it and rein it in and out on command. SOS doesn't have a leader to buy or a structure to undermine. The resistance doesn't need to hold meetings, pass motions, collect dues, and pay dividends. The guerillas don't wear badges, wave flags, or blow trumpets. It's the dog that doesn't bark one must beware of.

All Miller knows for sure is that someone is taking a bite out of his pie every day. Even salaried employees are working against him as they see the writing on the wall. Only top executives in the Rapture Club will be spared the axe.

I got news that isn't news to anyone who's been listening. There is no guarantee. The only promise is that wealth will flow to power. As individuals, we don't have a chip to bargain. Labor's power is collective.

Rosemary's Baby
(March 29, 2006)

Because there's a record of them screwing us.
—"Shareholder Lashes Out,"
Detroit Free Press, **March 17, 2006**

The Special Attrition Program (SAP) is a Delphi pension. Delphi is bankrupt. The only animal that will eat an opossum is a human. So it should come as no surprise how many Delphi workers are taking the SAP despite the fact it appears to be hanging upside down from a limb that's about to crack.

After nine months in the back room, Shoemaker and Gettelfinger came out with a buy-off that looks like Rosemary's baby. And they act so proud of it.

After all this time only one thing is perfectly clear: the Shoe-Finger Duo don't have the bristle and grit to stand up to Wagoner and Miller. We need a gang of Bull Buckers at the bargaining table to get the job done right.

"The deal" is intended to reduce GM's liability and decimate the union. "You can go, you can go, you can go, the rest of you get screwed to the fence post."

The kiss-off is not a comprehensive, collective bargaining solution, it's every man for himself and damn the rest. "The deal" is anti-union to the core. Trust yourself, trust your brothers and sisters, but never trust "the deal"—it was conceived in fraud and wrapped in deception.

The buy-off is a boondoggle. Like the excitement of the gambler who doesn't count his losses, the allure of the buy-off relies on poor math skills and weak impulse control. Before you decide to take the money and run, add up how much you will lose over the next thirty years. Make an informed decision, not an impulsive one. We deserve all the information, not just the *Highlights*. We deserve adequate time to examine all the options. After nine months of heavy backroom breathing, there's no reason to treat the affair like a shotgun wedding.

The companies have complained for months that legacy costs are the reason for their failure. Now they propose that adding to the burden of the legacy costs is a solution. They can't have it both ways. Were they lying in the first place or are they lying in the second place? Honor and commitment don't mean squat to GM-Delphi. The devil is in the details, not the sales pitch.

Miller's latest proposal belongs in the shredder with the rest of his threats and deadlines. He didn't even take it seriously. It looked more like crib notes than a contract.

The Concession Caucus didn't distribute the first two proposals, but they are floating the third one like a backdrop for the buy-offs. But where is the UAW's counter proposal? Remember how the Con Caucus said, "We have a plan"? Is this it? A half-baked buy-off?

We can expect to hear "Your plant is going to close! Cut and run! There's no hope!"

Take it in stride. The chicken dance is a time-honored concession-bargaining tradition.

When Miller petitions the court to void the contract, the clock will start ticking. If the judge nullifies the contract, the *no-strike clause* will cease to exist. All bets are off then. No contract means *no holds barred*. Delphi workers will have the right to take matters into their own hands on the shop floor. We'll be pushed back to a situation similar to the 1930s. Without a contract, workers have the right to defend their interests with "protected concerted activity." Major disruptions will likely occur. Strike preparations will begin in earnest, with or without a vote. We can tell the Shoe-Finger Duo, "Don't call us, we'll call you when we're damn good and ready."

It's self-defeating to approve any deal that divides the union. Two tiers is too many. MIAs are unacceptable. Solidarity isn't idealistic, it's common sense. If we sell ourselves short with buyouts, buy-downs, or buy-offs, the debt will come due with a vengeance.

Workers' rights are defined by struggle, not by contract or law. You get what you are willing to fight for. Nothing more. If the Concession Caucus tries to give us the rush job, Vote NO. If they won't show us anything but the *Highlights*, Vote NO. If Miller voids the contract, work to rule and be prepared to ratchet up a notch. Delphi workers will have the opportunity to take solidarity and direct action to a new level. We may as well empty the arsenal. For most of us, it will be the war to end all wars. Let's leave a legacy we can be proud of, and ignore the chicken dance.

"Bankruptcy Is a Growth Industry:" Steve Miller's Speech to the Detroit Economic Club at the Masonic Temple
(April, 3, 2006)

I dressed in corporate drag: a dark gray suit and tie, black wingtips spit-shined, and a gold watch I bought on the street on my way to do business in the Temple. The watch didn't work but it sparkled, and appearance means more than substance when one is trying to pass inspection. I was about to hear Steve Miller give a speech to the Detroit Economic Club, and for a Soldier of Solidarity it felt like an out-of-body experience. There wasn't a trace of grease under my fingernails. All the bills in my wallet were laundered.

I was surprised by the light security. I coulda-shoulda stuffed my pockets with paintballs. I walked in unimpeded and took my seat at table #49. I introduced myself to the assembled guests: management types in "communications" at Metaldyne; a couple of thick skulls from GM Powertrain; an investor whose suit cost more than my car.

While the corporati wallowed in the warm sty of mutual flattery, the industrial landscape of Detroit disintegrated all around us and a cold rain descended on the luckless and the damned. The Third World status of Detroit's inner city is emblematic of cities all over the United States. The deterioration is not the accidental byproduct of capitalism's vaunted *cre-*

ative destruction. The destitution was engineered for a purpose: to control labor costs. Solidarity House is surrounded by sweatshops.

A levity of polite manners subdued the normal aggressiveness of the free-enterprise crowd, but my appetite was in a self-protective mode— wary and circumspect. I could have been described by security guards as the guy with "a small, dark look on his face."

I ate lasagna, salad, bread, and tiramisu. I felt warm and sleepy. The voices around me were soft. The ambiance was distinctly devoid of emotion or nuance. This must be what porkchoppers feel like all the time—amnesiac. I forgot about my comrades outside with picket signs. The wind hammered their faces with hard rain, but I didn't feel any pain, just a vague misgiving. I could see Miller. I estimated the distance as a peg from third base to first. I could have beaned him with a paintball. Mentally I approached the dais, leaped over the table, and strangled him with my bare hands. I imagined murdering the remaining corporati with kitchen utensils while women screamed in the background and their men fainted.

Then we pledged allegiance and prayed to Mammon.

Miller began his discourse with a spate of jokes intended to appear off the cuff. His imitation of self-deprecating humor and spontaneity reminded me of diagramming sentences with Sister Mary Gertrude. No one got it. He was playing for the crowd, but the hard edge of skepticism in Detroit is serrated like an old bucksaw. His punchlines couldn't bridge the kerf.

How does the old saw go? Those who can manage a business do. Those who can't file bankruptcy? Gauging the reactions of the crowd led me to believe the media hasn't tapped into Miller's noxious effect on investors, engineers, community leaders, and people who in one capacity or another are experienced in manufacturing. The victim of megalomania doesn't suffer, everyone around him does. The power of self-delusion is inestimable. When Miller looks in the mirror he sees a full head of hair, not a boiled potato.

The media portrays Miller as a "straight shooter." Someone who tells it like it is and lets the proverbial chips fall where they may. I don't believe I was the only one in the room who heard the contradictions, false analogies, and damn lies. For example, he said the steel industry under his direction "endured a painful restructuring, but has been restored to health."

Ninety-five thousand retired steel workers deprived of pensions and health care have not been "restored to health."

When he told us that "bankruptcy is a growth industry in America," he smirked as if he expected Detroiters would find his smugness amusing. I heard teeth grinding like a tranny that popped a drain plug.

He claimed the typical bankruptcy costs "about one hundred million a year in professional fees." He did not include the social costs.

If we provide enough carcasses, the vultures will flourish and the restructuring of America—lost jobs, lower wages, higher health care costs, and defunct pensions—will create new opportunities for bankruptcy, the premier "growth industry in America."

Welcome to Miller's World, where wealth is created not by labor in mining, agriculture, and industry, but by lawyers, which leads to the next question: fraud.

"I would just remind everyone that as embarrassing as that was to all concerned, the changes" (his handlers must have convinced him that "the changes" was more euphemistically charming than "accounting restatements") "had nothing to do with Delphi's cash rebalances or operating issues. Even with flawless accounting, we'd be exactly where we are today." Miller delivered this bold-faced lie with all the aplomb of a man telling children that they were delivered by storks.

Had investors known the truth, they would not "be exactly where they are today." Had workers known in advance that Delphi would sell parts to GM below cost, they would have raised a hue and cry and struck before GM could spin the scheme to jettison Delphi workers.

Miller bragged how well Delphi was performing in the categories of quality, delivery, and new business. So what's the problem? Labor contracts.

Delphi, he said, "inherited . . . tier-one labor contracts that are substantially higher than the prevailing union contracts throughout the US supplier industry."

He neglected to add that Delphi inherited, debt-free, all the property, patents, products, machinery, technology, and expertise of a premier tier-one supplier. Or that, minus racketeering, the profit margins of tier-one products are substantially higher than tier-two products. He neglected to mention that the pension was inherited fully funded and the labor contracts were not a surprise, like the rise in steel prices.

"Delphi's hourly labor costs have surpassed seventy-eight dollars for wages and benefits," Miller asserted.

"Seventy-eight dollars"? Every time Miller mentions labor costs we get a raise. Two weeks ago, it was seventy-six dollars. How does this work?

According to Delphi's *Total Compensation Summary*, distributed in 2002 and 2004, total compensation rose $1.31 per hour from 2002 to 2004. Since Miller took the helm it rises more than that every time he opens his mouth. The average hourly worker's total compensation in 2004 (the last year that Delphi mailed a *Total Compensation Summary* to every employee's home) was $42.36, which included social security taxes. How did we gain $35.64 since 2004? In Miller's World, accounting is a dramatic art.

The second reason for Delphi's failure was not racketeering (GM's demand that Delphi sell parts below cost), but rather "the decline in GM North American production volumes." Miller ignores the fact that Delphi's content per GM vehicle declined by design despite GM's contractual commitment to invest $1 billion in new business with Delphi. Instead GM chose to divest from Delphi and thereby undermine American operations and hasten the bankruptcy. Creative bookkeeping is the magic wand of "restructuring."

What is the solution? Miller cites "five big restructuring variables."

(1) Reduce wages and benefits and "address costly restrictions and work rules that inhibit productivity." In other words, break the union but preserve the bureaucracy as an arm of management to keep the rabble under control.

Miller said that when workers retired at "age sixty-five and then died at age seventy . . . the social contract inherent in these programs seemed affordable." In Miller's mind, now that we stand a chance of actually enjoying our fair share of those benefits, it's unreasonable.

He explained that in the old days "employers passed along the costs to customers." But now, "since their customers won't pay for it when they have choices," it's not viable. Miller asserts that "somebody has to pay," and it isn't going to be him and his gang of shrugging Atlases.

Miller's reasoning is fallacious. First of all, Toyota isn't selling vehicles cheaper than GM. So "choices" that customers make have nothing to do with health care or pensions. They make choices based on personal preferences, not an automaker's legacy costs. But more significantly, the customer is getting double-billed.

As Miller explained, when the promises were made, the cost was shifted to consumers. Where did the money go? Rather than fulfilling their responsibility to retirees by setting the money aside in a trust fund, GM squandered it. GM, like Delphi, spent our legacy on assets overseas and extravagant compensation for executives. Now Miller proposes passing the legacy cost on to taxpayers so that consumers will in effect pay for the same thing twice.

(2) "Financial assistance from GM sufficient to cover the transformation." To a sweatshop, I presume? Miller wants cash from GM. He wants walking-around money. He wants a new train set. Since he is the only player at the table with clean hands, he feels certain he will get it.

(3) " . . . be global category killers." He literally salivated over that garish phrase plucked from a B-movie trailer. The long and short of the "restructuring" is that Miller plans to cash out. He doesn't manage manufacturing enterprises. He isn't concerned with the long-term quality or efficiency of Delphi. He wants to chop it up, sell it off, and move on to the next carcass. This description of vulture capitalism isn't speculation on my part, it's Miller's track record.

For those of you who believe in political solutions, Miller cautioned, "in the final analysis there wasn't anything any state could do to offset the underlying economics involved." Capitalism is above the law, or, perhaps I should say, it *is* the law. The court serves perpetrators, not victims.

(4) Reduce "about 25 percent of our worldwide salary workforce . . . and eliminate up to 40 percent of our current corporate officer positions." This is typical of a Miller "restructuring." It's a quick way for him to make a million bucks and sleep well.

(5) Miller purports to "honor our accumulated pension obligations, thereby avoiding termination of our pension plan." Miller's plan requires "a way to stretch out our required pension plan payments" and make the pension contingent on achievement of certain goals, that is, wage and benefit reductions.

Miller warned, "I fear something like intergenerational warfare, as young people increasingly resent having their wages reduced and taxed away to support social programs for their grandparents' income and health care concerns." It was one point on which Steve and I may find agreement—two-tier wages are socially degenerate.

Miller's fear of "intergenerational warfare" did not prevent him from asserting that he wanted to "restore our underfunded pension plan out of future profits," which, by his design, is based on cutting wages for new hires. Workers, I may add, who will not have a vested interest in a defined pension for their elders, since they won't have one themselves. The "intergenerational warfare" Miller foresees is not so much a fear as it is a plan. Miller won't have to bust the union, because the union will self-destruct if it adopts two-tier as a solution.

The buyout whereby older workers are appeased with a "soft landing" is a time bomb, not an escape hatch. How can adding to the maligned legacy costs be a solution? As Mark Reutter wrote in the *Washington Post*: "There is little evidence that court-supervised reorganization produces a superior company. In fact, quite a few companies that come out of bankruptcy make a return trip, and there is growing evidence that the process diverts capital away from needed investments into the pockets of the restructurers" ("Workplace Tremors," August 23, 2005). Without national health care, it is likely that Delphi will return to court to dump the pension. The hourly compensation Miller proposes cannot cover the legacy costs. It's a sham.

Delphi is a test case. If Miller succeeds in breaking union contracts, bleeding pensions, and butchering the workforce while sheltering assets overseas, other multinationals, including GM, will follow suit. Bankruptcy will indeed become a "growth industry in America." Capitalism in the United States has evolved to the point where the courts routinely sanction the transfer of wealth from the masses to the few as a social convention.

Miller spelled it out plainly when he said, "What is at stake here is the basic social contract in our traditional industries." Miller intends to break that social contract so he can sleep well. Soldiers of Solidarity intend to give him insomnia.

In conclusion, Miller declared, "If we do this right, Delphi will remain one of the world's premier global automotive suppliers. . . . If we do it badly, Delphi may be broken up into small pieces, and America will have lost some of its precious industrial treasures."

Does he intend to "do it badly"? On March 31, 2006, Miller revealed his restructuring plan. Twenty-one of twenty-nine plants will be closed, sold, or consolidated. Is that not "broken up into small pieces?"

Contradictions, false analogies, and damn lies are Miller's stock-in-trade. The steel industry is healthy; pitting the young against the old will restore the underfunded pensions; all skill, knowledge, and valuable experience are clustered in the office; and the sale or closure of 75 percent of Delphi's US operations does not mean that Delphi "will be broken up into small pieces."

Miller insisted that the press only writes about the people who are angry at him. We don't hear about the people who are excited about Miller's World and his vision for the future. We don't hear about the people who want to make sacrifices for Miller's World. No, we just read about "those people" across the street who think that the Delphi bankruptcy is a fraud.

Yes, he had to acknowledge the Soldiers of Solidarity. He said his favorite picket sign was: "Miller Isn't Worth a Buck."

"It must have been a typo," he quipped. It was a proud moment for me. I made that sign.

My coconspirator, Juanita Cadman, has carried the sign in three protests in three cities.

The concept came from a coworker who prefers to remain anonymous, as do many in the dedicated ranks of the underground resistance. But he knows who he is, and that his message got through to Miller and the Detroit Economic Club, too. "Miller Isn't Worth a Buck."

If Words Were Bullets
(May 2006)

There was a knock at the door.

"You get it," my wife said.

"You get it," I said.

Sheila peeked between the curtains.

"They look like Jehovah's Witnesses."

She ran upstairs. They knocked again. I pretended I wasn't home. After a few minutes, I peeked between the curtains. I was eyeball to eyeball with a Messenger of the Law.

I slipped on my jacket, stepped out, and closed the door. Two nondescript Caucasian males: a blue suit, a brown suit, dull ties, white shirts, and eyes like ball bearings. I thought I had a plan.

"Can we ask you a few questions?"

"I'm just leaving. Got to hurry. 'Bye."

Then he showed me a badge: US Marshal.

I was raised Catholic, which is to say I feel naturally guilty. I believed my past had caught up with me auto-dogmatically.

"Did you write this?" the blond asked.

I looked at the printout: *Live Bait & Ammo* #71.

What could I say? It had my name on it.

"Did you intend to threaten anyone with this?"

I looked at the brown suit and then at the blue suit. They had identical grins, identical haircuts, and the superior air of white Christian men following orders. The blue suit pointed a manicured nail at a paragraph circled with blue ink:

I could see Miller. I estimated the distance between us as a peg from third base to first. I could have beaned him with a paintball. Mentally I approached the dais, leaped over the table, and strangled him with my bare hands. I imagined murdering the remaining corporati with kitchen utensils while women screamed in the background and their men fainted.

If words were bullets and corporate thieves were targets, I'd be a decorated deadeye dick instead of a factory worker with a histrionic sense of humor and a high-caliber ballpoint pen. I asked myself, "What would Cool Hand Luke say?" But I couldn't admit "a failure to communicate." I meant every goddamn word.

For a small dog I sure pull a lot of chain. This message from the Law was one of several efforts to harass and intimidate. On February 9, 2006, a local TV station made me the top story on the evening news. Grand Rapids news anchor Tom Van Howe accused me of scaring Toyota out of Michigan. The next day, the headline in the business section of the *Grand Rapids Press* blared: "Is Toyota Scared of This Man?"—replete with a picture of me wearing the same face I use to scare squirrels away from the picnic table. Considering how many workers were unemployed in Michigan, the story did create a hostile environment for me.

When I went into work that night, a machine repairman, Ted De-Witt, had torn my machine apart. "Go sit down," he said. "You're not going to work tonight." Since I ran the Final Assembly Bodine, the whole line shut down. Not only did Delphi lose tens of thousands of dollars in profit, they paid every worker on my line to sit down all night. The machine didn't start running until I left the building. Management got the message: when a worker is attacked, management will pay the price, and Soldiers of Solidarity will determine how much the price is.

The Cost of the Status Quo Is Always More
(June 6, 2006)

Cooperation, Concession, and Competition will save jobs and enhance the quality of our work lives when Elvis returns. Until then, SOS is convinced that taking control of the shop floor is a practical solution to an urgent need.

Power respects power, not punks. If you want a piece of the pie, you'd better be prepared for a piece of the action. And bring your own knife.

It's a good bet that before the King returns, Judge Drain will revoke the Delphi contract and the fulcrum of power will shift from the lawyers and the porkchoppers to the rank and file. Get ready. In lieu of a contract, the rules of the street apply. Office rats in union hats can talk book to the walls until the ceiling falls, but we've got gears to strip, wires to clip, and balls to break. Goodbye, contract. Hello, chaos.

The Concession Caucus will likely respond to the Judge's ruling by running a sham strike and then offering us a contract with the ruse, "We know it's a piss-poor deal, but it's better than the Drain." Send them back to the table. We've got more power than they bargained for.

Vulture capitalist Wilbur Ross said,

> The biggest question is this wild card of Delphi Corp. and then the union contract renegotiation next year. Those are two big landmines. Delphi's not going to totally shut down. But if a court does impose a draconian structure on the workers, you will at least see wildcat strikes. I just can't imagine if Steve Miller gets anything like what he's proposed, there will be peace and quiet. . . . I just think there's too much anger that's been built up and frankly even if the international union were to agree—and I don't think there's any great chance that it would—it can't control the individual workers well enough to get the settlement ratified ("Investor Sees Gold in Suppliers," *Detroit News*, April 19, 2006).

The rank and file is ready to rumble, but the Concession Caucus is leading the charge with a white flag. "We have made a conscious choice to put aside the adversarial approach," UAW vice president Bob King told an automotive conference in Detroit.

"King noted that the UAW has struck several agreements with major parts suppliers that relax union work rules and job classifications in factories to improve productivity" ("The UAW Takes a Cooperative Stance," *Detroit News*, April 20, 2006). King made this public statement the day after Wilbur Ross suggested it in an interview with the *Detroit News*.

No wonder Brother Bob King fails to organize new members unless an employer enlists him to help reduce labor costs. No wonder some of Gettelfinger's "most enthusiastic supporters are the top executives of the US auto industry" ("Union Leader Presides Over Painful Changes," *Washington Post*, May 15, 2006). The price of neutrality is always more than one bargained for.

In an effort to undermine the resistance and protect GM, the Concession Caucus frightens and entices Delphi workers to cut and run. As

Bob King indicated, remaining members will be coerced into conceding every hard-won work rule that makes factory life humane and gives individual workers a crumb of autonomy.

The Concession Caucus is signaling to their corporate partners they are ready to roll over, not only at Delphi, but across the board. The Con Caucus has already helped GM and Ford set a legal precedent to retract retirees' accrued vested benefits. No amount of concessions will save jobs or satisfy management's craving for ever-cheaper labor. Workers who compete with workers are playing Russian roulette for the bosses' amusement.

Productivity has propagated faster than tail on a rabbit farm, yet owners want to pound more plow horses into shares. Like they say on a narrow street in Manhattan, "One man's loss is another man's dividend." As long as we stick to the competitive agenda, we'll never win. The system demands a loser, and we've been tagged like pigs for the slaughter.

Former Democratic presidential nominee George McGovern advised unionists that the quest for "more" is no longer "a very effective strategy" ("The End of 'More,'" *Los Angeles Times*, May 22, 2006). At last, Democrats have revealed the flip side of NAFTA—the end of progress for the working class.

When Samuel Gompers was asked, "What does labor want?" He replied, "We want more schoolhouses and less jails; more books and less arsenals; more learning and less vice; more constant work and less crime; more leisure and less greed; more justice and less revenge."

McGovern, the old sawhorse of the Democratic Party, preaches that we should endeavor to cooperate with the ruling class in its quest for more jails and less schools; more weapons and less tools; more vice and less learning; more crime and less work; more greed and less leisure; more revenge and to hell with justice.

Justin Hyde, reporting on bankruptcy proceedings, writes: "John Sheehan, Delphi's chief restructuring and accounting officer, said if Delphi gets the changes it wants in its contracts, the company would save $9.2 billion by 2010, but would still need to find another $4.6 billion in cash. Of that amount, $3.1 billion is pension obligations, which Sheehan said the company was committed to honoring" ("Delphi expresses hope for contracts," *Kokomo Tribune*, May 25, 2006).

This statement to the court is worth paraphrasing. *If Delphi gets everything it wants the pension will still come up $3.1 billion short.*

So how long after Delphi gets everything it wants will the company be back in court? How long before Delphi retirees are cut adrift with a sardonic "Beg your pardon, didn't you read the fine print?"

Ron Gettelfinger, who promised to "hold the line on" and not permit employers to "shift the cost of health care onto workers," said he would not reopen the GM contract ("UAW Won't Reopen GM Contract," *Detroit News*, April 15, 2005).

Gettelfinger said, "If you concede a benefit, you figure it's gone. It would be hard to get it back. I've said before, I've been in negotiations a number of times over the years, I don't ever remember a company calling us up and saying, "Hey, you know what? We're doing so well since those negotiations, we feel like we shorted you guys and want to give you a little more." (Laughs.) "I know once it's negotiated away, it's gone" ("Leader Says Union Will Hear Out GM," *Detroit Free Press*, July 12, 2005).

Not only is it gone, Ron, but they'll be back for "more."

The Concession Caucus has made unprecedented concessions on health care and plant closings in the middle of a contract. The Con Caucus response to GM-Delphi's attack on workers is buy-offs and a series of classes on How to Live on Less; How to Retire When You Aren't Ready; How to Find a New Career; and meetings with financial advisors, the same professionals who didn't foresee the stock market dive in '99 and who sold Delphi employees' shares for five nickels and three pennies. The Con Caucus behaves like an arm of GM's Center for Human Resources, not a union.

The Con Caucus has no plan to fight back, because they are partners in the business and they view workers as a pain in the ass. The status quo has its costs, but those with status never pay.

NAFTA, a liberal agenda in conservative drag, succeeded in driving Mexican workers across the border, but where can we go?

The solution to our dilemma doesn't come from Karl Marx or Adam Smith, it comes from the playground. There are worse things in life than getting your ass kicked. There's putting your head down and walking away. If you let the bully take your lunch today, he will be back for "more" every day. We know the playground belongs to McGovern and his neoliberal cronies, but we don't have anywhere to go. We live here, and the only border we can cross to prosperity is the one from individual choice to collective action. The only way to beat the bully is to gang up on him. GM-Delphi's plan for success depends on our demise. Crash the celebration. When Drain pulls the plug, clamp the pipeline and throw down. We have nothing to lose but the boss's smile.

We Are All Temps
(July 20, 2006)

Before the end of the year, temps will dominate the workforce at Delphi. They make $14 per hour, they receive no benefits, and despite the fact that they pay union dues, they have no rights or privileges except one: they're eligible to vote on the contract.

Gettelfinger delivered. He gave Miller everything he asked for: a degraded workforce without a battle.

In regard to Delphi, Gettelfinger told reporters on July 17, "I think the attrition package got them where they need to be, and they act like nothing has changed."

He sold the cattle, and now he's surprised that Miller wants the ranch house and the barn?

Gettelfinger gives his corporate partners everything they want. Then he acts surprised when they want more. What did he expect? Where is the business savvy his corporate partners extol as the Finger's finest quality?

Gettelfinger insinuated there may yet be a strike at Delphi. Wagoner and Miller are certainly snickering. How do you organize workers who have no status in the company or the union? How do you convince them to strike when the local leadership and most of the members have jumped ship? The Good Old Boys weren't willing to fight. Now they expect temps to put themselves at the tip of the spear?

The Local 2151 Executive Board recommends holding an "Open House." They intend to invite the temps to come to the union hall two hours before their shift begins so they can eat snacks with the "leadership" and get a free T-shirt. The plan reminds me of that song Woody Guthrie sang about a soup so thin you could read a newspaper through it.

The silver platter that carried the severed head of our aspirations was polished back in April 2004 when the UAW International completed negotiations on a two-tier supplement for Delphi: $14 per hour, no COLA, no pension, and squat for benefits.

The International did not permit members of the affected local unions to vote on the two-tier supplement. I appealed the decision to the PRB.

For those of you who are unfamiliar with the acronym, the Public Review Board is a pantomime of "Justice Delayed," performed by puppets who with great humility describe themselves as "distinguished." Members of the PRB are selected and compensated for their services by the accused, the UAW International Executive Board. At every Constitutional Convention, a representative of the PRB testifies that they have never uncovered any corruption in the UAW.

The *Detroit News* reported that a federal jury found Donny Douglas, a UAW International Rep, and Jay Campbell, a Local Bargaining Chairman, guilty of "conspiracy to break labor laws and to extort favors from GM." The civil suit against the two men was dismissed because time limits expired before plaintiffs, members of UAW Local 594, could exhaust internal union remedies, including an appeal to the PRB. The judge inferred that *they should have known better* (Paul Egan, "UAW Officials Found Guilty," *Detroit News*, June 28, 2006).

In Amsterdam, the display of prostitutes in shop windows makes lechery appear socially acceptable and commercially legitimate. In the UAW, the Public Review Board makes treachery appear innocent and appeals for justice academically irrelevant.

An appeal to the PRB is an exercise in futility, but I couldn't resist the wordplay. My repartee with the wits in Sold-our-dignity House supplied a trove of certifiable quotes. For example, in defense of two-tier wages the International asserted, "The future hire group is a null class" (PRB Case #1504, p. 15, line 2).

The segregation of future union members into a "null class" is a harrowing prediction of the future of the union. The Preamble of the UAW Constitution avows that "the ideals and hopes of the workers who come under the jurisdiction of the [UAW]" are exemplified by the statement 'that all men are created equal,'" and that within the union "lies the hope of the worker in advancing society toward the ultimate goal of social and economic justice."

Where is the hope of a new hire in advancing toward the goal of social and economic justice if the union relegates him or her to second-class citizenship? New hires, the workers who embody the future of the union, have been disenfranchised in advance.

Two-tier isn't a collective bargaining strategy, it's a symptom of social decadence.

Article Two of the UAW Constitution states that our purpose is: (1) "To improve working conditions, create a uniform system of shorter hours, higher wages, health care and pensions; to maintain and protect the interests of workers under the jurisdiction of this International Union." (2) "To unite in one organization, regardless of religion, race, creed, color, sex, political affiliation or nationality, age, disability, marital status or sexual orientation, all employees under the jurisdiction of this International Union."

Two-tier sticks these principles in the shredder. Two-tier impacts all active, retired, and future members. If new hires are classified as a "null class," then one day they will in turn classify senior members and retirees as a "null class." The term is an existential coffin for the union.

The introduction of temps into Delphi and GM is a sign of things to come. The contract is *temporarily* suspended for a certain *class* of workers. The Concession Caucus is bending over backwards to help their corporate partners emulate the Toyota system of *permanent temps* which is, for all intents and purposes, a two-tier caste system for workers. Gettelfinger is backpedaling to the future.

Two-tier is wholesale discrimination against an entire class of people. Two-tier severs the solidarity between generations. Two-tier will destroy the union. Is that the plan?

The Concession Caucus not only accepts management's unilateral "right to manage" (Paragraph 8, UAW-GM National Agreement), they administer the degradation of the working class, because they do not believe workers have any value other than that dictated by the bosses. Gettelfinger and Wagoner's worldview is one and the same. In their eyes there is no alternative to the domination of capital over labor: certainly not mass resistance.

In Gettelfinger's address to the UAW Constitutional Convention, he described the challenges we face as insurmountable. His outrage was muted. His attitude was resigned. He skirted confrontation with management and stuck to the party line: cooperation.

The Concession Caucus always reverts to the same solution. They tell workers who to vote for, namely Democrats. They encourage workers to put all their hopes in the ballot box rather than direct confrontation at the point of production. The bait and switch diverts attention from the Con Caucus conviction that workers must sacrifice for the greater good, which they assert is the "Partnership" between company bosses, union bosses, and the Democratic Party.

The Partnership is pilfering the accrued vested benefits of retirees. The Partnership is slashing wages and benefits. The Partnership is undermining working conditions, including the eight-hour day, equal pay for equal work, and the integrity of a union contract which defines rules that give workers dignity.

Worst of all, the Partnership is degrading an entire class of workers by designating them temporary. How can we organize workers who have no status in the company, the union, or the political system? Active workers, temp workers, retirees, and the unemployed share a vital common interest. None of us have a status in the Partnership. We are all temps. We are all disenfranchised. We are immigrants in the land where we were born.

The King of Crap
(September 11, 2006)

When it comes to humor, you can't beat the truth. On August 21, 2006, *Apollo*, Delphi's official employee communication network, announced "Compliance Is Everyone's Business: An Interview with David Sherbin."

It's comforting to know that there exists a "Chief Compliance Officer" who, in his own words, encourages "any Delphi employee to call, write, or e-mail me with ideas, thoughts, and even complaints about the compliance program."

The knowledge that someone appointed by the Delphi Board of Directors has the will and the power to hold the unscrupulous accountable lends credence to the questionable, and trust to the double standard. A display of honesty in the leadership inspires the ranks with confidence to conform with the drill no matter how "irregular" it may appear on the surface, or beneath, as the case may be.

Since Mr. Sherbin didn't include his contact information in the interview, I called the Delphi Ethics Line and asked Sister Snitch to put me in touch. But I'm jumping ahead. First, some excerpts of the actual interview between Delphi's *Apollo* and the Chief Compliance Officer, David Sherbin:

Apollo: What do you mean by Ethics?

Sherbin: Ethics usually means a strong moral code and doing what is right. . . . What we need to assure is that the pressures of business and competition don't encourage any of us to take "short cuts" or "bend the rules just a little bit" to gain an edge. . . . Good people can make bad choices if they don't have a framework that helps them make the right choices, and we want to make sure at Delphi that people always make good choices.

Apollo: Why are we doing this now? Did we do something wrong?

Sherbin: My appointment and the development of a formal Compliance Program is more about doing things right than a response to any specific events or problems within Delphi. . . . We have had problems including certain accounting irregularities that led to our financial restatement. To make sure similar problems, or new ones, do not occur again, we must make compliance with laws, regulations and our own internal Delphi standards part of our corporate "DNA."

Apollo: How can we help?

Sherbin: Building a compliance culture is about each of us taking individual responsibility for our own compliance and collective responsibility for our team's compliance. It means we need to step up and say, "That's not right" when we see a potential violation . . .

Apollo: A lot of employees are nervous about using the Ethics Line. I hear a couple of comments consistently—"Do you really expect us to snitch on each other when we see things we think are wrong?" and "Nothing will happen if I call except I might lose my job." What are your thoughts on this?

Sherbin: . . . Raising critical compliance issues is not "snitching"—it is really protecting everyone's jobs. We try our best to maintain the confidentiality of the Ethics Line process, even when callers do not request it. I can also tell you that if we ever find out that someone has retaliated against a Delphi employee for calling the Ethics Line in good faith, we will take immediate disciplinary action, up to and including termination.

Just like *Apollo*, I have heard the same "comments consistently"—fear of snitching on peers and getting the old goose whacked. But I'm all for "protecting everyone's job." So I dropped a dime and used an alias.

Me: Hi. This is Ed Northern. I work for a Delphi plant in the United States.

Sister Snitch: Hi, Gregg. Let me guess. You work in Coopersville, Michigan, in department 988, B-shift, Line 5, Final Assembly Bodine. You are fifty-six years old, five-foot-five, 130 pounds.

Me: I'm bigger than that.

SS: In your sleep . . . married with three children, and your Social Security number is—

Me: Hey, I thought this was supposed to be confidential.

SS: My lips are sealed, and this conversation will be recorded for your protection.

Me: My protection against what?

SS: Getting your goose whacked for snitching on your peers and desecrating the good name of Delphi in public.

Me: Public?

SS: Everyone in Compliance will receive a copy of your taped confession for review and retaliation.

Me: From now on call me Ed, or Mr. Northern.

SS: Whatever.

Me: Delphi is selling scrap.

SS: Is that your compliance issue? Forgive me. I thought you had something juicy. What's wrong with making a little money on scrap? Are you against the profit system? Are you a communist? Don't you believe in recycling? What do you expect us to do? Throw money away?

Me: We already did throw it away. I don't know why or how they managed to keep these parts around so long, because we scrapped them out three years ago. But they've hauled a shitload of defective parts back into our shop, and workers have been ordered to black out the serial numbers and dates and etch new serial numbers and dates and then we ship them to—

SS: Sounds like job security. Are you against working for a living? When was the last time you pledged compliance to the flag?

Me: You mean allegiance.

SS: You can allege whatever you like, but the fact you made this call proves that you are not in compliance with the Delphi code of silence. Besides, the product you call scrap will be repurchased by Delphi. It's the accounting that confuses you, not the facts. All systems comply automatically in accordance with our Universal Reciprocal Process.

Me: Forget it. I have another complaint. Representatives from Delphi headquarters held captive-audience meetings in our plant at which they persuaded employees to invest their life savings in Delphi stock under false pretenses, and now the stock isn't worth crap.

SS: So what are you saying? We didn't sell enough scrap or we sold you a bunch of crap? What is it?

Me: Both! Scrap and crap are both violations of compliance.

SS: Look, if you hadn't wasted so much time complaining about scrap, what we told you wouldn't have amounted to crap. Compliance is nothing, in essence, but a disposition to yield to the will of authority. Since Delphi is the WILL and the WAY, you are the one indisposed to yield and thus ultimately responsible for the failure to aid and abet the delivery of scrap to customers in Delphi's Advance Complicity Program so we could buy it back at a mutually beneficial profit and thereby double the return on your investment.

Me: I never thought about it like that. Compliance is not in itself a defined standard, but rather the appearance of unquestioning conformity, and the Chief Compliance Officer is thus the King of Crap.

SS: Your complaint will be processed in the order it was received. Anything else, Gregg?

Me: Ed. I'm ED NORTHERN, for the record. I insist that you honor my confidentiality by referring to me by my allegorical alias: ED NORTHERN, patriot, Christian, and penultimate good old boy.

SS: Whatever. Are we done?

Me: Delphi is paying people out of the Jobs Bank account who are not in the Jobs Bank.

SS: So what? I thought you liked Jobs Bank. I thought all you guys liked the rubber room. I thought bouncing off the walls is what you do best.

Me: Paying workers out of the Jobs Bank fund when they are not actually in the Jobs Bank, but are actually continuing to function in their appointed positions, is what one might call an "accounting irregularity," or double bookkeeping.

SS: Are we talking about appointees or workers? Because they are not one and the same.

Me: We are talking about workers doing appointed jobs. Delphi has taken them off the payroll and put them in the Jobs Bank to make the operation look more efficient than it actually is. Then Miller complains about the cost of the Jobs Bank. It's a scam.

SS: According to the Delphi Employee Redundancy Program, appointees are categorically in the Jobs Bank because they don't add value to the product, and if it wasn't for nepotism, they would all be fired.

Me: I can't argue with you about the nepotism, but paying them out of a separate set of books is fraud.

SS: One moment. I am connecting you with the Chief Compliance Officer.

Chief Compliance Officer: I understand you used the F-word. Do you know what we do to employees who use the F-word?

Me: Is this where the compliance comes in?

CCO: I don't answer questions. I ask questions.

Me: Then ask yourself why Delphi should get away with underfunding the pension while simultaneously investing in assets overseas, which are sheltered from bankruptcy.

CCO: Congratulations, Gregg, you're a perfect candidate for our compliance program.

Me: My name is Ed. ED NORTHERN: Christian, patriot, and goddamn good old boy from—

CCO: And you have won, yes, you, Gregg, have won an all-expenses-paid adventure to Compliance Island, where you will experience total immersion in the Delphi Ultimate Manufacturing Strategy System (DUMASS).

Me: I don't want—

CCO: Don't worry. It's entirely virtual. You won't feel a thing.

Chapter Three

Where the Road Paved with Concessions Goes: The 2007 UAW-GM Negotiations

Delphi CEO Steve Miller encountered no resistance from UAW leadership as he radically downsized the parts company in the United States and took advantage of lower-tier pay for new hires. The Detroit Three automakers followed with demands for similar concessions from the union in the 2007 contract negotiations. Soldiers of Solidarity organized coworkers to sound the alarm and stand against any further givebacks.

That Our Children May Have Peace
(November 2006)

In the progress of politics, as in the common occurrences of life, we are not only apt to forget the ground we have traveled over, but frequently neglect to gather up experience as we go.

—Tom Paine

The bad news is, I have a long commute since I transferred back to GM from Delphi. The good news is, I'm working the road to rule. I drive slower than a mule with hot cargo and expired plates. Screw the oil companies. I get forty miles to the gallon. I relax like a poor man with a radio and nowhere to go. I lean like a lowrider whose vehicle *is* the destination. I pause in motion with an unlikely simile—a silo in the wind—knowing I've already arrived where I am. I treat the highway of American industry and commerce like a place of idleness and repose. This isn't Zen, it's revolt.

My time is worth more than money to me because I can't earn any more of it. I can only spend it wisely.

I work in a warehouse, which is a place where goods are stashed and money is made literally hand over fist. It's all in the turnover. We produce nothing. We add no value. We receive the goods, and we ship the goods, and the markup for the time between makes the loan sharks on Shake St. look like Saint Vincent DePaul. But the magnum of profit doesn't halt the speedup. We can't march fast enough for the General. There's only one solution: shoot the drummer.

Is it maximum profit or minimum conscience that drives our nation to compete for the lowest standard of living? Even children are sideswiped in the race to the bottom line. Schools are turned into sweatshops. Hospitals are managed like maquiladoras. Homelessness is mental health therapy. Prison is substance abuse treatment. Every program or agency whose purpose is to serve the public interest is underfunded, abused, and degraded. Our families suffer under the yoke of being double wage earners without disposable income or time to spend with their children. Meanwhile, Congress debates whether a minimum wage which snorkels the poverty line will ruffle the feathers and furs on Wall Street.

The madness of the method isn't just about money. The vultures already have all the money. They have plans for all the money you and I will ever make in our lifetime. They have plans for our pensions, our 401(k)s, the money that falls through the hole in the doughnut they call prescription drug coverage for senior citizens. They have plans to profit off the deaths of our brothers and sisters in Iraq and Afghanistan. It's not just about the money. It's about control.

When the debt comes due, when the dollar deflates, when property values tank, and the market collapses, what will the wealthiest of the wealthy do? Seize everything of value. Buy up the homes of workers for a dime on the dollar; snap up utilities at bargain basement prices; then jack up rents and rates in tandem. They'll commandeer all the hard assets, the natural resources, the oil, and the gold. Just thinking about it makes me drive slower.

And the slower I go, the more the knowledge of where I've been and where I'm going comes into focus. The more I listen to the radio spin circles around my vehicle, the more I notice what's missing from our conversation about the common good, namely the working class.

There is no *middle* class and no *lower* class in America. There are only workers who have decent jobs, and workers who don't have decent jobs. Those who do hold decent jobs are only one catastrophic illness, one plant closing, or one indefinite layoff from destitution. The victims of capital's creative destruction aren't strangers. They are working-class Americans made destitute by a system that requires unemployment to hold down inflation.

Lou Dobbs is wrong about the growing demise of the middle class in America. There is no middle class to demise. The mantle of middle-class status presumes a degree of security and upward mobility that does not exist. The notion of safety, draped like the boss's arm around one's shoulder, is based on the premise that hard work pays off and loyalty is rewarded. The middle-class dream is as dead as the deer I see splattered on the highway every day. There is no middle class for special workers. There is only a working class, and we—however special we may feel—all work in the same demoralized place, under the same relentless pressure to sacrifice our lives for the success of a godless corporation. Where will it end?

Despite expectations to make a billion dollars in net profit, Harley-Davidson in Milwaukee demanded the union impose a two-tier wage and benefit cut in order to secure *new* work. Union members voted the double-cross down soundly. But union leaders pursued a vigorous campaign to promote the competitive ideal. On the second try, the traitors' deal was narrowly ratified.

The soul of a union leader who pushes two-tier is darker than the pupil of a well digger's eye. Every union leader knows there's no water at the bottom of that hole. Two-tier is not just about money, it's about control. Harley-Davidson's extortion didn't stop at the doorstep of the union hall. The state of Wisconsin agreed to provide help with infrastructure improvements, training costs, and even capital. The assault on workers is state sponsored. Health, education, and social programs get slashed while the corporate blitzkrieg on the working class is subsidized. Mussolini would be impressed, but Tom Paine would shoulder the musket of conviction: "If there must be trouble, let it be in my day, that my child may have peace."

Two-tier is not just about the money, it's about who owns whose soul. The most effective way to break the spirit of the working class is to compromise our moral code by forcing a choice between fighting back or betraying what is most precious—our children.

We stand at the crossroad knowing full well where both roads lead. One road leads to dishonor and the other to the dignity of struggle. One road points to the hope and courage of collective action and the other to shame, despair, and isolation.

After such knowledge, what forgiveness?

Will reduced wages mean the work will be safer or more humane? Will reduced benefits mean more security? Or will it simply mean the collective power of workers will be harnessed to serve our masters' driving passion—maximum profit for minimum wage? The corpos must think we are dumber than horses. The yoke never lightens, the hardship never wanes, and the hope for retirement in dignity fades like a dope smoker's dream.

Last year, while Delphi was making headlines with threats and intimidation, Hastings Piston Ring, an auto supplier in northern Michigan, quietly and with the blessing of the federal court, cut off pension and health care for retirees. Production of piston rings didn't miss a beat and the profit kept pumping like a flathead eight on a straightaway.

Two-tier for new hires and a kick down the stairs for retirees. That's the refrain. Verses in between change the names but not the rhythm or the rhyme scheme.

Hastings Piston Ring, Harley-Davidson, and Delphi are not isolated cases. The degradation of the working class is chronic and contagious. We need collective action, not more concessions. We need to try our souls in the temper of our times that our children may have peace.

Where the Road Paved with Concessions Goes
(January 2007)

I used to enjoy road trips. The privilege of driving one's own vehicle—the comfort, the privacy, the independence—is, above all else, seductive.

Speed is power and power intoxicates faster than a boilermaker on an empty stomach. When I hit the open road, my mind hums with illusions of grandeur. Top it off with the whipped cream of rock and roll and I feel as bright as a maraschino cherry. I'll take all my meals to go.

The wanderlust of Americans is legendary. Our nation was conceived on the fly by desperadoes, fugitives, adventurers, runaways, gamblers, mercenaries, or—if you prefer them all mixed in a gumbo and served in a socially acceptable cup of a word—immigrants.

Pulling up roots and moving on is an American tradition. We are driven by our passion for change. We have come to regard excessive mobility as if it were a natural phenomenon, but the road was engineered and the object of our obsession for perpetual motion was manufactured. It's as if the boss said, "My way or the highway, and they're both the same."

We weren't born with a gene to drive like devils. There was a time when all travel was a means to an end, rather than a means to evade all ends and stifle the reflection of a life well lived. Who has time for reflection? We live in the fast-forward mode. Like dogs at the track chasing a mechanical rabbit, we race to keep up with the payments—gas, oil, insurance, maintenance—and the lease on a vehicle which conveys us to work so we can keep up with the payments on mortgage, phone, electricity, heat, and the latest, fastest craze.

The poor dogs never catch the mechanical rabbit that leads the race and we—no matter how much overtime we work—never make enough to relax and watch the dogs go round and round.

Race track owners have plans for all the money you and I will ever make. Which is why they persuade us to wager our savings on a 401(k) while the trade imbalance skyrockets and the national debt digs a hole to China. But who has time to speculate, much less extricate from the webbing of globalized gibberish that masquerades as editorial wisdom à la Flat Earth Friedman? It's not an accident that workers don't have time to think, let alone organize.

Workers from closed GM plants in Lansing are driving to work in Grand Rapids as former Delphi workers from Grand Rapids are commuting to GM plants in Lansing which, by the way, would have been a very cool city, the first to mass-produce the electric car, if General Motors hadn't killed it. Instead the brand-new GM plant in Lansing is mass-producing crossover SUVs, which is like Philip Morris inventing a new brand for the coffin nail.

I want off the merry-go-round.

According to the Bureau of Labor Statistics, a quarter of all work-related deaths last year were caused by highway crashes. Of course "work-related" does not include commuters, it only includes truck and bus drivers, sales reps, police, and others whose work entails long hours of daily driving. For the rest of us non-professional highway users, the leading cause of death by accident is not a slip, a trip, or a fall, it's a highway crash. The difference is, we are not, technically speaking, at work when we crash.

"According to the Federal Highway Administration, almost two-thirds of all highway fatalities are categorized as 'road departures,' as opposed to intersection or pedestrian accidents, an indication of tired drivers veering out of their lanes or off the road altogether" ("America's Most Dangerous Jobs," *Forbes*, November 6, 2006).

And what is the leading cause of death when an exhausted driver departs from the road? A rollover.

GM announced that it will voluntarily provide rollover protection on all vehicles in five years. Why not make vehicles that don't roll over in the first place? Because that would require a center of gravity that isn't four feet off the ground. Vehicles that don't roll over require aerodynamic designs, which likewise improve fuel efficiency. No dice. We will continue to roll over like loyal dogs dedicated to pleasing our gas masters because a safe, efficient, zero-emission electric vehicle is not what Americans want. Don't take my word for it, trust GM, the company that loses more market share every year.

Forget all that, it's past, it's gone. Behind the wheel, we all feel like lead singers. That's the magic. The predominant feeling of driving is characterized by the song "My Way." *My* hands on the wheel, *my* foot on the pedal, and all the comforts of numerically controlled climate at *my* fingertips. The best defense is a good offense, and the cliché carries over to the highway, where the biggest consumption monsters self-propel like mobile bomb shelters. But the My Way Highway leads to greater consumption, which leads to more work, which leads to treadmill fatigue, which leads to "road departures."

Who's leading whom on this highway to hell?

It's all about control: control over choices, communication, political action, or the lack thereof. The masses are asleep at the wheel while the wealth they generated is transferred offshore, and that troubling notion just crossed my mind like a Grateful Dead lullaby: "Two good eyes and you still don't see."

The plan to fail is a lucrative enterprise. No one could fail as successfully as GM-Delphi year after year without a plan to shelter assets overseas and break contracts—pensions, benefits, wages—in the United States.

The demand for more concessions is a pattern that repeats across the spectrum of manufacturing, transportation, construction, mining, agriculture, and service. The employers want more and the neoliberals are dishing it up, à la carte. *Work harder for less and we'll let you work longer.* That's the *new* New Deal.

The nation that kicked off the struggle for the eight-hour day is logging more hours than any modern industrialized nation on earth. Every household needs two wage slaves and every wage slave needs a vehicle to keep them on the treadmill. The turmoil is designed to foil collective action. The degradation of workers is not natural, accidental, or unavoidable; it's a plan. Put the jigsaw pieces together, and the picture is clear as glass and sharp as pain.

In 2004, the UAW Concession Caucus negotiated a supplemental agreement that cut wages in half, eliminated the pension, and reduced all benefits for new hires at Delphi. *Members were not permitted to vote on the deal.*

In 2006, the Con Caucus negotiated early retirements and transfers at GM-Delphi that accelerated the transition to a permanent lower wage at Delphi. *Members were not permitted to vote on the deal.*

In exchange for these sacrifices, UAW members won the right to walk away without a fight. Ron Gettelfinger, the UAW president who delivered the passive cooperation of union members and paved the way for more concessions, is an invaluable asset to the corporations.

Here are a few more pieces of the puzzle. Federal courts have consistently protected accrued vested benefits of retirees under a union contract. Gettelfinger pushed through takeaways from retirees, then filed a bogus lawsuit against GM in order to set a legal precedent. The lawsuit was counterfeit because there was no conflict. GM and the Con Caucus had already agreed to take accrued vested benefits from retirees who *were not permitted to vote on the deal,* and GM paid for the UAW's legal fees.

Now that the legal barrier has been removed, the Con Caucus is free to enforce the robbery of retirees in future negotiations. Pensions will be devoured by health care premiums and co-pays, and *retirees will not be permitted to vote on the deal.*

Corporate moguls served by neoliberal lackeys-in-waiting have plans for all the money you and I will ever make. They have plans to take away every damn nickel and dime.

Dave Yettaw, former New Directions leader and president of UAW Local 599, used to say, "The corporations are playing chess and the UAW is playing checkers." The company thinks three moves in advance and the lackeys-in-waiting respond with, "What is your pleasure?"

The answer is always the same, "More."

The Big Three will demand two-tier in 2007 under the cover of more flexible utilization of temps. The Con Caucus will promote this concession as "better than" what they led us to expect, and then claim we won "job security." Buyouts will spice the deal and accelerate the demand for temps. Members who think they have landed safely in retirement will stand by helplessly as accrued vested benefits are picked from their pockets. Retirees' hands will be tied because *they can't vote and they can't strike.* The endgame is right around the bend.

Slow down, Casey Jones, slow down. A highway paved with concessions can be fatal. Keep your eyes on the road and your hands on the wheel. Don't roll over. Slow down. Slow down, now.

Bar Codes & Boondoggles, Slogans & Goals, Subliminal Messages & Robot Control
(February 2007)

I've worked for GM and Delphi for twenty-eight years. Trust is not an issue, because there is no trust. We have a contract. The company violates the contract and we contest. That is the nature of our relationship. It's purely adversarial. The company pushes workers to do more for less and we push back.

In a capitalist society, it's inane to expect workers not to act like investors. We too seek the highest profit for the investment of our time, energy, and expertise. One thing you can count on in a capitalist society is that everyone wants the same thing: buy low, sell high. Getting more for less is the basis of the capitalist ethic. We didn't make the rule. We just work to rule.

The corpo-rats understand this motivation, which is why the competitive edge is pressed to our wrists. I say wrists because we are expected to do our own cutting. The company threatens to close the plant or outsource work if we don't become more competitive. How do we become more competitive? By bleeding jobs.

We bleed jobs by speeding up the line, increasing rates, ignoring hazards, two-tiering new hires, and outsourcing jobs to nonunion contractors who employ our brothers and sisters at lower compensation. If we succeed in this competition, we lose everything but the right to work. Then, for a perk, we get to vote on what we want to give up next.

Every competitive program requires a slogan, and the GM slogan of the year is: "Quality is job security." It sounds good, but actions, not slogans, reveal one's true intention.

I work in a GM warehouse. In my department, Order Selectors fill forty-seven orders per hour. They scavenge the shelves for parts, package and label them, and throw the packages into one of four bins, depending on the type of shipment. It's a lot to do in a short time.

Packages are regularly returned because they were thrown into the wrong bin. This is a chronic problem, but management does not attempt error-proofing. They prefer finger-pointing. Finger-pointing has not proven effective as an instrument of change, but the pantomime persists because the company is not really interested in quality, as that might lead to job security. The real goal is to increase job *in*security, which compels more frantic competition.

The solution to misplaced packages is simple. We need a color code. Four primary colors would do the trick. Instead, workers are expected to read bar codes. Scanners, not humans, were designed to read bar codes.

Humans were designed to read Hebrew, Arabic, English, even hiero-glyphics, but not ‖|‖|‖|‖|‖| .

To the untrained eye all bar codes look the same, but there are dif-ferences. For example, some bar codes are wider than others. Some are taller or thinner or shorter or longer or have other incremental variations. Attention to detail helps. But when you have sixty minutes to find, pack-age, label, and dispose of forty-seven different parts, you may miss a detail in favor of an expeditious toss over the left shoulder.

Management takes no responsibility for this chaos because "quality is job security" and job security is not a GM goal. If quality were the goal, each label would have a primary color to designate the proper mode of transportation.

Besides reading bar codes, the Order Selectors have to package the parts they scavenge from the maze of shelves and racks. Many of the pack-ages require tape, as opposed to self-stick flaps. Tape has a double value because it's not only time-consuming to apply, it's harder than hell to re-move. So we eat time on both ends—shipping and receiving—and we all carry razor knives, which makes everyone feel safer.

Some parts also require "over-boxing," whereby one box is put over another box. Since one box has proven to be inadequate protection, we use two boxes and double the inadequacy, double the time, and double the effort. It's a time-honored GM policy: *If at first the plan doesn't succeed, do it over and over and add red tape.*

But there's a good reason that the "over-boxing" doesn't protect "gen-uine GM parts" from damage, because, per management directive, Order Selectors are required to throw them.

Heave may be a more accurate description. Some of these parts—say, an alternator—are pretty heavy. Throw them six to ten feet and they crash. If they land on a thirteen-ounce plastic component—say, a tail-light—something has to give, and the box and the bubble wrap give like a water balloon on impact. But management claims they can eat the cost of damages, including the customers' anger, because they save money by eliminating a few jobs. You see, a more careful parts handling process might take more time, and since "Quality is job security" is a slogan, not a goal, we are hell-bent on destruction.

Another area of concern is selecting the wrong part or wrong quantity, which naturally makes one wonder: "What the hell are the bar codes for?"

Perhaps GM can't afford the software. A bar code's a boondoggle without the relevant software. If I had a computer at home like the ones they use in our warehouse, I would put it at the curb. I would put a sign on it that read FREE. And I bet my paycheck no one would take it.

The prevalence of antiquated technology leads one to wonder if the front office isn't sharing an abacus and a Ouija board.

When management want to close a plant, they stop investing, sabotage production, and blame workers for not being competitive. How do I know? I worked at Delphi.

But all is not lost. GM's Super Bowl commercial featured a robot that was fired for dropping a screw. The robot was shamed and rejected by its peers. The robot's struggle to adjust to the world outside GM was hopeless. After a series of unskilled, low-paying jobs, the robot was filled with such loneliness and despair that it committed suicide.

But it was only a nightmare. The robot woke up on the assembly line anxious as hell and eager to please.

The unsophisticated viewer may think this skit has something to do with dehumanizing workers for the sake of quality control and hyper-productivity, but insiders are aware that GM's CEO, Rick Wagoner, is known in official circles as "the Robot."

One more screwup, and the Robot will make the ultimate sacrifice for the good of the company.

And you thought the subliminal message was "quality is job security."

Delphi: A Dead Oracle and a Dirty Verb
(May 20, 2007)

Karen Healey, vice president of Delphi Corporate Affairs, speaks to the Economic Club of Lansing, Michigan.

After I wrote about Steve Miller's speech at the Detroit Economic Club, the FBI sent agents to my house. So allow me to begin this article about my recent experience at the Lansing Economic Club by saying I am not a threat to national security. Steve Miller and his band of vulture capitalists, on the other hand, are economic terrorists.

Steve Miller, the Delphi Board of Directors, JPMorgan Chase, Citicorp, and senior executives like Karen Healey, who spoke at the Lansing Economic Club, conspired to use the bankruptcy court rather than the much-extolled *free market* to break contracts with unions, suppliers, and customers; to evade responsibility to state and local governments from whom they coerced tax breaks for years while simultaneously exploiting the infrastructure and educational foundation provided by the body politic; to trash shareholders' contributions, including in many cases the life savings of loyal Delphi employees; and to tear down, sell off, and otherwise extract the value still inherent in a company that ranked "No. 1 on the *Automotive News* list of top 150 original equipment suppliers to North America with original equipment sales of $16.89 billion in 2006" in order to enrich themselves ("Delphi Posts $63 Million Loss for March," *Automotive News*, April 30, 2007).

Karen Healey, vice president of Delphi corporate affairs, compared herself to "Pollyanna" in the course of her corporate image-polishing. Why shouldn't she have a cheery outlook? She and other senior executives will reap stock options in a reconstituted Delphi worth 10 percent of its post-bankruptcy value plus $87 million in bonuses.* That's enough boodle to make the eternal pessimist tuck his tail up his ass and grin with both eyes. Sorry, Pollyanna, but an obscene metaphor is the only suitable description for such gross public misconduct. The bare truth is: vulture capitalists have no socially redeeming value.

Ms. Healey was in Lansing to gloss over fraud and conspiracy charges, massive mismanagement, rampant incompetence, and a trail of lies more convoluted than a snake's path through the Garden of Good and Evil. She must have felt relieved to see the Lansing Economic Club

---

* A bankruptcy judge later reduced the Delphi executive bonus payment pool to $16.5 million, plus $46 million in short-term incentive pay and $68 million in long-term incentive pay ("Delphi trims $85 million from execs' bonus fund," *Detroit News*, Jan 29, 2008).

wanted to be glossed over. Club members were busy devouring dehydrated fish squares smothered in mushroom soup. In my traditional Catholic up-bringing, we referred to such jailhouse fare as the culinary equivalent of penance. A Friday ritual wherein mortal sins were expunged through stoic chewing and beatific facial expressions. But it may have been chicken, pigeon, or opossum. Who knows what lurks beneath the mushroom soup, or a murky quarterly report?

In any case, I couldn't swallow the victuals or the BS that passes for oracle in an age when capitalism attacks not only workers, but investors. We don't need PR flacks. We just need the facts. Oh where have you gone, Jack Webb? Our nation turns its lonely eyes to you. I looked around, but there were so many cheap suits in the crowd I couldn't tell who was whom.

Delphi was a debt-free corporation in 1999 after it was spun off from General Motors. Delphi owned the property, the machinery, the technology, the patents, the products, and the research facilities outright. The pension was fully funded. Delphi had no retirees. Six years later Delphi claimed bankruptcy. Today the pension is underfunded by over ten billion dollars, and the stock is worthless.

While Delphi underfunded the pension and stockpiled debt in the United States, they purchased assets overseas that are protected from US bankruptcy laws. That's not a "corporate restructuring," it's a swindle.

Delphi intends to sell US assets, which they inherited tax free, to raise pocket money. Former workers at Delphi made decent wages, but when JPMorgan Chase and Citicorp agreed to finance Delphi's bankruptcy for an initial $4.5 billion, they set out to make a killing.

Ms. Healey's speech promised to tell us "What's Next for a Transformed Company," but the pretext seemed premature for a company that has yet to present a reorganization plan to the court, attain "consensual agreements" with its unions, resolve civil lawsuits by large-scale investors who were defrauded, litigate criminal investigations by the Justice Department, or appease its largest unsecured creditor and customer, General Motors. I may not be well educated, but I've got eyes, man.

"Bankruptcy," Ms. Healey smiled, "doesn't carry the stigma that it once did." Which is to say, vulture capitalists have no shame. Bankruptcy in Pollyanna's eyes has become a "cottage industry." I kid you not. She used that quaint phrase to describe the diabolically sinister shysters who conspire to rip off retirees, workers, investors, and taxpayers.

She said that Delphi is committed to "preserving" the pension plan "for both hourly and salaried people" by "freezing it" and "fully funding it."

Preserve by freezing? Does Pollyanna think we're talking about string beans? Delphi underfunded the pension in 2001,'02,'03,'04,'05,'06, and '07. Now we are supposed to believe that after the vultures pick the bones clean, the pension will be preserved and fully funded through the magic act of freezing?

She assured us that Delphi "has a concrete plan" which she couldn't disclose because "we are still in a very delicate period with negotiations." Delicate indeed. Delphi only lost $11 million on US operations in March 2007. If Delphi hadn't paid $10 million in fees to the "cottage industry" that advises the crooks and $37 million in bonuses to retain the incompetents, Delphi would have shown a $36 million profit in the United States in March. If Delphi had reduced salary staff at *half* the rate they cut hourly workers, they could have saved, by conservative estimates, an additional $24 million for a total profit of $60 million in one month just in the United States. But they don't want to show a profit yet, because the vulture capitalists want more concessions from the unions. What passes for delicate in Pollyanna's world is called *cutthroat* on the street.

Despite the cloak of confidentiality, she assured us that they are "working very hard to get out of this process as quickly as we can." Since Miller initially bragged that Delphi would be out of bankruptcy in early 2006, I think it's fair to say that Miller lost control of the process and the only "concrete" in his action plan is the dead weight at the top. The brash, antagonistic, arrogant *provocateur* who paraded around the country like a corporate crusader in 2005 hasn't ventured from his spider hole in over a year.

Healey very concretely said, "We are committed to *not* comment publicly on these decisions with important stakeholders, but I can tell you we are *passionately* committed to a consensual resolution" (italics *hers*). Consensual is a curious word considering the other parties are crying fraud, lawsuit, fraud, criminal conspiracy, fraud, ripoff, fraud, racketeering, fraud, betrayal. Did I mention fraud?

She said, "We have reduced cost structure across all our US manufacturing organizations." She didn't admit they want more concessions from union members, because every nickel they wheedle from workers will bolster their bonuses. As David Barkholz reported, "The savings are substantial. In the first quarter alone, the Delphi Steering Unit saved $28 million from having a lower-paid workforce, the company revealed in its first-quarter financial filing this week. The unit represents just 10 percent of the $6.7 billion in Delphi sales posted in the first quarter. So the companywide savings would have been much greater in the quarter. Delphi spokeswoman Claudia Piccinin declined to provide total savings" (*Automotive News*, May 9, 2007).

Delphi PR flacks want it both ways. They want to "polish the halo," as Pollyanna professed, but they don't want to be honest. After her speech about the transformation of Delphi, I spoke to Ms. Healey face to face. When I questioned her about the report in the *Automotive News*, she got flustered. "I don't know where they get their information," she said.

"From your quarterly report," I replied.

"Analyst Kirk Ludtke said Delphi's first-quarter results show 'clear evidence of a turnaround in the company's financial performance.' That is especially so in light of declining North American sales at GM, Delphi's largest customer, said Ludtke, who works for CRT Capital Group LLC in Stamford, Connecticut" ("Union Cuts Help Delphi as Salaried Cuts Lag," *Automotive News*, May 9, 2007).

The *Automotive News* is a conservative and credible source. On the other hand, we know from experience that Delphi executives are liars. How many times were employees in captive-audience meetings encouraged to buy Delphi stock on the basis of false reports? Why should we believe them now? Why should we make more concessions? They already robbed us twice. Any counterproposal from the UAW should demand more compensation, not less. New hires deserve more because they make all the sacrifices, they do all the work, and they don't have a pension to look forward to. New hires deserve more. Lots more.

Ms. Healey confided that Delphi intends to cut 25 percent of the salaried workforce, plus "40 percent of office work positions would also be eliminated." But Delphi doesn't want to follow through with salary and other administrative cuts until after they wrest more concessions from the unions.

Dave Barkholz calculated in the *Automotive News* article: "If an additional 7,500 salaried workers had been cut, Delphi would have saved an additional $562.5 million, assuming a $75,000 per person cost."

Seventy-five thousand dollars? Sounds like a conservative estimate, considering Miller's contention that UAW members averaged $138,000 per year. One billion dollars would be a more accurate estimate of the savings/profit.

On top of these savings, Delphi anticipates selling, consolidating, or closing twenty-one of twenty-nine plants in the United States. If Delphi transfers the legacy cost back to GM or the government's Pension Benefit Guaranty Corporation (PBGC), what is the profit margin on the sale of an asset they never paid for? And where will the money go?

The same place it has always gone. Money isn't lost, it changes hands; in this case, from the working class to the vulture class. Chrysler workers would be well advised to study the game plan. They're about to get Delphied.

When Conviction Is Irrelevant
(July 7, 2007)

General Motors' contention that health care costs $1,500 per vehicle is a false analogy. Since retirees outnumber active workers five to one, five-sixths of the $1,500 figure is for retirees. Thus, the real cost of health care for active workers is $250 per car, which is in line with Toyota's costs.

The real issue is corporate accountability. If I didn't start saving for retirement until after I retired, no one would be impressed with my investment strategy. Yet that is exactly what GM did. They promised deferred compensation to workers in the form of lifetime benefits, but didn't invest money to cover the anticipated expense. Why? They never intended to make good on their promise. They aren't stupid, they're dishonest. Matter of fact, David Cole, the son of a GM president, backs me up on this. "In business, lying is one of the things you do all the time" ("Cutting Up DCX Not a Done Deal," *Detroit Free Press*, May 23, 2007).

The number of GM vehicles made in the United States has nothing to do with the cost of health care. If GM returned production of vehicles from China, Korea, Mexico, and Canada to the United States, the cost of health care would not go down. In fact, the total cost would rise as new workers were added to the payroll. Besides, the conclusion that we need to build more cars in the United States to balance the equation of active and retired employees never occurs to the pencil squeezers, because GM does not intend to build more cars in the United States. Instead, GM intends to sell us on the idea of concessions in order to subsidize the transfer of assets overseas. Don't buy it. A concession contract depreciates faster than ink dries.

Furthermore, the assertion that we do not pay health care premiums is a lie. Between 1976 and 1999, seventy-three cents—not adjusted for inflation—was diverted from our cost of living raises to pay for health care. Gettelfinger has negotiated an additional seventy-nine cents in COLA diversion to offset the cost of health care. On top of that we sacrificed a 3 percent raise that averaged eighty-three cents for a total $2.35 per hour.

For the sake of conservative estimates and easy math let's round down to two bucks flat per hour. Eighty dollars per week. Four thousand dollars per year donated by each and every GM-UAW member for health care, not including overtime or adjustment for inflation.

But it doesn't make a damn bit of difference. We could work for free, and GM wouldn't sell any more vehicles. In fact, GM would sell fewer vehicles, because their most loyal customers couldn't afford them.

Does GM really have a cost disadvantage of $2,000 with Toyota and Honda? If so, it's primarily because they have to put money on the hood to move metal off the lot. Add in recall and warranty costs, and you'll find GM is underestimating the cost disadvantage, but none of the above is labor related.

Nor is the total cost of health care restricted to labor. The health care sum also includes salaried employees, salaried retirees, Rick Wagoner's daily pedicure, and Bob Lutz's* facial peels. For all we know, the total cost of health care could include hourly maintenance on robots.

---

* GM's design chief at the time.

The question we should be asking is, "What is the total *cost of mismanagement* per vehicle?" If we make health care concessions to cover their asses, we will lose our own. Every time we agree to shoulder more of the costs through COLA diversions and increased out-of-pocket expenses, GM is encouraged to demand more concessions. As long as we are willing to pay, GM has no reason to demand accountability from management or national health care from Congress.

Other than customary lip service, the UAW has not shown support for national health care, either. Why? Because the Con Caucus would rather get in on the action by controlling a multi-billion-dollar VEBA. UAW office rats could skim hundreds of millions in administration fees, just like they do with Joint Funds. They won't need union dues. They'll happily slurp cream off a VEBA.

Reporters write about "VEBA" as if it was a mysterious force heading our way. Just because we only see a fin in the water doesn't mean the shark hasn't arrived and we don't know its intent. When the UAW filed their phony lawsuit against GM in 2005, the court sanctioned the UAW's right to concede benefits for retirees, and GM paid the legal fees. Retirees used to have defined benefits guaranteed for life. With a VEBA retirees have a defined contribution, and a diminishing contribution at that. As administrator of the VEBA the union becomes the arbiter of concessions. Office rats have a vested interest in protecting the capital they live off of, just as they do the strike fund. The Con Caucus protects capital in the strike fund because they use the interest to propagate their species. It's like an HMO that profits by denying health care.

It's hard to convince an old fisherman that the fin he sees in the water is not a predator he should be wary of. But the persuaders in this case have a huge advantage. When the company and the union work together, conviction is irrelevant.

A Practical Solution to an Urgent Need
(August 7, 2007)

GM-Delphi is the leading manufacturer in the fastest-growing automobile market in the world—China. The rapid expansion is fueled by the marriage of cheap capital fleeced from US labor and cheap labor marshaled by a Chinese police state.

It was a marriage made in hell.

But a marriage made with the purest of motives: profit. When the leading "Communist" and capitalist states decided to exceed Wall Street's expectations, all the walls came down. No expense—life, liberty, or reputation—was too great to impede the pursuit of profit.

At the height of America's dominance in the world economy, GM made promises of lifetime benefits to workers, and the US government made boogiemen of communists. The Red Scare worked like a stove match. Union officials routed the radicals from their ranks and bound labor's fate with apron strings and no-strike clauses. In both events, war and treachery, victims were workers who died in combat or got the short stick on both sides of the Pacific.

What corpos call *restructuring* is simply a transfer of wealth from the working class to the investing class. Every concession we make subsidizes the transfer of assets. This isn't speculation, it's history repeated in one industry after another: steel, textiles, appliances, electronics. We are not only losing jobs, we are losing labor's accumulated wealth.

Bankruptcy in the US auto industry is not an accident; it's a business plan. The government does not appear to have an industrial policy, but the transfer of labor's legacy wealth to offshore accounts is the policy in practice.

Every kid on the American playground knows how it feels to be at the top of the teeter-totter when your partner finds a new friend.

When the economy crashes and the entire working class is impoverished, we will understand the true *legacy cost*. The legacy of treachery and deceit. The legacy of union-management partnership. The legacy of war after war after war. The legacy of a government that stands down while corporations trash communities as surely as Hurricane Katrina trashed New Orleans.

The corpos declare that legacy costs curb investment, but they conveniently ignore the legacy profits that GM-Delphi invested in China, Mexico, Latin America, India, Korea, Russia, Eastern and Western Europe. Profit is our legacy, too. The destruction of America's industrial base is not a random consequence of globalization, it's an investment strategy.

The older generation may be able to preserve their retirement benefits in the short term, but the declining value of the dollar will degrade their standard of living as the trade imbalance teeters and war catapults our national debt over the star-spangled horizon.

The VEBA won't save America's flagship industry or throw an inner tube around retirees when the cost of living rises faster than false hope dies. We don't want VEBA, we want universal health care, not only for our own generation, but for our children and grandchildren.

The challenge we face is too big for piecemeal fixes and private portions. Every time we cut a deal that deprives the next generation—as in two-tier and VEBA and buyouts that close plants—we underwrite the corpos' three-act play: Isolate, Whipsaw, Liquidate.

If the UAW doesn't demand the right to strike over outsourcing and plant closings, GM will accelerate its exit plan. If GM achieves two-tier in this contract, it will bust the union in 2011. If the UAW permits GM to strand retirees with a buy-down VEBA, you may as well continue working as long as you can still maneuver the walker and the oxygen tank through the turnstiles. Caterpillar had a VEBA, too. It's broke.

Autoworkers have an opportunity in 2007 to invoke the crisis that could provoke dramatic change in health and industrial policy. We can avoid the confrontation, but we can't escape the consequences of cowardice. If we fail to act collectively, we'll be picked off separately. Solidarity is not an ideal; it's a practical solution to an urgent need.

A Cat Named Job Security
(September 3, 2007)

The cat is out of the bag. Chris "Tiny" Sherwood, president of Local 652 in Lansing, confirmed that the UAW is negotiating a two-tier wage for new hires.

The tradeoff? "Job security."

You'd have thought that job security cat was at the bottom of the river by now, securely anchored with a bag full of broken contracts, but the promise of job security has more lives than a loan shark has lies.

"We won't go to a two-tier wage unless we get something out of it," Tiny said. "That would have to be something like job security" (Barbara Wieland, "Two-Tiered Pay Plan Figures in GM Talks," *Lansing State Journal*, August 24, 2007).

"At the Saturn complex in Spring Hill, Tennessee, local UAW officials have tentatively agreed to let workers earn less than half the $28-an-hour wage of veteran GM workers to staff an onsite parts-sequencing operation," wrote David Barkholz in *Automotive News*, where he broke the story revealing that two-tier is here but the UAW calls it "organizing" (Dave Barkholz, "UAW Budges on 2-Tier Wage," *Automotive News*, August 20, 2007).

Now that the UAW has lost two-thirds of its membership, the Con Caucus is unveiling their Southern Organizing Strategy: Work for Less.

Here's how the cat is skinned. The Con Caucus convinces employers to let them reorganize their workforce at lower wages. Outsourcing indirect labor and subassembly jobs and then reorganizing them at lower wages is like trading a dollar for seven dimes and calling it win-win. "It may be a way to help keep union jobs," said Sherwood (*Automotive News*, August 20, 2007).

GM must pay Tiny a lot of overtime for these bite-size snacks of wisdom. Barbara Wieland reported in the *Lansing State Journal* that "in 1982, there were about 23,000 people working for GM in Lansing; now there are about 6,000" (Barbara Wieland, "Rabble Rouser," *Lansing State Journal*, June 18, 2007). In other words, roughly 70 percent of GM's most loyal customers—employees—are out of work in Tiny's town. Nonetheless, Tiny thinks more cooperation with the corporate agenda will save union jobs.

In her article, Wieland states, "In the same time (1982–2007), market share has fallen from 43 percent to about 25 percent." I wish one of the wizards in GM's marketing department would calculate the employee to market share ratio. There may be a correlation here.

Of course, there's more than one way to drown a cat.

The Concession Caucus has always believed in a multilevel approach to givebacks and they aren't willing to rest on the laurels they won at Delphi and Visteon. Big Three automakers and the UAW are staging rallies around the country in "hopes the grassroots effort will help beat back" fuel economy mandates (David Shepardson, "Carmakers Hold CAFE Rallies," *Detroit News*, August 15, 2007).

Apparently, company-union leaders haven't read reports that contend declining sales are a result of US auto companies' failure to build vehicles customers *want*, as in, *fuel efficient.*

The strategic impact of a corporate-orchestrated "grassroots" campaign against better fuel economy is like drilling a hole in the bottom of a boat to let water out. It may slapstick a smile on everyone's face, but it won't sell cars or save jobs. Unions and corporations should be campaigning together for national health care—a solution that would help workers, manufacturers, and customers. Instead, corpos and their partners in the Concession Caucus are singing "VEBA Las Vegas" as bilge water rises to the oarlocks and the deck chairs slide overboard.

The VEBA scam gambles retirement security on the UAW's chances of beating health care inflation by playing the stock market. But the only way to beat health care inflation is to buy stock in pharmaceutical companies and then raise co-pays on retirees.

The Con Caucus promotes VEBA on the premise that retiree health care will be safer in the hands of the union *if* the company goes bankrupt. Of course, a VEBA partially funded by equity in the company leaves just enough apron string to hang oneself in the event of bankruptcy.

Cars that burn more cash than workers earn won't sell. A plan to **V**andalize **E**mployee **B**enefits **A**gain won't sell. Two-tier won't save union jobs, it'll sell them to the lowest bidder. Don't let the Con Caucus put our union on the auction block. Send negotiators back to the table with a clear ulti-matum. Autoworkers must profit from their labor, or nobody will.

Highball the Strike
(September 25, 2007)

At the press conference to announce the UAW strike against GM, Get-telfinger stood before the microphone like a deer in the headlights and said he didn't want to strike. He felt "pushed off a cliff." He said, "No one wins a strike."

Should rank-and-file members have to remind the president of the UAW that everything we ever gained—from union recognition to COLA and Thirty-and-Out—was won in a strike?

Gettelfinger reiterated concession after concession after concession that he has negotiated on behalf of GM. Then he expressed surprise that the sum total didn't add up to a positive, and that GM wasn't more coop-erative. How is it he never learned that when you roll over, again and again, management takes you for a punk, not a partner?

How should we regard a union leader who waves the white flag in the first hour of a strike?

Gettelfinger turned to Cal Rapson, UAW vice president in charge of the GM Department, and asked him if he wanted to say anything. Rapson sat on his hands and shook his head no. I have never seen a more abom-inable lack of leadership. Rapson put seventy-three thousand workers out on the street and he had nothing to say to them? Rapson should be taken off the job, denied workers' comp, and placed on extended disability for lack of backbone.

Gettelfinger suggested that he had been "naive" about GM's inten-tions. The loss of innocence is tragic in children, not old men. Everyone in work boots knows GM intends to take back everything they can.

Gettelfinger admitted that he had approached GM about a union-con-trolled health care plan—VEBA—two years ago. He never consulted UAW members and retirees about his VEBA idea. He consulted with Lazard Ltd.

and came up with a plan to help the folks on Wall Street, who live off unearned income and union office rats who need a desk to rest their feet on.

Local union leaders shouldn't have to field all the phone calls from distraught retirees. The retirees who won strikes back in the day deserve to have an information meeting where Rapson and Gettelfinger explain how an underfunded health care plan is going to protect them. They deserve answers to their questions straight from the horse's mouth. Anybody who wants to screw around in the back room and deliver Rosemary's baby should be prepared to attend the baptism by fire, not pass the buck off to local officials.

Reporters, analysts, and rank-and-file UAW members have openly speculated that the strike is a ploy. If it's short and sweet, we should be suspicious. We gave up $2,000 a year *minimum* for the last VEBA. We stand to lose more in four years of a concession contract than we would in a sixty-day strike.

Ask yourself some questions while you picket. Does a VEBA make you eager to retire or determined to work as long as you can? Can you trust a scheme that's long on promises and short on cash? Can you keep your head above water without COLA? Is it a good idea to sell out new hires? Can we retreat to victory?

The corporations want to take away everything we ever earned. The union president responds by calling a strike and then saying, "No one wins a strike."

That's a setup.

If we want to win, we have to highball the strike and demand no end until VEBA is off the table, full cost of living is restored, retirees get the health care they earned from the company, temps win equal status as union members, and we gain the right to strike over outsourcing and subcontracting.

Don't back down. If they come back with a tentative agreement in a matter of days, be prepared to send them back to the table. Nothing like a boot to the backside to straighten a spine.

Vote to Send Bargainers Back to the Bargaining Table
(September 27, 2007)

Gettelfinger dropped it into reverse, popped the clutch, and drove "over the cliff," as he said in a televised announcement.

Seventy years of progress ended in a solidarity-shattering, two-tier crash.

In 1970, the UAW won a sixty-seven day strike at GM. The struggle paid off: Thirty-and-Out and uncapped COLA. In 2007, after a two-day strike, Gettelfinger capped COLA, froze wages, cordoned off a two-tier zone for new hires, and gave GM a 30 percent discount on retirees' health care—$35 billion for a $50 billion debt.

Which leads us to the $15 billion question. Who will make up the difference?

GM execs laughed all the way to the bank.

"While the devil will be in the details, our first reaction is that GM captured a much broader set of concessions than we previously antici- pated," JPMorgan Chase analyst Himanshu Patel said in a note. GM shares "rose as much as 9.7 percent" (Bloomberg News, September 26, 2007).

Indeed, the devil is in the details, and GM workers know they will not know those details until after ratification. The rush to ratify is a sure sign that the Con Caucus doesn't want members to examine the contract too closely or debate it among themselves before they cast a vote. Hence the slogan, "Vote NO until you KNOW the whole truth."

Don't imagine that GM will pull up to Solidarity House with a Brinks truck and pile cash into wheelbarrows for the mystical VEBA. GM is expected to fund the union-controlled trust with a combination of cash, stock, and promissory notes. As VEBA fund managers, the UAW joins the sharks and parasites in the insurance industry and will assume GM's role as the gatekeeper—the collector of tolls, which will be auto- matically deducted from pensions or extracted in co-pays.

The Finger-Wagon Accord amounts to a massive transfer of wealth from retirees to GM coffers. "In effect, the new agreement allows GM to cap and move off its books to an independent trust, a more than $50 billion debt owed to the UAW for retiree health care" (*Wall Street Journal*, September 26, 2007).

Retiree health care will no longer be a defined *benefit*. Instead it will be a defined *contribution* capped at approximately 30 percent less than its projected cost. A neat discount if you can get it.

"For GM, restructuring the UAW health care legacy burden should help free the company to pursue Mr. Wagoner's strategy of accelerating growth outside the U.S." (*Wall Street Journal*, September 26, 2007).

Labor's legacy wealth will be transferred to assets overseas, and GM's job security pledges will go in the trash with the rest of their promises. In 1980, there were three hundred and fifty thousand UAW members working at GM. Today there are seventy-three thousand. Job security pledges litter every contract we've had since 1980.

Job security in the Finger-Wagon Accord will "depend on whether local unions at the factories agree to local contracts that make the plants more competitive. GM has been pushing local unions to agree to money-saving work rule changes, or so-called competitive operating agreements," company spokesman Don Flores said. "The local deals . . . cover a wide range of topics, including the number of job classifications and restrictions on nonunion labor allowed to work inside plants" (*Detroit News*, September 26, 2007).

There's a reason that competitive operating agreements (COAs) at Delphi have not been implemented. They don't want us to see how bloody the practice of cutting jobs to save jobs can be.

Active workers will give up the cost of living that our retirees fought and won for us in 1970. The COLA has accrued $2.08 as a result of the last contract. COLA adds a dollar in overtime pay and amounts to over $83 a week in straight time: a bare minimum of $4,300 a year which will not accrue in the new contract. But that's just the beginning of the UAW's transition to nonunion conditions.

"GM will implement a two-tier wage system for workers not doing core manufacturing" (*Detroit News*, September 26, 2007). Two-tier is a symptom of union decadence—a blatant act of discrimination against a whole class of workers. In the old UAW, there was no such thing as non-core workers. We were union to the core. A union that degrades workers is self-destructive, not competitive. If sacrifices are necessary, they should be shared equally by all classes and all generations, starting with the captains of industry.

COLA diversion, coupled with a wage freeze, means that top-tier workers will enter negotiations in 2011 at the same base rate as 2007 but surrounded by lower-tier workers hungry for a piece of the pie.

Divided, we beg. United, we vote NO. Send bargainers back to the table with a clear mandate: from new hire to retired, we are one union.

Chapter Four

The Perfect Capitalist Disaster

The UAW's 2007 agreements with the Detroit Three rolled back decades of gains. The UAW gave up wage progression, and diminished layoff protection, job security, and tuition reimbursement. The UAW transferred more health care costs to workers and retirees and diverted even more cost-of-living adjustments to offset the cost of health care for the companies.

For future hires, the UAW cut wages in half, reduced insurance benefits, and eliminated defined benefit pensions and health care in retirement.

The knife was driven deeper when the UAW agreed to reductions in paid absence and in the power to choose when vacation was permitted. Across-the-board takeaways in compensation weren't enough. The company insisted on rubbing workers' noses in the feces of union dignity by reducing break time.

The decision to eradicate work rules, which the company claimed impeded production, was, in effect, a transfer of power from workers to bosses. Reduced classifications gave more power to the boss and less autonomy to the individual worker. The starkest example was the zero tolerance attendance policy. Regard for one's humanity was excluded from any evaluation of a worker's attendance.

The UAW's support for rollbacks in fundamental compensation affirmed the bossing class contention that workers were worth less, and that—despite enormous gains in productivity—workers contributed less to the value of the product.

The 2007 UAW contracts set the stage for an attack not only on manufacturing workers, but all workers, including those in the public sector. Whereas the UAW once set the benchmark for progress, 2007 signaled that the UAW would now set the standard for the degradation of the working class.

The UAW 2007 agreement was a watershed moment in America. When UAW office rats took a dive, the American Dream went down for the count. Hard work doesn't pay, but the rewards for white-collar crime compound, time after time.

Less than two years later, GM and Chrysler followed Delphi into bankruptcy proceedings overseen by the Obama administration. As part of the agreement the UAW agreed to, and members at GM and Chrysler ratified, even more sweeping concessions that slashed compensation and eliminated decades of work rules. The agreement includes a ban on strikes through the next contract and stipulates that UAW contracts conform to competitive industry standards—that is, those of nonunion autoworkers.

When the Union Turns Against You
(January 2008)

I've been quiet since the UAW contracts with GM, Ford, and Chrysler were ratified. I've been quiet but not inactive. I've had my ear to the ground, listening to the sound of a slow train coming.

Workers are stressed. Pressure is relentless. Management adds tasks to jobs already overloaded, speeds up the line, raises rates, runs rampant over work rules, violates seniority, disregards production standards, harasses, intimidates, and disciplines. When members call out the union and demand a grievance, more often than not, the rep says, "They can do that. You're lucky to have a job."

I hear from young workers at Delphi earning wages below the industry average who feel passionate about the union. But they report that the union doesn't back them up. They feel abandoned. Worse, they feel attacked. "What do you do when the union turns against you?" they ask.

Some of the older workers are resigned to buyouts, but they worry about the future and they feel ashamed of the legacy that's been squandered for the sake of cooperation, jointness, and teamwork. It's apparent that the "corporate restructuring" is not about product, process, or design; it's about breaking the spirit of unionism and degrading workers. You can retire but you can't hide. The systematic attack on working people isn't a sign of economic recession, but rather regression to an older, more vicious time.

The corporations are waging an all-out war against workers. We're getting hammered on the shop floor. And all that Gettelfinger and the Con Caucus can come up with are new ways to surrender.

The UAW International's commitment to corporate restructuring at the expense of workers, both union and nonunion, is an abdication of the right to represent anyone but their business partners. The deduction of dues from paychecks does not a union make. If Michigan becomes a right-to-work state, Ron Gettelfinger has no one to blame but himself.

As a former employee of Delphi, I know the cost of restructuring and the toll it takes on workers and communities. I know how restructuring breaks unions and decimates solidarity. I know who chose to fight, and I know who chose to betray the fight.

In 2003, the Concession Caucus negotiated a two-tier supplement at Delphi. Gettelfinger said the two-tier wage was needed to make the company competitive and save jobs. Within four years, twenty-seven thousand out of thirty-three thousand union members were eliminated at Delphi, and the remaining workers were brought down to the lower wage and benefit scale.

Gettelfinger & Co. were not deterred. They brought the same contract to GM, Ford, and Chrysler in 2007. Don't be surprised if they open it up for more concessions in 2009. Ronnie's on a roll. On Valentine's Day, the *Automotive News* will host a $50-a-plate dinner to honor the auto companies' favorite sweetheart, the president of the UAW, Ron Gettelfinger. The corpos will be licking their fingers and snickering into their napkins. The captains of industry have good reason to feel delighted.

Contracts negotiated by the Concession Caucus divide and subdivide workers into antagonistic factions: the old and the new, the core and the non-core, the active and the retired, the temporary and the permanent, the skilled and the unskilled. Con Caucus contracts are designed to destroy solidarity. It's no wonder Gettelfinger is the favorite valentine of the corporati.

As ramifications of the new UAW contracts bulldoze the membership, workers will take their vengeance out on local union leaders. Anyone who supported this yellow-dog contract will be thrown out of office. If you've considered running for local union office, beware. Local leaders, however well-intentioned, will become the administrators of a union-busting program; the enforcers of core and non-core assignments; the excusers of seniority violations; the mollycoddlers of a ruthless restructuring. You'll find yourself saying, "I don't like it either, but they can do that. You're lucky to have a job." One may as well apply for supervisor and try to reform GM from within. Same difference.

The UAW is a one-party state, hard-wired to undermine solidarity, corrupt good unionists, and defend the corporate agenda. If we mistake the Concession Caucus for a legitimate union with workers' interests at heart, we'll be led to the slaughter like sheep that are sheared before they are butchered.

The UAW is a mess. It appears that the Concession Caucus led by Ron Gettelfinger is on the ropes, knees buckling and head spinning. Unless you see it from their perspective—successful implementation of the corporate agenda—in which case they are right on the money. The members may be confused and demoralized, but the bureaucracy is progressing rapidly toward the restructuring objective: replace top-tier workers with second-tier and temporary workers. The transfer of over fifty billion dollars in legacy wealth earned by workers to Con Caucus control, in the form of an unregulated VEBA, completes the transaction.

Money isn't lost, it changes hands. And when it changes hands, someone has to pay.

The bargaining committee at Freightliner in North Carolina stood up for their members' rights. Management fired them. The UAW International put the five fired UAW leaders on trial, despite the objections of the local union membership. The local union found them not guilty, so the International kicked the Freightliner Five out of the union. What was their crime? Fighting the good fight. The International is bent on destroying local union leaders who resist the corporate agenda.

UAW members who are laid off, or on disciplinary leave, should be alerted that you must notify the local union financial secretary *in writing* that you are eligible for good standing without payment of dues. Otherwise, you will be removed from the roster after six months (UAW Constitution, Article 16, Section 19). You must do this every month thereafter. Because if you are not a member in good standing, the union can drop your grievance, and no one will find the body. The Con Caucus aren't interested in retaining members, they are cleaning house for their business partners. Every top-tier worker is on the tip of the broom and headed for the dustbin.

What do you do when the union turns against you?

Collective action outside the corral of the compromised grievance procedure is our only recourse. Bullies don't deserve courtesy. Traitors don't deserve respect. When union-management goons run over the work rules, show contempt for the local union, and wipe their feet on retirees, there are no rules of engagement to uphold.

My people have an old saying: "If you haven't quit fighting, you aren't defeated."

Who are *my people*?

My people are black and white, old and young, men and women, communists and democrats. In sum, people of all persuasions united by one common bond—the old religion. Not the Con Caucus genuflection to the idol of competitiveness, but the old-fashioned, shoulder-to-shoulder, back-to-back, worker-to-worker solidarity that won everything that Gettelfinger & Co. betrayed.

We're all in this kettle together. Every working person is our natural ally. Senior workers have an obligation to defend new hires. We gave them the broken legacy of two-tier, and it's our job to amend it. Bring them up, or they will bring us down.

As I listen to the rumblings on the shop floor, I recall that I've felt overwhelmed and under siege before. But however steep the odds, I never felt alone. My people will never stop fighting. Deep in their bones, they know there's no seniority date for equality and no retirement from solidarity.

The Expectation Stick
(July 2008)

Management did away with rates in my workplace. The new standard is "expectations." No need to explain what that means. Everyone who works for a living is familiar with the short end of the expectation stick.

The switch—from rates to expectations—bars unbiased evaluation by quantifiable results (production rates) and legitimates arbitrary judgment by unqualified assessors (supervisors).

Expectation is not a valid standard of measure; it's a bully whip, a 40-inch yardstick, an optical illusion that leads us to an overwhelming question: when has management ever met our expectations?

By every standard of measurement, General Motors has failed the expectations of shareholders, dealers, customers, and workers.

I work in a GM warehouse. Not only is the storage space underutilized, we store empty containers. How can workers make up for the decision to stockpile empty containers and reward executive failure? For that matter, can any amount of concessions on behalf of labor ever make up for the decision to build products based on the diminishing expectation of cheap oil?

Incompetence and mandatory redundancy aren't unique to GM. Everyone who labors rather than speculates for a living feels the relentless pressure to work harder, faster, and longer to make up for bad management. Teachers and nurses are as understaffed and overtaxed as lineworkers.

Capitalism disdains all rules and regulations, but everyone is familiar with its expectations. For example, business expects to transfer all increased costs to the customer and expects workers to absorb all increased costs without a raise, because (according to conventional expectations) even a minimal raise in the minimum wage will cause inflation.

The premise of this unrealistic expectation is counterfeit. Wages don't cause inflation, wages chase inflation. That's how the economy is planned.

The basic maxim of business is "buy low, sell high," yet workers are expected to sell themselves short and pay top dollar. Management expects workers to sacrifice the profit from their labor in order to ensure the profit of speculators. The pundits of expectation deem self-sacrifice the patriotic duty of every red-blooded American worker. Or else.

Mark Perry, a shill funded by the anti-labor Mackinac Center for Public Policy, stated in his blog *Carpe Diem*, "Flint's manufacturing sector is dead, and it has now officially become a service-sector economy" (June 22, 2008).

Perry, citing unspecified "economic theory," blames unions for "losses of market share, employment, and output." According to Perry and his associate hacks in the business press, if we were willing to work in subservient conditions for substandard wages, we could have all the manufacturing jobs we want.

But Mark Perry, like auto-industry analysts David Cole and Sean McAlinden, among others, conveniently ignore the fact that management never ceded the right to manage. GM's unilateral right to manage is not an unidentified "economic theory," it's Paragraph 8 of the UAW-GM National Agreement. Management determines the designs, the technology, the process, the marketing, and the cheap nonunion suppliers who drive up warranty costs.

Unions didn't undermine the success of GM's North American Operations in the auto industry. Productivity gains exceed compensation. We make twice the product we did thirty years ago, with half the workers. The value-added labor we contribute adds less than 10 percent to the total cost of the vehicle. The other 90 percent belongs to management.

Profits generated from North American Operations funded investments overseas and carried those foreign investments when they lost money throughout the eighties and nineties. GM didn't treat those losing investments like redheaded stepchildren. GM protected and nurtured those foreign investments because they were part of a long-term plan to divest from the United States and throw legacy obligations overboard.

What did you expect? Patriotic capitalism?

Ford, GM, and Chrysler are preparing to "delphi" (*v.* to sabotage, undermine, bankrupt, mismanage, and recklessly abandon) North American Operations. The post-bankruptcy plan has already been agreed to by the UAW Concession Caucus, just as it was with Delphi. Two-tier is in the dugout and ready to take the field.

The Con Caucus traded the prospects of the next generation for the security of a VEBA, a health benefit for retirees that was under-funded 30 percent from the get-go. Now the UAW is loaning $1.7 bil-lion to GM from VEBA money it hasn't yet pocketed. Do they expect us to believe this swap is on the up and up? GM did not make a binding reciprocal commitment to secure union jobs. We see the give, but where's our take?

In the 2007 negotiations, the UAW had the opportunity to compel the auto companies to advocate a national single-payer health care system as the only viable means of survival for manufacturing in the United States. (All of our foreign competitors have single-payer national health care. Shouldn't US companies have the same competitive advantage?) In-stead, the Con Caucus let them off the hook with the VEBA scheme. Rather than acting like a social movement union for the benefit of all workers, the Con Caucus chose to behave like a business.

Trouble is, the auto companies won't honor their debt to the VEBA unless the UAW agrees to more concessions and plant closings. Via VEBA, the UAW has become a full partner in the exploitation of workers. The corruption engendered by union cooperation with management is spreading like a socially transmitted disease.

Buzz Hargrove, the president of the Canadian Autoworkers union, negotiated concessionary contracts with the automakers prior to the Canadian Autoworkers' national Bargaining Convention. Before the ink dried on the fast-track deal, GM announced it would close another plant represented by the CAW.

Should the Canadian Autoworkers have expected something differ-ent from a president who brokered a deal with Magna Inc. to set up a company union that would operate without the nuisance of elected union representation or a grievance procedure?

In the wake of a new UAW contract, Ford is closing plants in the United States and expanding in Mexico. Both Ford and GM will import small, fuel-efficient cars from South America and Europe as they close plants in the United States. Chrysler has signed a deal with Chery Auto-mobile in China.

Those who have observed how history unfolds in the present know the future isn't a wild guess. We're going to get the short end of the expectation stick—broken promises and legal excuses.

The social contract is in shambles. All the rules are broken. Now is our chance.

From the ashes of the old, from the scrap of heaps, from the scream of a free-market economy plunging off the cliff, comes opportunity. Every vehicle on the road is obsolete and will need to be replaced. We are on the cusp of a new technology driven by market forces out of control. Someone will have to do the work required to build new transportation and energy-efficient accommodations. As Sheikh Zaki Yamani, a former oil minister from Saudi Arabia, once said, "The Stone Age didn't end because there were no more stones. It ended because people became more intelligent."

It isn't simply the shells of old heaps that will have to be towed to the scrap yard. The institutions—corporate, government, union—that brokered the self-destructive contrivance called neoliberalism are obsolete and need to be replaced.

We, the people, have expectations, too.

A Perfect Capitalist Disaster
(August 2008)

What appears to be a catastrophe in the auto industry could be the perfect storm for GM, Ford, and Chrysler. They've wanted to close plants and jettison dealerships for a long time. The 2007 contracts with the UAW gave the auto companies an unrestricted license to close plants because of conditions "beyond the control of the Corporation" such as "market-related volume decline." Now they are ready to open the gift that is the contract.

Unlimited plant closings, coupled with time limits on the Jobs Bank, mean the Con Caucus has delivered the union's head upon a platter. But I am no great prophet, and this is no great matter of speculation. Everyone knows "market-related volume decline" is in sync with the goal to close plants and cancel commitments to dealers.

The 2007 GM-UAW contract listed nine plants to be closed for certain, and one to be "closed or sold." But that was before the perfect capitalist disaster. Now, poaching is legal and the game are penned in.

Manufacturers didn't push free trade agreements because they expected to export from the US. They never expected to export anything but jobs. The objective of free-trade agreements was to close factories in the United States, invest offshore, and import products formerly *made in the USA* back to the US market. The current capitalist crisis gives auto companies a perfect opportunity to bankrupt North American Operations and become major importers.

GM and Ford, like Delphi, invested profits overseas (foreign assets are protected under US bankruptcy law) rather than pumping dollars back into US plants. Chrysler does not have extensive investments overseas, but they have made a deal with Chery Automobile in China and they could partner with another foreign automaker to import small cars to the United States—unless Cerberus, the private equity fund that owns Chrysler, prefers a fire sale. In either case, we can't deny that the dogs from hell are at the gates.

Some speculators feel that, unlike Delphi, it would be too risky for GM to declare bankruptcy, because consumers would not buy vehicles from a bankrupt company. But Americans buy tickets to fly on bankrupt airlines maintained by disgruntled mechanics and depressed pilots. Why wouldn't they buy a car from two bankrupt companies: Delphi and GM?

Under bankruptcy protection, GM would continue to operate some plants in the United States. The disaster scenario would enable them to accelerate the transition to lower-tier workers and extort greater concessions from the UAW. Bankruptcy—like a boxer taking a dive—is a business plan.

There is simply too much cash to be skimmed by reneging on VEBAs and pensions. If they can't pay, as they say, who will have to pay and pay and pay? I've said it before, and I'll say it again. Money isn't lost, it changes hands. We are about to experience a massive transfer of wealth. It will be the most enduring legacy of the UAW's partnership with the corporations.

The VEBA was sold to UAW members as an insurance policy against the specter of bankruptcy. What the Concession Caucus didn't explain is that the health of the VEBA depends on the profitability of the company. Because they didn't get the money up front, the VEBA is essentially a promissory note. If the company goes bankrupt prior to an actual transfer of cash, the VEBA is busted flatter than a penny on a railroad track.

The security of retirees depends on the success of the VEBA. In turn, the VEBA depends on concessions from workers and plant closings. Some would attest that the UAW has a serious conflict of interest. But members know better. There is no conflict. The sweethearts have already made their bed.

Steve Miller, who is managing the perpetual failure at Delphi, said in a speech to the Detroit Economic Club on June 4, 2008, "One of the biggest factors in a decision to put new investment offshore is the punitive effect of health care costs on job creation in America."

Miller told the audience that after Delphi emerges from bankruptcy, he would like to take a role in solving "the country's number one domestic political and economic issue [health care]." He thinks he knows how to take waste out of health care.

Look at what's left of Delphi and Bethlehem Steel, and then ask yourself if you want the likes of Miller fixing health care. Miller's idea of waste is workers. Or more to the point, the cost of workers and retirees who, as he said in a previous speech, *live too long*.

One of the areas of waste that Miller cited during his speech was malpractice lawsuits. Miller is suing the Appaloosa hedge fund for backing out of an investment in Delphi. Apparently, due diligence exposed Miller's reorganization plan as flimflam. Miller didn't hesitate to file a frivolous lawsuit to force a hedge fund to invest against its better judgment.

What sort of businessman coerces someone into investing?

Miller has spent the last three years wasting money on fruitless legal proceedings and rewarding Delphi executives for continuous failure. If we don't mount a counteroffensive to wrest control of health care from parasites like Miller, we will lose more than VEBA. Our lives are on the line.

We're not affordable. We live too long. Miller and his vulture capitalist cronies want to fix that. Manufacturing workers have lost too many jobs and made too many concessions. Retaliation is in order. We know how to take the waste out of the system—cut out the middlemen. We don't need them. They do not perform any value-added function in the delivery of health care. They are more than a burden. They are a moral hazard.

Why should duffers sporting cologne that costs more than a doctor visit be allowed to skim money from doctors, nurses, hospitals, clinics, medical supply companies, and patients? We don't need the middlemen. Give them six months' severance, and offer to retrain them for work in the foundry.

Health care is ground zero of the perfect capitalist disaster. Miller & Friends want to fix health care so retirees don't live too long and the private insurance industry keeps making jackpot profits. He and his class of vulture capitalists want health care that restricts access by workers and retirees and specializes in serving those who were never exposed to the hazards of hard work.

One way or the other, the perfect capitalist disaster will be a catalyst for change.

Concessions We Will Gladly Make
(November 2008)

Our Republican friends on Capitol Hill want to make us take concessions until we're earning less than workers in foreign auto plants in Alabama. Trouble is, as soon as we reach parity with the Work-for-Less states, the competition will lower the limbo stick. And they'll keep lowering it until all workers are face down in the dirt.

But many of us agree that the Jobs Bank is a hoax. At the last GM plant where I worked, management put forty people in the Jobs Bank and assigned one person to watch them do nothing. The rest of us had to work mandatory overtime to make up for the lost production.

Why would a company pay people to sit down and do nothing and then pay other employees time-and-half to make up for what the do-nothings weren't doing? It doesn't make sense, unless you are keeping two sets of books. One for the company and another for the Center for Human Resources, a tax-exempt, nonprofit corporation that administers funds for the Jobs Bank and reimburses salaries, benefits, and expenses for UAW International Reps.

The purpose of the Jobs Bank was never to save jobs. The purpose was to silence protest. The Jobs Bank is, in effect, a hypnotic drug—like Ambien. It puts workers to sleep while their jobs are outsourced. This isn't an opinion, it's a numerical fact. The Center for Human Resources, with the cooperation of the International UAW, has overseen the reduction of hundreds of thousands of good-paying jobs.

It's counterintuitive to pay workers for not working. Unemployment is a drain on the economy. It's nonproductive. It keeps all boats from rising by depressing wages. But for trickle-downers, there's an upside: degrading workers curbs inflation. Likewise, the Jobs Bank has an upside for the companies. It mothballs workers, gets them off the books, and curbs demand for real job security—meaningful work.

There's only one reasonable solution to the wastefulness of Jobs Bank and unemployment compensation: jobs. There is a lot of work to be done at GM since Hurricane Wagoner hit. The government could invest in rebuilding the manufacturing base. How long did it take the auto companies to retool at the onset of World War II? We've done it before, and we can do it again. But this time, let's beat the fossil-fuel burners into cutting-edge transports.

Under the current proposals by the Detroit Three, government loans would be used to close plants and cut jobs. How does it help communities or the larger economy to reduce the workforce and undermine the tax base? Any government assistance should be tied to job creation, which is why we would gladly concede the Jobs Bank, a proven job killer, and replace it with a plan to create meaningful work.

Another concession we could gladly make is in the area of UAW appointees who get paid to keep the rabble unaroused. We could save a lot of money by kicking those slackers off the gravy train. For every UAW appointee carrying a clipboard, GM has a white collar working hard to double the redundancy. We can afford to concede the UAW appointees. Put them back on the line and reduce overtime in favor of full employment.

We can also concede the twelve hours of double-time the bargaining chair gets to sit home on Sunday. Let's concede that payoff. Instead of the company paying union officials to hide in their cubbyholes, let's put them back to work until they are called out and actively investigating a grievance. We don't need union oafs who are beholden to the boss for sheltering them from the discomfort of labor.

There are plenty of concessions UAW members are willing to make. We will give them Ron Gettelfinger's mustache. We will give them Bob King's phony apprenticeship. We will give them UAW vice president Cal Rapson's nepotism. We will give them UAW vice president Jimmy Settles's extra chin. We will give them UAW vice president General Holiefield's bag of wind. We will give them UAW secretary-treasurer Elizabeth Bunn's deer-in-the-headlights stare. We will gladly give up the Center for Human Resources and the hundreds of millions in payola connected to joint funds. We'd be glad to flush the waste out of the system.

But we won't give up what we have earned. We won't give up our pensions, benefits, wages, or work rules. And we insist that the United States finally live up to world-class standards and provide health care for the whole working class.

In Defense of American Workers
(December 2008)

If you had an opportunity to address Congress about the auto bailout as a rank-and-file UAW member, what would you say? Would it go something like this?

> I am not testifying before Congress today to request that American tax-payers loan Detroit automakers twenty-five billion dollars so they can close factories and permanently lay off thousands of workers. I am not here to support the Detroit automakers' intention to import half the vehicles they sell in the United States, as do foreign competitors like Toyota, Honda, and BMW. I am not here to advocate that American workers compete for the lowest wages in the world. Quite the opposite. I think we should compete for the highest wages.

I stand before you to advocate for a national industrial policy that supports and sustains the expansion, rather than the destruction, of the middle class. I stand before you to advocate for an industrial policy that strengthens our economy, strengthens our national security, and makes the American Dream of a higher standard of living attainable for an ever-expanding number of citizens. I am here to advocate that Congress recognize that the working class is the backbone of this nation and that the success of our nation as a whole depends on the health and well-being of our most valuable natural resource, the American worker.

In the last thirty-five years, the income of American workers has declined precipitously while prices for health care, education, housing, food, and energy have steadily increased. Americans are working more hours with fewer vacation days than workers in any other modern industrialized nation. Even though we are working longer and harder, our incomes are not keeping up with inflation. Fewer and fewer American workers have pensions or health insurance. America, once known as a nation that took pride in its expanding middle class, today has a reputation for degrading workers and pursuing a competitive race to the bottom.

Some members of Congress propose that the best solution for the Detroit automakers is bankruptcy. They propose that the automakers should dispose of their obligations to retirees, as if retirees were somehow unworthy of the deferred compensation they earned with steadfast loyalty and honest labor. If Congress sanctions the refusal to honor contracts, it will become a defining moment in the history of our nation, a moment of legislative infamy.

Civil societies rely on trust, not treachery. Civil societies rely on government to restrain predatory capitalists and to mediate class conflict. If the highest legislative body in the nation endorses contempt for contractual commitments, where will it end, and who can be held accountable? Such a precedent will not stop with autoworkers. Every retiree and every working person who hopes to retire will feel threatened by the willful destruction of contractual agreements.

Historically, unions have had a positive impact on our society and our economy. When unions negotiated improved wages and benefits, they expanded the middle class and set a standard that lifted all workers. The expansion of the middle class created a vibrant economy that benefited business and government. Business reaped the rewards of an upwardly mobile workforce. In turn, a growing economy enriched the tax base and allowed government to lower tax rates for businesses and wealthy investors.

When unions negotiated pensions and health care for retirees, it was considered deferred compensation. Workers sacrificed higher wages in return for a secure retirement. The companies passed the cost on to consumers, but the companies didn't invest those higher profits in a trust that would provide for retiree health care. Instead, they indulged themselves and their shareholders. Corporate malfeasance should not be rewarded with a congressional pardon.

If companies are allowed to break contracts, the debt will be passed on to taxpayers in the form of corporate welfare. If government assumes responsibility for all or part of those expenses, it will, in effect, charge the consumer twice. Once when the car is purchased, and a second time when taxed to compensate for the companies' misappropriation. CEOs should not be allowed to justify increased prices as an incumbent expense of a union contract, then pass on the cost to taxpayers when the bill comes due.

I am a UAW member, but I would be remiss if I did not speak up for our brothers and sisters at Toyota and the other "transplants." The workers at foreign transplants in the United States do not have a defined pension. They have a 401(k). They have seen the value of their retirement savings destroyed by unscrupulous and irresponsible financial policies, or the lack thereof, through no fault of their own. Workers at the transplants do not have health insurance in retirement. They will be forced out of work by injury or company policy before they are eligible for Medicare. They too deserve a national industrial policy that respects their labor.

Foreign automakers have the advantage of national health care for workers in their home countries, but in the United States, they treat workers like disposable commodities. They work them 'til they hurt them, then they throw them out the door.

My advocacy for a national industrial policy that ensures retirement in dignity is not limited to union members. All American workers deserve health care and security in retirement, equal to or better than that enjoyed by workers in Europe and Japan. The United States should raise the standard, not pursue a race to the bottom.

I am not here to ask Congress for a handout, but rather a well-deserved hand up. It is imperative that we rescue the flagship industry of our manufacturing base. Our economic health and our national security are at stake. But it is not fair to bail out the privileged and neglect the plight of the average worker. Medicare for All, as advocated in John Conyers's bill, HR 676, is one remedy that would address the unfair competition that plagues manufacturing in the United States. Medicare for All would help all employers, all workers, and all consumers.

Furthermore, any bailout that is not contingent on job creation would damage our economy. America needs a vibrant middle class and a revitalized industrial base to stabilize our economy and strengthen our national security. Any bailout that supports the innovative malaise in our industrial sector or rewards companies for investing overseas while simultaneously breaking contracts with American workers is tantamount to sabotage.

I am not here to apologize for workers who constitute the backbone of America. We have never failed. I am not here to beg on behalf of the men and women who fought the wars, built the roads and bridges, manufactured the goods, delivered the services, and transported every conceivable product from its origin to its destination. I am here to demand the respect and dignity we deserve.

For too long, Congress has legislated in favor of capital over labor. The preference has not served our national interests. As Abraham Lincoln said in his first annual message to Congress in 1861, "Labor is prior to, and independent of, capital. Capital is only the fruit of labor, and could never have existed if labor had not first existed. Labor is the superior of capital, and deserves much the higher consideration."

The Detroit automakers need a bridge loan to survive the current credit crisis. But another bailout that neglects the working class would be a fatal mistake. We will not survive the worldwide recession afflicting our economic security if we fail to defend the people who have never failed their nation.

Legacy Profits Outweigh Legacy Costs
(December 19, 2008)

After the first bailout was voted down, President Bush warned that if we didn't hand over seven hundred billion dollars, the house of cards would fall and all the king's cronies couldn't put it back together again. Since all the cronies on Capitol Hill had a face card in the deck, the pyramid scheme was reinforced with unctuous indignation and promissory notes.

But on the day the Bureau of Labor Statistics (BLS) reported that we lost five hundred and thirty-three thousand jobs, more than in any month in the 124-year history of the BLS, President Bush shrugged and essentially said, What's a few million more?

With poker face in place, Bush told the TV machine, "I'm concerned about investing taxpayers' money in companies that might not survive." Which may lead the common citizen to wonder: What's the difference between Citibank, AIG, Bear Stearns and a company like General Motors? Sweat, products, torn ligaments, products, constructive labor, products, herniated discs, products, practical skills, products, carpal tunnel and—did I mention—"products" as opposed to unsecured securities, uninsured insurance, and debt financed with debt?

Credit where credit is due: Bush is the biggest bullshitter on the planet.

Like most folks who work for a living, I think management is organizationally impaired, logically deficient, structurally unsound, impractical, and dedicated to the pursuit of deception. General Motors is no exception, and Congress is like GM without a budget.

If Congress had had the integrity to raise taxes on gas like Europe and Japan, the market would demand fuel-efficient vehicles. The failure of Congress to legislate responsibly tipped the table in favor of our competitors. Congress was shortsighted and is as much to blame for the glut of SUVs as the Detroit Three—Alibi, Plea, Deny—and their sidekick with the runny nose.

What was Gettelfinger doing there? Alibi, Plea, and Deny wanted to show Congress how well trained he was. As usual, the working class, the one party who bore no responsibility for this colossal failure, wasn't reserved a place at the table. Unless you count the one on the leash.

Republicans, who paraded "Joe the Plumber" on the campaign trail, demonstrated that they despise labor in general and organized labor in particular. They accused UAW members of making too much money and bargaining successfully for health care and pensions. They referred to retiree benefits as "entitlements." As if we didn't earn those benefits. As if the nature of our work—production, as opposed to paper shuffling—rendered us ineligible for deferred compensation. As if people who actually produce a good or service don't deserve such basic amenities as health care. As if dignity in retirement was reserved for those who never got grease under their fingernails. As if a wage that allowed you to pay the bills on time and send your children to college offended the capitalist creed. As if legally binding contracts with workers were toilet paper. As if the right to bargain collectively was illegal.

Their analogies to the transplants were deceptive. The main reason the transplants aren't organized is that they pay as well or better than UAW contracts. The accusations of undeserved legacy costs ignore the other side of the ledger: legacy profits. Profits that were pocketed by executives, doled out to shareholders, and invested overseas at the expense of American workers and the deferred compensation they earned. Legacy profits far outweigh legacy costs. From 1994 to 2003, GM made $104 billion in profit, not including investments in new plants overseas and acquisitions of foreign companies like Fiat. How much was set aside for retiree health care?

A portion of legacy profits should have been invested in a trust to ensure that the burden of retirement benefits wouldn't be shouldered by the next generation. But according to the capitalist custom of class privilege, sharing profits with workers is derided as uncompetitive, while sharing profits with management and investors is lauded as just rewards. For the rich, money is an incentive; for the poor, it's a moral hazard. The diversion of profits to nonworking people is the fundamental fraud of the free-market system.

The Republicans' unbridled contempt for workers revealed an underlying agenda: the humiliation and degradation of labor. We weren't criticized for incompetence. We were maligned for earning a good living. We were vilified for violating their fundamental belief that we aren't equal as a class.

When it comes to wages, there is no bottom to the bottom line. They won't be satisfied until we are all on our knees and begging to work for food. In their eyes, unequal status under the law doesn't stop with immigrants. All workers should be at the whim and mercy of their employers. All workers should be an underclass.

Their underlying agenda is to manipulate "Joe the Plumber" for political democracy while they deprive the working class of economic democracy. What good is the right of citizenship if those rights are revoked as soon as you punch the time clock? What is the value of the right to vote for rich people to represent you if you can't support your family?

Their real agenda is to bust unions, like Reagan did to PATCO,* and turn collective bargaining into collective concession-making. Their real agenda is to strip the working class of health care, steal their pensions, and whipsaw them with the threat of termination.

Keep Your Eye on the Rabbit
(December 2008)

When you believe in things you don't understand, you suffer.
                    —**Stevie Wonder, "Superstition"**

Bush's bailout for the Detroit Three is a $17.4 billion bow on a prepackaged bankruptcy. Chump change for fast-track union busting.

The bailout is conditioned on the UAW agreeing to a nonunion contract. That means: elimination of COLA; deep out-of-pocket expenses for health care; conversion of pensions to 401(k)s; no Jobs Bank or SUB pay; complete disregard of seniority rights; and retiree health care in hock to company stock.

Bush's bailout turns the feds into hired guns. Hired to shake down the union at no cost to the company. Why hire lawyers to pilot your company through the kangaroo trails of bankruptcy court when you can get a Car Czar to chop the shop for free?

The real chumps in this exchange are taxpayers. Lower wages won't lower prices or stimulate demand. The only thing lower wages guarantee is increased competition for increasingly lower wages. Toyota has already

---

* The air traffic controllers' union destroyed by President Ronald Reagan during a 1981 strike.

revealed plans to slash compensation (Jason Roberson, "Toyota Sweats U.S. Labor Costs," *Detroit Free Press*, February 8, 2007).

When a nation exports the means of production, recession turns into depression by design. Depression gives the companies leverage to restructure rapidly. The depth and breadth of restructuring in the auto industry will exert downward pressure on compensation in all sectors of the economy. Eventually, workers won't be able to afford autos, let alone homes or health care.

In order to better understand the scam, we need to step back and examine the long-term trend. We didn't arrive at this juncture by accident. GM is poised to take full advantage of this latest capitalist disaster. GM manufactures vehicles in thirty-five countries. They're prepared to compete for the lowest wages in the world.

The UAW Concession Caucus typically justifies concessions because GM has lost market share. But market share is the top hat, not the rabbit. The two principal trends to track are productivity and sales. Accountants can lie about everything else.

GM's share of the market looks smaller because the market has grown. In fact, GM's sales have remained steady while productivity has leaped off the charts.

In 1992, GM had 34 percent of the US market and sold 4.4 million vehicles. In 2005, GM's US market share fell to 25.7 percent and GM sold 4.5 million vehicles. (The rabbit didn't shrink, the top hat got bigger.) In 2007, GM sold 4.5 million vehicles in North America and lost more market share. Keep your eye on the rabbit, not the hat.

What's most shocking is the enormous jump in productivity.

In 1992 GM employed 265,000 UAW members. In 2005 GM employed 111,000 UAW members. In 2007 GM employed 73,000 UAW members and sold as many vehicles in North America as ever. Let me do this again. Without the top hat this time.

1992: 4.4 million vehicles and 265,000 UAW members

2005: 4.5 million vehicles and 111,000 UAW members

2007: 4.5 million vehicles and 73,000 UAW members

When you remove the top hat the rabbit looks pretty fat. The trend is clear. One would think that higher productivity would mean higher profits and thus higher wages. But GM invests heavily in the craft of creative book-keeping. Higher profits are transferred offshore into assets protected from bankruptcy, and masters of illusion point to the rabbit in the hat and shrug.

If figures lie and liars figure, what's a Gettelfinger? In 2005, Ron Gettelfinger and his Concession Caucus insisted that UAW members must open the contract and give more concessions to make up for lost market share. In 2007, the Con Caucus pulled the same stunt.

If productivity increases phenomenally, why are workers responsible for lost market share? How will concessions increase market share? Isn't market share the purview of the marketing department?

There's another aspect to marketing: that is, convincing the public that workers are overpaid despite a long-term trend that indicates extraordinary productivity and stable sales volumes.

Concessions can't buy security when the company is bent on exporting jobs instead of products. And if market share is the only measure that matters, all the concessions and company-union collusion that the Con Caucus has preached for twenty-five years are abject failures. But US market share is not the sole criterion for success in a multinational corporation.

In 2007, GM sold more than nine million vehicles worldwide for the third consecutive year.

Let me say that again, without the top hat.

In 2007 GM *sold more than nine million vehicles* worldwide for the *third consecutive year.*

GM plans to become a major importer to the United States, just like Toyota, but they need help. They're counting on government assistance to help them close factories, disarm resistance, and downsize domestic operations until the rank and file is small enough to snuff out as discreetly as a cig.

If all goes according to plan, GM will employ about the same number of UAW members at the end of 2009 as Delphi did when it was spun off in 1999. Delphi is not going to exit bankruptcy, but it is well established in Eastern Europe, Asia, Mexico, and South America. Likewise, GM is poised to dump retirement obligations onto taxpayers, cut wages in half, drive dealers out of business, and import 50 percent of the vehicles it sells in the open US market by 2010.

The Car Czar will enable the Detroit Three to gain all the advantages of bankruptcy—broken contracts—without the encumbrance of litigation.

When the finance companies came to Congress with their tin cups extended, no one scrutinized the compensation of their workforce or suggested that they were overpaid. The evident bias clarifies the class conflict. In the eyes of Congress and professional parrots, blue-collar workers do not deserve to be in the middle class. We don't deserve to own homes, take summer vacations, send our kids to college, retire with dignity, or have unrestricted access to health care.

GM not only wants to import cars to the United States, but also sweatshop standards. GM is ready to lead the industry to the lowest level, but they need help from the Con Caucus and the government to convince workers to lower their standards. The president of the UAW stands for concessions.

To paraphrase an oracle: don't believe in people you can't understand, or you will suffer.

Most of us learned early on the American playground that when someone knocks you down, you get up and kick his ass. If the bully is too big, you organize and the whole gang kicks his ass. The UAW Concession Caucus, led by Ron Gettelfinger, prefers to roll over every time the boss glares. He's already waving his white hanky and promising to behave nonunion.

He's pulled this trick too many times. Shame on us.

If You Want to Rise Up from the Ashes
(February 2009)

All this speculation about what the UAW is going to give up next neglects one well-documented fact: the contract. The deal went down in 2007. It's over. Gettelfinger & Co. are sweeping debris from the halls of infamy and locking the door on their way out. One doesn't need a bloodhound to follow the trail; it's well documented.

The fact is, the UAW was marching sheepishly into a nonunion contract when Senator Bob "Loud Dog" Corker shot his mouth off and blew the cover. Now Gettelfinger has to act coy and say things like, "What's competitive?"

What's the point in playing dumb? The train has left the station. While UAW members were busy splurging their signing bonuses, the carnies were pulling the stakes from the tent. The deal went down. The prize is a union with less ferocity than a stuffed animal.

New hires were sold out so the Con Caucus could throw old hires a rabbit foot. The Thirty-and-Out incentive for retirees set new workers back thirty years. Turnabout is not only fair, it's inevitable. When the VEBA goes bust, retirees will be rubbing the rabbit foot and looking for work.

How did we get fooled again?

We didn't. We know the truth, but like alcoholics, we don't want to admit it. The government, the corporations, and the unions are working together to degrade workers. We don't want to admit it, because such knowledge would demand action, and action would banish stupor, and stupor is our drug of choice. Every drunk has a rationale, however flimsy, and we, the union, have a history of flimsy excuses and weak choices.

We chose to buy into the dog-eat-dog system and abandon solidarity. We stopped bargaining for the common good. We stopped standing together. We traded jobs for wages and ultimately sold out the next generation for a sip of delusion—the delusion that capitalism would save us from the ravages of capitalism.

The buy-in was gradual and diabolically methodical. It started with something as simple and attractive as home ownership. My own hometown is a prime example.

In the Furniture Strike of 1911, the city of Grand Rapids was brought to a halt. One of every three wage earners was directly employed in the furniture factories. Hundreds more labored in shops that supplied the furniture manufacturers. After a long and bitter struggle, the strikers caved. The furniture workers' union in Grand Rapids never recovered.

Big Bill Haywood, a cofounder of the Industrial Workers of the World (IWW), visited Grand Rapids during the strike. Two years later, an IWW article entitled "What's the Matter with Grand Rapids?" analyzed the strike. The author asserted that one of the main reasons the strike was lost was because too many workers were homeowners. They would never risk losing their private property. They had an investment, a stake in the big tent of capitalism.

Grand Rapids had the highest home ownership rate for a city of its size in the nation. Trouble was, the industrialists controlled the banks and the wages. The debt-to-income ratio was not only too high, it was *adjustable.* Mortgages had to be paid off or refinanced every one to three years (Jeffrey Kleiman, *Strike! How the Furniture Workers Strike of 1911 Changed Grand Rapids*, Grand Rapids Historical Commission, 2006).

After the success of unions in the Great Depression era, employers required new tools to tame workers. They didn't dig too deep to find their scheme.

The first rule of the street is: Never fight a man who has nothing to lose.

The rulers made sure workers had something to lose.* Later, new tax-deferred vehicles such as 401(k)s were devised to entice workers to invest in the stock market, where value was directly proportionate to downsizing and outsourcing. We were cordially invited to buy in, and—in the interest of long-term financial security—be partners in the business of exploiting workers.

Conflict is fundamental to change, but when we are mostly concerned about our individual economic security rather than the security of our class as a whole, we are more likely to settle for the safe bet and the status quo. Hence, the conflict avoidance of buyout is the preferred option. When you have investments in the stock market and a mortgage to consider, class conflict is out of the question. Social and economic security is perceived as an isolated, individual decision, not a collective one.

The latest Special Attrition Program (SAP) is a bludgeon. As factories close, the Jobs Bank is dumped, and the possibilities for transfers vanish, workers will have little choice but to cash in their chips, because the Con Caucus does not have an agenda independent of the corporation.

Since the buy-in has collapsed, it only makes sense that we should now buy out. Buy out and go away.

---

* Workers were enticed to invest in homes with the easy credit and IRS deductions on mortgage interest and property taxes.

Go away, quietly. Go away, powerless. Go away, helpless, isolated, and *de*-classed.

The bottom of each page of the SAP alerts the reader that the provisions are "subject to the terms and required approvals and certifications set forth in the Loan and Security Agreement entered into between GM and the United States Department of the Treasury."

They're all in on it: union, management, and government. The latest capitalist disaster doesn't alter the corporate agenda, it accelerates implementation. It wasn't always this way.

The sitdowners of '37 were not invested in the capitalist system like we are. They didn't fight to preserve their investments. They fought for power—power for the whole working class.

The UAW is not a force to be reckoned with today. Everyone with seniority is headed for the door. They think they can buy out as easily as they bought in. They don't understand that capitalism won't save them. They haven't been liberated, they've been exiled.

The UAW's slow slide into muddled irrelevance will never trigger resurgence. If you want to rise up from the ashes, you have to stand in the line of fire—like the sitdowners, like the civil rights marchers, like the many honorable men and women in our long history of struggle who died like criminals, so their children might live in peace.

They're Closing In
(February 16, 2009)

The Detroit Three cite legacy costs as their biggest competitive disadvantage. Their solution? Add to the legacy costs by retiring more workers faster with buyout packages subtracted from the pension.

When the market crashed, the government loaned the Detroit Three money on the condition that they close factories, cut jobs, and slash wages. Then, the government passed a stimulus bill to create jobs. The irony failed to earn a grin in Rust Belt states.

GM estimated its retiree health care costs at fifty billion dollars and committed half that amount—$24.1 billion (and promises)—to a union trust fund (VEBA). Now the government demands that 50 percent of the 50-percent-underfunded trust be replaced with stock worth less than six rolls of toilet paper.

It's illegal for a company to invest more than 10 percent of pension assets in its own stock. Why should a VEBA be different? Over and above the question of legality, the government's proposal compromises the union's ethical capacity to represent workers. The union will have a vested interest in the company's stock. But you haven't heard the punch line.

GM is planning a government-run bankruptcy. The union won't be left with an investment for retiree health care. The union will be left holding a bag of chicken necks.

And the slapstick at Chrysler makes the situation at GM look like romantic comedy.

Government mandates neglect the fact that the Con Caucus already ratified contracts that will ratchet working conditions down to nonunion levels by 2011. Well actually, the company-government didn't neglect the Con's con, they just want to pop the clutch and hit the wall at maximum RPM.

The government is strong-arming workers into accepting terms that will achieve the benefits of bankruptcy without litigation. The wage scale will become nonunion; the VEBA won't last a decade; on-demand will replace the eight-hour day; the pension is underfunded; the Detroit Three will close dozens of plants and import half the cars they sell in the United States; all without the hassle and haggle of bankruptcy.

A real union solution would advocate for all workers, not just an isolated gaggle in the gated community of the UAW elite. A real union would reject the VEBA demolition derby and put all its energy into John Conyers's HR 676 bill, which would insure everyone equally, not just the privileged. A real union would resist buyouts and job cuts by demanding a shorter workweek to offset reduced demand.

The company-government-union cartel prefers to reduce labor costs by curtailing Supplemental Unemployment Benefits (SUB), thereby pushing more workers into early retirement or foreclosure. The plan will result in more desperate workers lining up for fewer desperate jobs. It's a bust in the chops to the working class, but a boon to bankers and bosses as high unemployment depresses wages and curbs inflation. Screw that.

We deserve a union solution: a collective action that unites rather than divides workers.

If the union demanded a short workweek in exchange for SUB, all affected workers would remain employed and equal. When the market goes up, workers would return to a forty-hour week without diminished wages. A real union could back the talk with a one-day walkout and send an army of unemployed workers on buses to Washington with a petition to convert closed auto plants into nationalized manufacturing centers for energy independence. But don't expect the Caucus that negotiated two-tier to unite the union. Collective action is not their agenda. They're collaborators, not organizers.

We can debate economics until the pyramids collapse, but there's a chronic and undeniable tic in our current fix: class conflict. Bankers get handouts without conditions, but a blue-collar industry in need of a loan—because reckless bankers destroyed the economy—gets boiled in a vat of Republican venom and ordered to return for more of the same in ninety days.

I'm no fan of management. The Detroit Three are grossly mismanaged and overcompensated. They deserve a dressing down. But workers aren't responsible for the failing economy or the sinking of the flagship of American industry. Bankers, bosses, and bureaucrats failed, not workers. It's like the Pentagon procurement racket. War profiteers get no-bid contracts worth hundreds of millions of dollars. Soldiers get shot, killed, traumatized, and maimed. It's a bad deal. We deserve better.

We deserve a union that represents all workers, everywhere, equally—including our brothers and sisters in arms. Bring our soldiers home, now. We've found the enemy. They're closing in.

Business-as-Usual Unionism Is Dead
(February 23, 2009)

The crisis in auto isn't quarantined in Detroit. Every manufacturer in the United States is afflicted. Likewise, the crisis in the UAW isn't restricted. All workers and retirees, union and nonunion alike, are impacted by unemployment, falling wages, insufficient health care, and social insecurity.

Business-as-usual unionism is dead. Any bargaining goal short of victory for all is an injury to workers everywhere.

Now is an opportune time for the UAW to "step up to the plate," as Gettelfinger likes to say, and demand a solution that benefits all workers, their families, their neighbors, and their employers. The era of bargaining for segregated privilege is over. A government subsidy for Big Three retirees, as Gettelfinger suggested in his *Washington Times* op-ed, is socially irresponsible, economically unfeasible, and politically dead on arrival ("Reviving the domestic auto industry," *Washington Times*, February 22, 2009).

Gettelfinger's whim fails on two counts: first, to galvanize the unorganized; second, to aid manufacturers struggling to survive.

The UAW is in a unique position to leverage a practical solution to an urgent need. The fulcrum is production. The power to produce is an economic fundamental our country can ill afford to ignore. Health care reform, not concessions, is pivotal to industrial revival.

Manufacturing in the United States doesn't suffer from a lack of skill or productivity. It suffers from a pandemic patchwork of lame excuses for health insurance. Our major competitors were never burdened with an albatross that compares to the private insurance rackets strangling American business. The notion that a federal subsidy for the Detroit Three can waylay the reckoning is naive.

Our unhealthy dependence on private insurance not only strangles businesses, big and small, but city councils, county commissions, boards of education, and entire state budgets as well.

Workers and retirees all across the nation need a union leader with the guts to say, "No amount of concessions by workers will save manufacturing in the United States. We demand that Congress pass a universal single-payer health plan. A plan that emulates the best practices of all our major competitors. A plan that puts the best interests of all Americans ahead of special interests. A plan that will restore the competitiveness of our manufacturing sector and provide a broad and diverse base of employment opportunities for everyone."

The important question isn't how much it will cost, but rather how much it will save, and how fast we can save ourselves from the private insurance drain on our economy. John Conyers's bill, HR 676, will provide cost-effective universal single-payer health care. The savings are three-pronged. Employers will save, workers will save, and health care providers will be saved from scaling the ramparts of paperwork erected by insurance companies that maximize profit by obstructing coverage.

The automakers' major competitive disadvantage is legacy costs. HR 676 will level the playing field. Workers will gain both earning power and bargaining power. Quality and efficiency will improve as doctors spend more time treating disease and less time navigating the commercial reefs of private insurance. Everyone will benefit. HR 676 even provides for workers displaced from insurance companies.

HR 676 will stimulate the economy, not only by putting more disposable income in workers' pockets and investment dollars in manufacturers' budgets, but also by creating jobs as demand for primary health care increases.

We've been indoctrinated by the insurance lobby into believing that more access to health care will drive costs up and the quality of care down. The fact is, the only health care criterion in which the United States leads is cost. Our competitors cover more people for less money and outperform us in every qualitative measure of health. Private insurance, not medical expertise, is the debilitating factor.

Private insurers have a profit motive to limit choices and access to health care. Private insurers have a profit motive to layer health care costs with administrative fees and luxurious salaries. Private insurers have a profit motive to persuade us that treating patients at the most cost-effective point of intervention—primary care—rather than at the most expensive point—emergency rooms—is inefficient and morally hazardous. Nothing could be further from the truth.

We've been duped. We pay more, we get less, and manufacturing in the United States has been mortally wounded in the process. We need one nation with one health care plan. We need one union to step up to the plate and say we won't back down until every man, woman, and child has equal access to the health care they deserve.

Two-Tiered Too Long
(March 2009)

The credit crisis jammed the automakers' restructuring plan like a semi jack-knifed on the highway. But the rescue plan reveals a more insidious malady than credit default swaps and pimped-out politicians. Namely, two-tier.

Two-tier has morphed from a union concession in collective bargaining to a standard American bias. Two-tier is a whopping bonus to the rich and a "moral hazard" whip to the poor. Two-tier delivers bailouts to the investor class and foreclosures to the outsourced class.

Two-tier is not a cure, it's a curse.

Two-tier demands more jails and less schools; more arsenals and less tools; more greed and less leisure; more revenge and less justice.

Two-tier is not a solution to economic crisis. Two-tier is a symptom of social decadence.

Master Madoff couldn't devise a more sinister method of bankrupting a family every hour of every day than our two-tier system of health insurance. But health care for profit is just another symptom of social decay in the land of the free marketeer and the home of the wage slave.

People express outrage when executives at AIG are rewarded for failure, but Delphi workers are used to it. Every three months for the last three years, Judge Robert Drain has awarded millions of dollars in bonuses to the very executives whose mismanagement and fraud drove Delphi into bankruptcy.

Who believes the government will manage GM and Chrysler differently in a so-called "surgical bankruptcy?"

We know where all the cuts will come.

Workers take pay cuts, job cuts, benefit cuts. Executives take home cash in wheelbarrows.

The crisis in manufacturing can't be quarantined in Detroit or amputated with buyouts. Every manufacturer in America is on the gurney. We are merging into the ranks of nations who are neither self-sufficient nor independently wealthy. No one needs or desires to import our financial wizardry.

Manufacturing in the United States hasn't failed from a lack of skills or productivity. It was waylaid by a lack of political will to provide (1) universal single-payer health care and (2) investment in products that confront the dual challenge of environmental crisis and energy independence. Government support for more concessions, rather than long-term investment, means more of the same. Two-tier is the predicate of class conflict.

A society that degrades rather than rewards labor is self-destructive, not competitive. Two-tier may prevail in the precincts of law and yellow-dog contracts, but sooner or later the underclass will push the pendulum back.

Some of us aren't waiting for leaders to emerge.

When Magna Inc. and its UAW partners presented workers at New Process Gear in Syracuse, New York, with an ultimatum—accept more concessions or the plant will close—workers voted to close. Twice. Within weeks of the first vote Magna was back with another offer, but workers had had enough.

Every crisis has a bottom.

Bottom isn't a wage cut, a speedup, or an unfair labor practice. Bottom is the point at which one worker says to another worker, "Enough is enough," and together they begin pushing back.

Are we there yet? Are we ready for a national strike? Are citizens ready to defy the corporate state? To occupy Congress?

Not just yet, but I wouldn't park on the tracks.

Our soldiers are coming home, and they've been two-tiered too long.

When We Are Led to Believe a Lie
(April 6, 2009)

If you believe the *Motley Fool* and other stock advisors in the business press, 90 percent of GM's losses can be attributed to the UAW, which accounts for 10 percent of a vehicle's cost.

The math may seem a bit obtuse, but the politics is clear as fizz. The UAW's disproportionate responsibility for the automakers' unprofitability is based on the same sort of accounting wizardry that led GM to claim they lost $39 billion in November 2007 due to "deferred tax credits."

If it smells like BS and it looks like BS, trust your common sense and skip the taste test.

Thanks to corporate welfare, GM accumulated more tax deductions than they could take in a year. So they deferred the tax deductions and booked them as an asset until the asset got so fat it attracted the attention of auditors who asked, What's beneath this fig leaf?

Wagoner was quick to assure the Fools not to puzzle their pretty heads. The $39 billion wasn't actually a loss of cash, he said, since it never had a tangible, marketable existence. It was merely an accounting gimmick—a fancy—like paper wings.

The Fools refer to compensation like pension and health care as "welfare," despite the fact that unlike "deferred tax credits," the compensation was earned by productive labor.

It's no wonder the Fools are having trouble figuring out what part of GM is losing what, how much, and why. They ignore the obvious and thumb their noses at analysis. For example: GM sold 4.4 million vehicles in the United States in 1992 and employed 265,000 UAW members. GM sold 4.5 million vehicles in the United States in 2007 and employed 73,000 UAW members.

A company can't make productivity gains as astounding as that and lose money on labor. Something else is shaking the timbers. Maybe we should question the competitiveness of executives. How do they compare with their Japanese counterparts in compensation and achievement? Or more precisely, who's controlling the money?

Since GM sold as many vehicles in the United States in 2007 as they did in 1992 and employed 192,000 fewer UAW members, profits should be way up by any accounting standard. Unless, of course, profits were siphoned off into investments overseas, dividends, bonuses, or unaccountable black holes of financial rigmarole. In 2005, GM paid Fiat two billion dollars to get out of a "put option" that would have required GM to purchase Fiat.

GM sold over nine million vehicles worldwide in 2005, '06, and '07. If GM lost money on sales that enormous, Wagoner wouldn't have been awarded a $23 million payoff. He would've been put up against the wall and shot. What does the Board of Bystanders know that we don't know?

For starters, GM manufactures vehicles in thirty-five countries. GM has been expanding in emerging markets for twenty years and hasn't let up on the gas. In September 2008, GM launched construction of a $250 million corporate campus in Shanghai. GM invests about one billion dollars per year to expand production in China. In April 2008, GM announced a plan to build a $200 million engine plant in Brazil. GM opened a second plant in India in September 2008. It also announced plans to double the number of dealerships and service centers throughout India. In November 2008, GM opened a $300 million plant on the outskirts of St. Petersburg, Russia. In March 2009 a venture partly owned by GM through its Korean subsidiary Daewoo announced a plan to open a new car plant in Tashkent, the capital of Uzbekistan. Alongside this international expansion GM announced the closure of twelve plants in the United States in 2007. In 2008 GM added five more to the list of plant closings.

GM is on the march but according to the folks who call $39 billion in "deferred tax credits" an asset, the UAW must get leaner and *welfare* for blue collars workers should be axed so *unearned income* for the leisure class can get jacked up.

The $39 billion asset was a boondoggle. It never existed, not even as an unhatched egg, let alone a chicken. It wasn't a loss of cash, it was an auditor's correction of crooked bookkeeping. But it helped steamroll the union and trumpet the demand to dump legacy costs. Labor's legacy of profit was invested outside North America, but that shouldn't make the debt uncollectable. Labor deserves to benefit from the investment of its legacy profits. Labor has a legitimate lien on capital.

Soldiers of Solidarity has been saying this since 2005, when Delphi first filed for bankruptcy. Delphi transferred assets overseas. They insisted that assets outside the jurisdiction of US courts were profitable but untouchable. When Delphi proposed to cut wages in half and eliminate retirement benefits, we warned that Delphi was the lead domino, and the wage and legacy cut would ripple through the economy. We warned that the restructuring would spiral down and that its impact on the economy would be profound and permanent.

It doesn't require a degree in economics to figure out that workers making fourteen dollars per hour don't buy new cars. They don't buy homes and they don't invest their savings in the stock market. They live paycheck to paycheck. Restricted income leads to boycott by default. The economic blowback won't end with the Detroit Three.

When GM's labor costs reach parity with Toyota, Toyota will ratchet wages down again. The automotive industry is too entrenched in our national economy not to have a cascading impact on wages throughout the country. The dominos won't stop falling at the end of the assembly line. They'll keep tumbling until every domino is down.

If the Detroit Three can't sell cars to their own workers, it doesn't matter how cheap they buy labor. The market is going down. It's the paradox of thrift. When savings aren't invested at home, in production as opposed to speculation, it reduces demand and inhibits growth.

The double whammy of free trade and de-unionization in the United States compounded the thrift paradox. The savings extracted from cheap, nonunion labor were invested overseas. The companies' thrift strategy undermined their most loyal customers—employees and communities in the United States.

What can workers do? What's our alternative? Strikes are worse than useless when the company wants to reduce inventory.

We are left with one option: the wallet vote. We aren't buying your crap anymore.

We won't buy anything we can't eat and we'll be growing our own. We aren't investing our life savings in banks or stocks or bonds. We are opting out of the system controlled by crooks and liars. In a rational society, workers could petition the government to invest in productive enterprises that create jobs, but we don't have a socialist democracy. We have a government controlled by moneychangers and pissant politicians.

Unaccounted-for billions are turned over to private financial institutions. A pittance is dedicated to temporary job creation, and nothing is invested in manufacturing. Stop-loss loans that require collateral damage—layoffs and plant closings—as a condition of remission do not constitute investment. The arsenal of democracy has been outsourced to China, Brazil, and Uzbekistan.

Stuffing pockets at AIG, Bank of America, and other default swappers is not investing, it's speculation—it's casino capitalism. It's a massive transfer of wealth from the working class to a cadre of people who live off unearned income.

Zero dollars have been invested by our government in regenerative, productive, industrial capacity. The paradox of thrift is self-defeat. If government funds aren't used to promote the prowess and ingenuity of manufacturing in the United States, we won't see recovery, we'll see depression in capital letters.

The US market didn't dry up naturally. It was raped and plundered. Unlike the *Motley Fool*, we know the perps aren't the ones with dirt under their fingernails. The government has not, to date, gone door-to-door confiscating guns, but the oligarchy is methodically stripping the nation of toolmakers.

We are led to believe a lie when leaders degrade labor in honor of false profits.

Preserve your skills. We're going to need them.

Right Back Where We Started
(April 29, 2009)

Sometimes one can't see the precipice for the pitfalls. When you've lost a job or taken a steep pay cut; when your pension is threatened and your backup plan nose-dives; when you're faced with foreclosure or stuck in an abandoned neighborhood; when your biggest investment in life just lost half its value despite all the time, love, money, and labor you put into it; when you're forced to relocate but can't afford to uproot; when you're too young for Medicare and too old not to have pre-existing conditions that exclude you from health insurance; when you've followed all the rules, only to find that the rules have changed; when one or all of the above applies, it's understandable that you may cling to your private barrel of anxieties as the current hurls you down the Niagara.

Understandable, but useless. The barrels that we cling to—contracts, unions, pensions, promises, IRAs, VEBAs—will not protect us. Workers' rights are not defined by law or contract. Workers' rights are defined by struggle. Empty barrels won't protect us from the precipice, and there's no turning back. The United States is not in a recession. We're getting "restructured" and "rationalized."

The good news is, the barrels that once provided an illusion of safety are smashed to smithereens. From the wreckage, we can clearly see that either we all rise up together, or no one walks away with dignity, let alone a living wage. The good news is, no one—not the salaried workers, the knowledge workers, or the retirees—will be spared. The carbon monoxide of "too-bad-for-them-but-I'm-okay" complacency has blown away. Catastrophe demands unity. The good news is, our history can lead us.

Money isn't lost, it changes hands. It's not a conspiracy, it's capitalism. The transfer of wealth from labor to capital didn't begin with the current crisis. We can trace it back to Caterpillar, Staley, Bridgestone, and every lockout since then.* We can trace it back to the offshoring of steel, rubber, textile, and electronics; to restructured airlines that pilfered pensions; and the presidential termination of PATCO. We can trace it back to narrow interest bargaining and lunch-bucket politics that allowed the corpo-rats to pick us off, one isolated union at a time. We can trace it back to southern tenant farms and garment sweatshops in Manhattan. What's new isn't the method, but the magnitude. All workers in all sectors are under the whip this time.

The Delphi bankruptcy characterizes the contemporary strategy and serves as a template for what the Detroit Three and subsequent industries

---

* A reference to the strikes at lockouts centered in Decatur, Illinois, in the mid-1990s.

can expect. Recently, Delphi abolished health care and life insurance for salaried retirees. The switch enabled the company to report to the SEC that it "swung to a $566 million net profit from a $577 million loss a year earlier" (*Autobeat*, May 13, 2009). Easy money. Unearned money. Lots of it.

Next they will liquidate the salaried employees' pensions. What's to stop them? Capitalism is the law.

GM and Chrysler may not achieve all their goals in the quick-rinse bankruptcy controlled by the feds, but they'll be back in court to finish the job, just like Delphi. Observe how history repeats itself.

Base wages at Delphi were negotiated by the UAW in 2004, eighteen months prior to bankruptcy: fourteen dollars per hour and no pension. Base wages at the Detroit Three were negotiated by the UAW in 2007, eighteen months prior to bankruptcy: fourteen dollars per hour and no pension. One coincidence leads to another. The die is cast.

Each new UAW contract promises security in exchange for concessions from workers. The latest UAW Concession Con promised to deliver members from bankruptcy and plant closings. As soon as it was ratified, Chrysler went into bankruptcy and announced more plant closings.

But the nail in the coffin is the agreement to settle the contract in 2011 by arbitration based on nonunion standards. That isn't a contract, it's a death warrant for the UAW. What could be more clear? The Concession Caucus has effectively decertified the UAW.

The union agrees not to strike and commits to a goal that nullifies any benefit to union membership. This is the price we pay for company stock in a VEBA? The UAW signs confidentiality agreements with the companies and leaves members in the dark. Read the actual contract language.

Read it and weep. Weep for the unsung heroes, who risked everything they loved in the depths of the Great Depression so the next generation might labor in dignity. Weep for the youngsters, who tread in the footprints of the generation who chose to collaborate with management and sold their birthright for a bowl of maggots that the clipboards call joint programs.

Read it and revolt, like the heroes of America's civil rights movement who faced guns and clubs, police dogs and fire hoses, pimped-out politicians and judges controlled by cowards in hoods so their children might live in dignity.

Read it and recognize that UAW members have lost their voting rights. We're right back where we started. Sometimes, where we started is the right place to be.

Recently my wife Sheila and I ventured "down to the crossroad" in Clarksdale, Mississippi, for the annual Juke Joint Festival. Every year it seems there is one old standard that predominates—that bands play at every juke joint we frequent. Each year it's different. This year, it was *Big Boss Man* by Jimmy Reed. Over and over again, we heard:

> *You got me working, boss man*
> *Working 'round the clock*
> *I want me a drink of water*
> *You won't let me stop.*
> *You big boss man*
> *Can you hear me when I call?*
> *Oh, you ain't so big*
> *You just tall, that's all.*

The blues are essentially subversive. Every blues song, like every river, has an undercurrent, a subtext, a bass line shackled to oppression and resistance. A song like *Baby Please Don't Go*, for example, isn't just another song about love. It's a song about slavery and addiction; it's a song about poverty and injustice; it's a song about fear and violence and solitary confinement. And like every old blues, it's a song about the struggle, the struggle to be human in an inhuman world—like Detroit or Buffalo or Cleveland, North Carolina. Or a meatpacking plant in Postville, Iowa, that treats workers like animals, and where the feds arrest those workers under regulations as cruel and uncivilized as Fugitive Slave Laws.

We're right back where we started. The authorities turned fire hoses and police dogs on the children in Birmingham, Alabama in 1963 and arrested them, just like the police beat and arrested children trying to escape the textile strike in Lawrence, Massachusetts, in 1912. The struggle isn't between North and South, black and white, native born and immigrant; it's between labor and capital.

When we try to take back what belongs to us, they will beat us and arrest us, and we will know exactly where we stand—on the precipice.

When Workers Lead the Way
(May 26, 2009)

The most important repercussion of the GM and Chrysler bankruptcies will be the formation of a new union. Obama fired the CEO of General Motors, but he decertified the UAW. There's nothing as hopeful as a plowed field.

An arbitrator, rather than collective bargaining, will determine the next UAW contract with the Detroit Three. Per the UAW-GM-Chrysler 2009 Agreements, the arbitrator's benchmark is parity with nonunion transplants. The UAW is effectively debarred.

Let's be clear on this point: UAW officials are not the victims of government interference, we are. The UAW Con Caucus always acted like the only downside to their job was representing members. Gettelfinger probably suggested that the government appoint an arbitrator so office rats could concentrate on their golf.

When the Con Caucus rep at one contract information meeting was asked what bargaining leverage we would have without the right to strike, the Con said, "Strikes are a thing of the past. We can bargain in good faith."

A second Con jumped to the mic with the contract *Highlights* in one hand and pounded the podium: "This is our ticket, our chance to live to fight another day."

The crowd grumbled. Fight with what? Our hankies?

When the Cons were asked if members would be allowed to vote in 2011, one Con said, "Of course."

"What happens if we vote it down?"

"Then it goes to an arbitrator."

According to the podium-pounding *Highlights*, members will get a chance to vote, but if they don't approve of "wage and benefit improvements based on maintaining an all-in labor cost comparable to its US competitors including transplant automotive competitors," an arbitrator will impose the nonunion standard and the Con Caucus reps will bow out "in good faith." Holy sheep.

UAW members at the Detroit Three will be no better off than nonunion workers in 2011. They will not be bound with golden handcuffs to UAW contracts. They'll take pay cuts. Pensions will be frozen and Thirty-and-Out abandoned. That's not opinion; it's what "maintaining all-in labor cost comparable to its US competitors" means. We'll live to fight another day, but it won't be under the leadership of the UAW Con Caucus.

The gloves are off. The 2009 contract was ratified under duress. The 2011 contract will be imposed without a legitimate vote of the membership. That's not union, that's indentured servitude. I would not want to be in the shoes of the next UAW office rat who tells a lineworker that he's lucky to have a job.

The banksters who destroyed the economy with criminal negligence and reckless indifference were not forced to make concessions. They didn't lose bonuses or retirement packages. Their contracts are sacred.

But retirees who purchased a health care plan with thirty years of hard labor and COLA diversions don't have a contract that the government respects, because the government doesn't respect labor. And members who pay union dues don't have reps that the company respects, because the government has outlawed collective bargaining for autoworkers at GM and Chrysler.

The US government gave control of Chrysler, an American icon and the creator of Jeep, to Fiat for no money down. The US government sponsored the GM scheme to import cars so they could compensate for plant closings in America. A wino could come up with a better plan.

Ikki Yamakawa, a reporter from Japan's largest daily newspaper, interviewed me in my home. I asked him if the Japanese government would ever pay Toyota to close factories in Japan, ship the means of production to Indonesia, and import the autos back to Japan for sale. He didn't answer me. He just laughed.

Americans are suckers. Everybody knows it.

In the United States, we don't protect manufacturing, but we zealously protect the health insurance industry, a money-sucking parasite whose only product is paperwork. GM claims that health care costs more per car than steel: an estimated $1,500 per vehicle and climbing. Rather than change to a more efficient single-payer system, our government helps companies export jobs to countries that have national health care. The financial wizards never miss an opportunity to compound the trade imbalance.

Recently, I encountered some Tea Partiers (TP) at a protest. They despise the government, but they were all waving American flags. One vocally gifted TP chanted, "Power to the people." They were protesting health care reform. They didn't want it. One TP held a sign that read: "Go to high school. Get a job. Buy your own health care."

These are confusing times. Folks are angry. We have legitimate reasons to distrust the government, the corporations, and the unions. When our fellow workers in the Tea Party discover that a high school diploma won't land a job that can pay for health care, they're going to need a plan.

A confrontation is in order. Power to the people is in order. A summit where we can discuss an economic policy for We the People is in order.

Necessity, not philosophy, drives change. We won't get change by whining. We won't get change by waiting for Congress to pass laws that make union organizing safe. We won't get change waiting for the lackey-in-waiting, Bob King, to remember the purpose of unions. We won't get change following rules designed to keep us pacified and powerless.

We'll get change when Congress is afraid to pass laws that hurt working people. We'll get change when the president of the UAW is back on the line wishing he had an extra six minutes of break time. We'll get change when UAW members overthrow the Concession Caucus by force. We'll get change when we break all the rules that keep us chained to the heart attack machine that cranks money out of poverty, illness, and war.

We'll get change, real change, when workers lead the way.

They're Scheming While We're Dreaming
(July 2009)

Sometimes it gets so bad one can only imagine it will get worse. Many UAW members believe the New GM will cut wages again; Ford will demand more concessions; and Fiat will cannibalize Chrysler.

Workers are not unreasonable. The past has shown that contracts are designed to be broken as soon as they don't benefit management.

On the other hand, retired salaried workers from Delphi have learned that team members are a lower class than union members. The unwritten promise they received in lieu of a contract sheathed a knife—a default dagger that cut out the heart of capital's most loyal guards.

Who will defend the palace now?

Experience is to education as a lead pipe is to a forehead.

Loyalty to the boss is a patsy's game. Nobody in the wild world of business does business without a contract except for the patsies who work without a contract.

But what's a contract without an enforcer?

Fish wrap.

Salaried retirees from Delphi have a sound ethical argument, but their legal legs are weak in the knees. Attorneys are selling them professional fish wrap disguised as legal advice.

The UAW secured pensions and health care for retirees only because they could enforce the contract with a strike. The court, like the Corps, bows to power, not pity. The unorganized get whatever the company is willing to pay—and what it's willing to pay is anything but ethical.

Delphi was designed for bankruptcy. GM switched pension credits from the GM plan to the newly formed Delphi plan. As soon as the spin-off was complete, GM pulled the plug. GM canceled contracts with Delphi, re-sourced with other suppliers, and demanded cuts in prices that forced Delphi to sell below cost. Bankruptcy wasn't a sign of failure, it was a business plan.

The Delphi fraud—led by a team of former GM executives—enabled General Motors to dump pensions and health insurance for tens of thousands of retirees. Salaried retirees from American Axle who had spent the bulk of their careers at GM discovered that their pensions were lumped into the Delphi plan, despite the fact that they had never worked for Delphi. When they filed a lawsuit, they learned it was legal. After all, they were nonunion. They delivered their services without a contract, in which case paternity does not apply.

The corpos and their hired pens are scheming while we're dreaming. They con employees into calling themselves *team members* instead of union members, and *associates* instead of workers. Corporate think-tankers disassociate workers from identifying with their class, and convince them the conflict between labor and capital is a thing of the past.

The first rule of writing is: *call things by their names.*

The first rule of business is: *confuse the rubes.*

Workers' rights—whatever the worker's walk of life—are won by struggle, not loyalty to the company or its political parties. Which leads us to some relevant questions:

1) How can we enforce the contract since the UAW gave up the right to strike until 2015?
2) What's the advantage of nationalism when the Corps are multi-national and borders keep unions confined to hostage negotiation, that is, severance rather than global expansion?

Capitulation over the right to strike is not new to the UAW Concession Caucus. They promoted the nationalistic *Buy American* program to union members, but refused to strike over outsourcing. They negotiated company neutrality in card-check organizing drives, but gave up the right to strike for a contract once the workforce was organized.

UAW office rats exchanged the walk for the talk and turned contracts into fish wrap. But their own pockets are stuffed with bennies: double pensions, 100 percent reimbursement for health care, travel expenses, and all the summer vacation they want.

Likewise, politicians wear flag pins and pledge allegiance to the lobbyists with the most money. Hence, the US exports jobs and bans the importation of medicine from Canada. Nationalism confines unions to the back yard, legislates a captive market for drug companies, and gives corporations free rein to trample workers' rights worldwide.

How is it that when unions form alliances with unions in other countries, it's communism, and when corporations invest in China it's free-market capitalism? They're scheming while we're dreaming. Rather than calling a spade a spade, they choose to confuse the rubes.

In the worst of times, people come together. Unlikely alliances collide and form new constellations of power. Salaried workers who witness the power of organized labor to protect its members understand the value of unions like never before. At the same time, activists know unions can do better and are busy dismantling the barriers—like nationalism and employment categories—that subdivide workers, tether organizers, and handcuff collective bargaining.

If organized capital can force the government to pay off investors' gambling debts and open borders to the unregulated flow of capital in pursuit of the lowest wages, then organized labor should likewise cross borders, expand alliances, and force the government to recognize the right of salaried workers to unionize in pursuit of happier outcomes than broken promises, foreclosures, and canceled health insurance.

Organized capital advances every time organized labor retreats. Workers at transplants like Toyota and Honda can expect the lead-pipe wake-up before the year ends. At which point UAW members can compete for lower wages, or reverse the trend.

Where do we begin?

Defend new hires. No more tiers. No more whipsawing. One union, one contract.

We need a national pattern contract that covers wages and benefits, including supplemental unemployment pay for all autoworkers in both assembly and supply.

A national pattern contract would take labor out of the competition. All benefits should be universal and portable and cover all UAW members under the national pattern agreement. Furthermore, all UAW members should have preferential hiring and transfer rights to all other companies represented by the UAW, regardless of point of entry. Portable benefits and transfer rights would provide a practical incentive for workers to join the UAW.

You don't think nonunion workers would join? Wait till they get the combination wage cut–speedup punch. The school of hard knocks doesn't graduate patsies. But we need a real alternative to attract new members, not fish wrap labeled "local contract with a no-strike clause."

To that end, the UAW should maneuver the expiration of all UAW contracts to coincide. Isolated strikes are suicide. Separate and unequal contracts for Ford, Chrysler, GM and every supplier in between undermines collective bargaining. We need one union with one contract.

Whipsawing lowers the standard of living for all workers. If we allow the Corps to divide us, isolate us, and treat each local unit or—as in the case of salaried workers—each individual as a separate entity, the Corps will continue to drive down wages, benefits, and working conditions. A national pattern contract with a national benefits fund could give organized labor momentum and open the door to a truly international union response to multinational corporate assaults.

We can't confront organized capital with a working class that is categorically disorganized. We can't confront multinational corporations with a union confined to local negotiation.

One union, one contract is not optional, it's imperative. The alternative is extinction.

Delphi's salaried retirees have confirmed the value of corporate promises and professional fish wrap. Concession after concession has confirmed the devaluation inherent in selective bargaining.

"It's time," as Jerry Tucker said, "to put the backbone back in the UAW." If the UAW isn't up for a spinal adjustment, it's time to organize a new union based on real union principles: one union, one contract.

Welcome to Juarez
(September 2009)

Where the cops don't need you and man they expect the same.
—Bob Dylan, "Tom Thumb's Blues"

In *Juarez, the Laboratory of our Future* (1998), Charles Bowden quoted Nicholas Steele, former head of Ford in Mexico, as he gushed with admiration for the Mexican government's control of workers: "But is there any other country in the world," Steele said, "where the working class… took a hit in their purchasing power of in excess of 50 percent over an eight-year period and you didn't have a social revolution?"

We are about to find out. In 2007 UAW members took a 50 percent cut in pay for new hires at the Big Three automakers. In 2009 the UAW gave up cost-of-living raises, annual performance bonuses, and the right to strike. The domino that went down in Juarez is cascading through North America.

For twenty-plus years, foreign automakers in the US pegged compensation at rates that discouraged union organizing, but that benchmark is rolling in the dirt and UAW office rats are running for cover beneath the skirts of Wall Street's whores—lawyers, politicians, and chief executive officers.

Maybe you haven't paid attention to the mayhem coming out of Juarez, that bright city on the hill that held out the promise of a new century of progress. But it's hard not to notice the dislocated anger massing at the gates of shuttered factories in the North. It's hard to ignore the plight of retirees, whose future was foreclosed on while Congress fiddled with health care reform and sheltered economic terrorists from harm. It's hard to turn your head when your child is facing a dead-end job market. It's hard to pretend hard times are someone else's load when "the vagabond who's rapping at your door is standing in the clothes that you once wore" (Bob Dylan, "It's All Over Now, Baby Blue").

Instead of a national strike, we stuck it to the next generation of workers: low wages, no cost of living adjustment, no pension, no health care in retirement, and boot-licking union officers eager to do the boss's dirty work.

No one is coming to save us. And the victims won't be eulogized as heroes in some patriotic songbook with a picture of the Alamo on the cover and punchy blurbs from "union-friendly" politicians on the dust jacket. Labor's war memorial will be a white flag embossed with tire tracks.

The president of Toyota said the weak US currency made it difficult to return to profit on an unconsolidated level. "When you get to this level, it makes it difficult to return to profit on sales growth alone," he said ("Toyota Head: Returning to Profit Hard with Weak Dollar," Reuters, October 2, 2009). That means wage cuts for workers at Toyota. That means plant closings, layoffs, and speedups for workers at Toyota. And that means the next UAW contract—pre-set to match Toyota—will be worse than the last unless the rank and file sandbags the office rats and retirees crash the 2010 Bargaining Con* in Detroit with overwhelming force.

We can do that.

We've got the numbers, and we've got the bayonet of greed pointed at our backs. They've already drained pension funds and 401(k)s. They've crippled health care reform and torpedoed s. If you haven't suffered foreclosure, you've lost half your equity. Everyone can see where this is going. Vultures are circling the car crash.

The price of oil can only rise as sources deplete and China and India demand their fair share. Our economy runs on oil, not credit cards. And since the dollar hasn't gained real value in thirty-eight years, what can workers expect from the bosses? Bonuses? Raises? Vacation pay?

UAW activist Frank Hammer put the countersink to the last nail in the coffin of nationalism when he said, "With the expansion of globalization, we are all foreign workers."

Welcome to Juarez.

Epilogue

The Last Word

The Canadian labor economist Sam Gindin once said, "If workers don't believe that change is possible because of their experience in the union day to day, forget about politics."

Politics is the cart. Work is the horse, the driving force. If we can empower workers where they live and work every day, then and only then can we organize a real resistance, a real union, a real social movement. Then and only then can we, as Jerry Tucker said, "put the backbone back in the UAW."

The UAW legacy of resistance and rebellion, its core culture of confrontation and direct action, has been replaced by a program of cooperation with the bosses. UAW officials promoted partnership, nicknamed "jointness," as a strategy to save jobs and stop plant closings, selloffs, and outsourcing. The mollycoddle strategy failed for workers, but succeeded for bureaucrats. We didn't save any jobs. We didn't stop any plant closings. We didn't dam the flood of outsourcing. The membership of the UAW has been cut off at the knees and UAW president Bob King is still trumpeting jointness as if it was the key to Solidarity Heaven. The man believes in himself. Trouble is, King's self is organizational delusion incarnate.

The only jobs that were saved by cooperation with the boss were union staff. A culture of favoritism, perks, and backroom deals replaced the culture of collective struggle. Porkchoppers were empowered and the membership was plundered. We've lost three-fourths of our members while foreign automakers set up nonunion shops on our turf and independent parts suppliers treat the UAW like a Salvation Army band without horns. No wonder. The UAW *is* a tax-deductible charity organization.

Almost a third of UAW officials have their salaries and expenses reimbursed by the companies through independent non-profit corporations. That is, funds dispersed from the company circle the spin-and-rinse cycle of an S-corporation, then flow down the funnel into porkchoppers' pockets clean as a dishwasher's knuckles. It's all legal, but the ethics would stifle a laugh from the devil.

Steve Rattner, the Car Czar, oversaw a restructuring that effectively decertified the UAW as a bargaining agent for workers by inserting a no-strike clause in the bankruptcy addendum. Little did the naive neoliberal know that the no-strike clause was initiated by King in exchange for neutrality agreements with employers back when he was vice president in charge of organizing more than a decade earlier. It worked so well for King and his business partners that he intends to expand the no-strike posture. Besides, UAW officials use interest from the strike fund for operational expenses. They don't want the principal depleted frivolously.

Since the International UAW is a one-party state, and members are increasingly deprived of the right to vote against contracts, either by stipulation or threat of reprisal, it is generally understood by the rank and file that the union is the enforcement arm of management.

How King expects to organize new members baffles those who believe that unions exist to represent workers. King has no such illusions. Rather than follow the standard union dictum to take labor out of the competition, King intends to hitch the union's wagon to the profit-sharing roller coaster.

While the press narrates the exodus of American manufacturing jobs, Asian and European automakers are setting up shop in the United States where labor grows cheaper by the day and our reputation for weak unions precedes the procurement with sycophantic fanfare. A case in point: after UAW members at a GM plant in Saginaw—formerly Steering Gear, now Nexteer—voted down a concession contract, union and management teamed up to coerce compliance.

Once the concessions were in place, the factory was sold to Tempo, an auto parts supplier, and Pacific Century Motors, an affiliate of the Beijing Municipal Government. At first, the Chinese were hesitant about Michigan's reputation for strong unions. UAW vice president Jimmy

Settles intervened. "Settles convinced them that the union was flexible and could do what was necessary to deliver the productivity Tempo needed, at a wages-and-benefits cost that would enable them to compete" (Tom Walsh, "Ficano's Trips to China Get Jobs as Souvenirs," *Detroit Free Press*, July 10, 2010).

Autoworkers didn't lose out to foreign competition. We lost control of the union. The UAW became a highfalutin nonprofit corporation, and workers got the short end of the expectation stick. Jobs are here, but the UAW failed to organize because officials were concentrating on their putts at the UAW Education Center golf course when GM stacked the deck and cut the deal. What happened to the rank and file made no difference to the managers of the new UAW franchise.

Originally, GM manufactured all its own components. They bought from themselves and sold to themselves and made a profit at every flip of the wrist. Why outsource? Why break up the cartel? They didn't. The same people still own the cake and eat it too.

GM took money out of the right-hand pocket, put it into the left-hand pocket, and said, "Look! A new company! Delphi! Lear! American Axle!"

We see the same managers in the same suits mouthing the same words out of both sides of the same mouth. The name of the game isn't competition, it's *Monopoly*.

In 1987, I worked at a GM plant that made fuel injectors. We also assembled fuel injectors for Bosch, one of GM's major competitors. Bosch was building a nonunion plant in South Carolina, but they weren't up to speed, so we helped them.

In 1988, Roger Penske bought some component businesses from GM. He whipped the mismanaged process into shape, distracted union office rats with cheese and crackers, and imposed a two-tier wage on workers. Then he sold the business to Bosch. Then he sat on the Board of Directors at Delphi. Then Bosch closed the UAW plant they bought from Penske and moved the jobs to their nonunion plant in South Carolina. Then GM outsourced work from Delphi to Bosch to accelerate the union-busting process.

Competition is for workers. Bosses don't compete. Bosses make deals.

At the UAW Bargaining Convention in 2002, UAW president Ron Gettelfinger chose Stephen Girsky, an analyst for Morgan Stanley, to be the keynote speaker. In 2005 Girsky worked as an advisor to GM's CEO and chief financial officer. In 2009, he began to serve on the GM Board of Directors and as a trustee for the UAW-VEBA, a health care trust for retirees.

Seating arrangements change, but the same people control the game, and they have plans for all the money you and I will ever make in our lifetimes.

Back in the nineties, when unions lobbied against free trade laws, the corporations resisted. Why? They could have retained a greater market share with protective trade barriers. They could have preserved their most loyal customers—employees and their families. Instead, they insisted we compete in the global market. Then they bought shares of foreign car companies and urged workers to compete with other workers by cooperating with the boss. They, the company bosses and the union bosses, appealed to patriotism. Buying American was a pledge of allegiance.

Many workers were deceived into thinking that buying American would save jobs. All it did was divert anger and make believe that foreign workers—both inside and outside US borders—were the enemy. Meanwhile, politicians removed barriers to globalization, imposed injunctions on unions, and reinforced the replacement of strikers. We bought American and the Corps bought whatever they wanted in Mexico, Europe, Asia, and Latin America with profits earned by American workers. Foreign workers didn't steal our jobs. The bosses exported them while porkchoppers pointed fingers across the border to cover their guilt.

The charade would make Jerry Springer blush. UAW president Bob King instructed three UAW regional directors to give bouquets to Hyundai officials in protest over the treatment of temp workers in Korea. The ploy may contain some veiled allusion to bread and roses, but the reference was lost on thousands of temp workers in the UAW who pay dues even though their status is one step below Jim Crow—that is, the discrimination is based strictly on class, not race. The bossing class no longer bothers to disguise its contempt for workers with a color code.

The ruling caucus in the UAW has perverted the union into an arbiter of degradation for workers. An entire generation of autoworkers has been systematically deprived of dignity and fair compensation. Wages and benefits for new hires were cut in half, and now King promises nonunion *employers* that the UAW can help them, too.

Forty years ago, workers controlled the shop floor and the union hall. It was our turf. That sense of empowerment wasn't confined. It walked out into the streets. The culture of struggle infiltrated the community. The Corps were threatened. The Corps had to devise a way to dismantle that core-to-core conflict between the values of solidarity and the values of dog-eat-dog capitalism. The Corps put down the club and proffered the carrot. They were charming in their approach. Bosses loosened their neckties and rolled up their sleeves. "Let's all get along," they said. "Let's work together." The shakedown was lubed with sweet talk and enticements.

The first indication that you are about to be date-raped is an appeal for cooperation. The come-on, inviting us to be partners in the business, was worth less than a perp's promise. Slowly, carefully, resistance was stripped from the UAW, and the force of rebellion turned against the fall guy—foreign workers, both in and outside the United States. Workers were duped into fighting other workers instead of the boss. We were ordered to double up and dumb down.

In 1903, Frederick Taylor, the man who masterminded the dummy-down approach to manufacturing, said, "All possible brain work should be removed from the shop floor." He reduced each task to its simplest function and diminished each worker to an indistinct cog in the process of production. Today, the fad is lean manufacturing. The Lords of Lean claim that it's all about working smarter, not harder. They contend they only want to get rid of the waste. By waste, they mean that moment between movements when a worker catches her breath.

The Lords proclaim it's a revolutionary system that offers workers a humanly fulfilling alternative to mass production. Alas, no evidence was presented to support this fist-pumping prediction. The International Motor Vehicle Program at MIT spent five million dollars on a five-year study, and researchers never asked a lineworker what he or she thought. They call that empowerment. Whereas a worker's idea of human fulfillment may range anywhere from a six-pack to a spiritual conversion, management's idea of fulfillment usually involves a pencil and a clipboard or something exceedingly dull, stupid, and boring. Lean is nothing more than an intensification of Taylorism. Whereas a worker used to have one dumb job, he or she now has four dumb jobs—one for each limb. This is what they mean by fulfillment.

The evangelizers of lean methodology spew an intoxicating jargon—*revolutionary*, *humanly fulfilling*, *alternative*, *empowerment*. You'd think they were trying to sell us on socialism, not some goddamned mind-numbing-carpal-tunnel-twisting-repetitive-trauma-disorder.

Whenever I am faced with a perplexing, stubbornly complicated communication problem, I ask myself, "What would Woody Guthrie say?" I think Woody would say that two people can use the same word and mean two different things. Take the word *cooperate*, for example. Workers understand that cooperate means to work together. But in the mouths of managers it means, "You do whatever we tell you."

Lean is nothing but Taylorism squared and extrapolated. Taylor's reduction principle is now applied to whole industries. Complex manufacturing facilities are whittled down to their simplest functions by outsourcing every nonessential task. Piece by piece, work is removed from the bargaining unit and outsourced to ever smaller and more specialized nonunion suppliers. The union isn't busted, it's disrobed, one piece at a time. So slowly, it's almost painless.

UAW strongholds have been strip-mined and abandoned. Union families have been severed from their communities, their history, their sense of belonging and continuity. I know GM gypsies who have worked in nine different plants. Their attitude cuts through bullshit faster than a ripsaw splits pine.

The UAW Concession Caucus has infected the ranks with a malaise of apathy, futility, and powerlessness more insidious than anything the Corps, the mob, or the government could have imposed all together. With bricks of patterned helplessness cemented with cynicism and spackled with distrust, the porkchoppers built a storm wall of complacency. But the deception, betrayal, and corruption of the UAW Concession Caucus is smashing holes in the storm wall.

When Bob King tried to promote the no-strike clause, among other concessions, to Ford workers at Local 600 (his home local) in Dearborn, Michigan, workers booed him off the stage and sent the contract to a crashing defeat. When UAW International reps tried to sell a concession contract to GM workers at Local 22 in Indianapolis, they were booed off the stage and members sent the contract to another crashing defeat. When the UAW International tried to unilaterally deceive and impose the bankruptcy addendum on five sites newly purchased by GM, workers forced the company union to abide by the successor clause in their contract and pay the raises and performance bonuses they deserved. When the UAW International and Magna Inc. threatened to close New Process Gear in Syracuse, New York, unless they agreed to more concessions, workers told them to go ahead and shut the plant down—three times.

Perhaps we've hit bottom, that point where workers say, "Enough is enough," and start pushing back.

As I write this on January 22, 2011, the UAW is launching another organizing drive at the transplants. Given Bob King's employer-centric rhetoric, I don't think the office rats could organize a square table and four chairs if you gave them a hint and a blueprint. But I know for a fact there are fighters in those plants, and they know more about unionism than all the bureaucrats in King Bob's entourage.

In April 2004, volunteer organizers from the Toyota plant in Georgetown, Kentucky, contacted me. They told me that an anonymous antiunion group—*Truthfinders*—was using excerpts from *Live Bait & Ammo* to defile the labor movement. After researching me further, they realized that I was just the type of union man they needed.

I drove down to Georgetown and listened to some of the finest, bravest, toughest union men and women I've ever met. The volunteer organizers on the front lines who square off with the boss and his herd of turkeys day after day are the real prizefighters of the labor movement.

I asked Mark Kinney why he was willing to run the risk. Mark turned a place mat over on the restaurant table. He drew five concentric circles. He pointed to the smallest circle in the center. "This is Toyota." He labeled the circle surrounding Toyota, *Georgetown*. The next circle, *Kentucky*. Then, the *United States*, and finally, the *World*. "What we do here," Mark said indicating the inner circle, *Toyota*, "affects everyone. If we fail to organize, Toyota will suppress everything. Wages in Georgetown, and Kentucky, and all over the United States will be impacted; suppliers, temp workers, the tax base, the general economy, everything."

What do we have to teach Mark Kinney about unionism? No one who works for a living has to "find" the truth. The truth hits you on the nose every day you go to work.

I went to work for the volunteers. I wrote *Ammos* and letters for and about them. I wrote a detailed four-page analysis and rebuttal called *Truth for Truthfinders* in which I exposed the lies, manipulations, and fallacies. Brother Allen Nielsen in Norwalk, Ohio, provided them thousands of free copies from his home printing press. I subscribed to the weekly organizing flier, *Outside Track*, by Tom Felicicchia, a rank-and-file volunteer whose work overshadowed the UAW's organizing department. Most importantly, I learned that the genuine union spirit can't be boxed and labeled and put on a dusty shelf in Solidarity House. There's a fire that burns in the hearts of workers that can't be snuffed out.

Like our old friend Dave Yettaw said, "You can defeat a leader, but you can't defeat the idea."

January 22, 2011

Afterword

In the summer of 2011, two years after the government bailout of General Motors and Chrysler and their subsequent bankruptcy, the business press was celebrating the return to profitability of the US auto industry. The "new GM," having rid itself of dozens of unprofitable operations, tens of thousands of workers, and "legacy costs" such as retiree health care, was making money once more, thanks to sweeping cuts in workers' compensation through changes in overtime pay and the ability to hire many new workers at around fourteen dollars per hour—half the top twenty-eight-dollar UAW wage.

Moreover, GM, which employed nearly half a million members of the UAW in the 1970s, had reduced its UAW workforce to around fifty thousand. Local union contracts, which had been for decades the UAW members' main protection against speedup, unsafe working conditions, and arbitrary action by management, had been replaced by "competitive operating agreements" modeled on work rules in US plants operated by nonunion competitors such as Toyota, Nissan, and Honda. In fact, the terms of the government bailout stipulate that GM and Chrysler's labor contracts set for renewal in 2011 match the pay and working conditions of those nonunion operations. Strikes were banned until the expiration of the next four-year contract, with binding arbitration designated as the only means of overcoming an impasse.*

The impact of all this on autoworkers was scarcely mentioned in an enthusiastic *New York Times* article on the Sonic subcompact car built at

---

* Nick Waun, "Will Auto's Three-Tier Wages Be on the Table?," *Labor Notes*, July 13, 2011, www.labornotes.org.

an assembly plant in Lake Orion, Michigan.* There, some 40 percent of workers make the fourteen-dollar wage—including a large number of workers whose pay was cut without a vote in their local union. Workers from independent parts vendors labor inside the plant for even less— around ten dollars per hour. Yet none of this sparked outrage among leaders of a union founded on the principle of equal pay for equal work. On the contrary: According to UAW president Bob King, these union concessions were vital to the health of GM—a company in which the union is a part owner through stock held in a health care trust fund. "We are committed to the success of the company," King told the *Times* reporter. "We had to talk about a business model that makes sense."

King's comments highlight the transformation of the UAW, the subject of Gregg Shotwell's *Live Bait & Ammo* newsletters collected here. Combining scabrous commentary with a literary flair, *Live Bait & Ammo* unfailingly amused, exposed outrages, and inspired. A selection appears here edited only for clarity and length.

But more than an account of past labor fights, *Live Bait & Ammo* is also an organizing tool for future battles. By evoking the best fighting traditions of the UAW and the labor movement, Shotwell has passed on to a new generation of working-class militants an example of how to give voice to the rank and file—not only in day-to-day struggles, but in the aspiration for a more just society in which workers will finally enjoy the fruits of their labor.

Lee Sustar
Labor Editor, SocialistWorker.org

---

* Bill Vlasic, "With Sonic, G.M. Stands Automaking on Its Head," *New York Times*, July 12, 2011.

Index

Also from Haymarket Books

Subterranean Fire: A History of Working-Class Radicalism in the United States • Sharon Smith

This accessible, critical history of the US labor movement examines the hidden history of workers' resistance from the nineteenth century to the present. Workers in the United State have a rich tradition of struggle that remains largely hidden. *Subterranean Fire* brings that history to light and reveals its lessons for today. ISBN 9781931859233

The Civil Wars in U.S. Labor: Birth of a New Workers' Movement or Death Throes of the Old? • Steve Early

From forced trusteeships to hostile inter-union raids, the labor movement has been gripped by a civil war that threatens its very existence. Steve Early argues that these polices are an extension of the strategy of labor-management collaboration that must be replaced with rank-and-file initiative if American labor is to halt its long decline. ISBN 9781608460991

Fields of Resistance: The Struggle of Florida's Farmworkers for Justice • Silvia Giagnoni

In Immokalee, Florida, the tomato capital of the world—which has earned the dubious distinction of being "ground zero for modern slavery"—farmworkers organized themselves into the Coalition of Immokalee Workers and launched a nationwide boycott campaign that forced McDonald's, Burger King, and Taco Bell to recognize their demands for workers' rights. ISBN 9781608460939

Live Working or Die Fighting: How the Working Class Went Global • Paul Mason

The story of the rise of the worldwide working class is a story of urban slums, self-help cooperatives, choirs and brass bands, free love, and self-education by candlelight. *Live Working or Die Fighting* celebrates workers' common history of defiance, idealism, and self-sacrifice. ISBN 9781608460700

Revolution in Seattle: A Memoir • Harvey O'Connor

In this moving political memoir, journalist and activist Harvey O'Connor captures the courage and defiance of workers on the march against the carnage of the First World War and the dramatic inequality that marked the era. In particular, O'Connor's remembrances of the Seattle General Strike of 1919 showcase the potential of working people to transform society and illuminate the vibrancy and militancy of the early American labor movement. ISBN 9781931859745

About Haymarket Books

Haymarket Books is a nonprofit, progressive book distributor and publisher, a project of the Center for Economic Research and Social Change. We believe that activists need to take ideas, history, and politics into the many struggles for social justice today. Learning the lessons of past victories, as well as defeats, can arm a new generation of fighters for a better world. As Karl Marx said, "The philosophers have merely interpreted the world; the point, however, is to change it."

We take inspiration and courage from our namesakes, the Haymarket Martyrs, who gave their lives fighting for a better world. Their 1886 struggle for the eight-hour day, which gave us May Day, the international workers' holiday, reminds workers around the world that ordinary people can organize and struggle for their own liberation. These struggles continue today across the globe—struggles against oppression, exploitation, hunger, and poverty.

It was August Spies, one of the Martyrs targeted for being an immigrant and an anarchist, who predicted the battles being fought to this day. "If you think that by hanging us you can stamp out the labor movement," Spies told the judge, "then hang us. Here you will tread upon a spark, but here, and there, and behind you, and in front of you, and everywhere, the flames will blaze up. It is a subterranean fire. You cannot put it out. The ground is on fire upon which you stand."

We could not succeed in our publishing efforts without the generous financial support of our readers. Many people contribute to our project through the Haymarket Sustainers program, where donors receive free books in return for their monetary support. If you would like to be a part of this program, please contact us at info@haymarketbooks.org.

Shop our full catalog at www.haymarketbooks.org or call 773-583-7884.

About Gregg Shotwell

Gregg Shotwell, a machine operator turned rebel writer, worked for thirty years at General Motors. His shop-floor fliers grew legs of their own. Workers all over the country and abroad downloaded *Live Bait & Ammo* and commandeered company copiers to spread what Gregg calls "the vigor of truth and the ruth of rebellion." His growing notoriety led reporters in his hometown to question: "Is Toyota scared of this man?" UAW bureaucrats pretend he doesn't exist, but auto industry analysts and reporters cite his work, and online labor media like *Socialist Worker*, *Labor Notes*, and *MRZine* post his articles, poems, and satires with unreserved enthusiasm.